‘A keystone resource and delightfully written gu[illegible] positive psychology, but also for those experience[illegible]

Dr Aaron Jarden, *Un[illegible] Melbourne, Australia*

‘Simultaneously a delightful treasure box packed with care by Jolanta Burke, and an elevating guided tour of important ideas, research findings, applications, and approaches that make positive psychology what it is. Set aside more time than you planned, and prepare to keep reading “just one more”.’

Professor Michael Steger, *Colorado State University, USA*

‘Masterfully chronicles Jolanta Burke’s journey through the evolution of positive psychology. With an intriguing blend of personal narratives, practical applications, and essential academic perspectives, this book presents foundational studies in a refreshing, captivating style infused with humour and authenticity. It is highly recommended as a pivotal resource for scholars of positive psychology.’

Dr Christelle Liversage, *North-West University, South Africa*

‘Dr Burke is a capable guide for those interested in touring positive psychology. She shines a light on the most important concepts, reveals landmark publications, and offers personal anecdotes that add passion to the topic.’

Dr Robert Biswas-Diener, *author of* Radical Listening, *USA*

‘Thoughtfully structured and highly accessible, the book covers everything from the fundamentals of positive psychology to its applications in education, health, and the workplace.’

Dr Hans Henrik Knoop, *Aarhus University, Denmark*

‘By distilling essential research studies into an engaging and practical format, the author provides readers with a rich understanding of the field’s development while fostering its application in diverse contexts. This book is a must-have guide for positive psychology enthusiasts.’

Dr Andrea Giraldez-Hayes, *University of Cambridge, UK*

‘Dr Jolanta Burke masterfully bridges academic rigour and practical application in her essential book *The Foundation of Positive Psychology: A Compilation of Key Studies, Theory, and Practice*. As a seasoned chartered psychologist, Dr Burke delivers a comprehensive yet engaging resource that serves as both a guide to the evolving landscape of positive psychology and an inspiration for its real-world application.’

Dr Tayyab Rashid, *Harvard University, USA*

‘She was able to explain very complex things simply, while respecting their complexity! It gives us an excellent overview of what positive psychology covers. It is undoubtedly the best synthesis in the field. It’s a book for everyone!’

Professor Charles Martin-Krumm, *President of the European Network for Positive Psychology, France*

'Dr Jolanta Burke masterfully curates essential research in positive psychology, bridging the gap between theory and practice. A must-read for those looking to deepen their understanding of positive psychology.'

Dr Ana Paula Nacif, *University of East London, UK*

'Jolanta has done the hard yards, gathering a wealth of knowledge and distilling it into one inspiring and practical resource. Read it cover to cover, or dip in and out as the moment calls – you'll uncover golden nuggets, fresh ideas, and hidden gems to spark your curiosity and energise your work.'

Dr Annalise Roache, *The Coaching Toolbox, President, New Zealand Association of Positive Psychology*

'What makes it leading-edge is that it delivers even beyond this promise by delving explicitly into territory that positions positive psychology within the complexities and challenges of the current climate along with a future focus that acknowledges a multidisciplinary view, embraces the importance of widening cultural approaches, emphasises issues of diversity and inequality and adopts a systemic perspective.'

Dr Ceri Sims, *Buckinghamshire New University, UK*

'The book manages to integrate two worlds that are often far apart, which makes it even more fascinating and special: scientific rigour and a personal touch. The special touch comes through personal stories that are as charming as they are deep in reflection and knowledge. All is sweetened with sparkling humour, so the journey into the positive psychology science is particularly charming. A must-read, for sure.'

Dr Helena Águeda Marujo, *University of Lisbon, Portugal*

'This much-needed resource fills a critical gap in the positive psychology literature, making it indispensable for scholars and practitioners seeking to deepen their understanding and contribute meaningfully to this dynamic field.'

Lucy Airs, *Anglia Ruskin University, UK*

'This book is what I imagine sitting at Dr Jolanta Burke's kitchen table to be like, hearing short bursts of digestible information on literally any aspect of positive psychology, made real with relatable stories from her life!'

Kate Brassington, *Zest Coaching and Consulting, Luxembourg*

'With her latest book, Jolanta serves a rich menu of positive psychology resources and practices. *The Foundation of Positive Psychology: A Compilation of Key Studies, Theory, and Practice* will no doubt become a one-stop-shop for students and enthusiasts alike.'

Laura Kinsella, *Senior Wellbeing Manager, Irish Life, Ireland*

'Dr Jolanta Burke's *The Foundation of Positive Psychology* is a remarkable blend of science and practicality, offering transformative insights into the field of wellbeing.'

Marta Cwiertnia, *HR Consultant, Life and Executive Coach, Ireland*

'This is a wonderful exploration of the science of wellbeing and positive psychology. Beautifully written, it "broadens and builds". Broadens in terms of expanding the breadth of wellbeing understanding while building capacity for more sustainable wellbeing strategies.'

Dr Mark Rowe, *Founder and Lifestyle Medicine Doctor, Thought Leader on Healthy Leadership, Burnout Prevention and Sustainable Wellbeing, TEDx and Keynote Speaker, Ireland*

'Burke offers a very fresh and transformative perspective that resonates across professions dedicated to human flourishing. Both broad and deep, yet highly accessible, this book is destined to become a cornerstone for students and scholars alike, inspiring a new generation of practitioners to approach their work with positivity and purpose. This new book represents what we have come to know Jolanta Burke's writings for: "Seminal, Engaging, and Accessible".'

Dr Conor Mc Guckin, *Trinity College Dublin, Ireland*

The Foundation of Positive Psychology

The Foundation of Positive Psychology: A Compilation of Key Studies, Theory, and Practice is a milestone text which serves as a comprehensive handbook for positive psychology. It offers a compilation of over 200 seminal papers that provide a balanced overview of the nature, origins, and evolution of the discipline. Across five chapters, readers will embark on a journey, delving into pivotal studies, theories, and practical applications that have moulded this dynamic field, exploring the promotion of positive psychology across various disciplines.

Every introduced publication in the book follows a consistent structure: providing a summary of key findings, an exploration of the paper's significance, and an examination of the practical implications and applications for professionals. The narrative goes beyond merely spotlighting cornerstone papers; it also traces the evolutionary path of contemporary ideas. Moreover, it confronts present tensions, lingering enquiries, and inherent limitations within positive psychological research while simultaneously envisioning hopeful pathways for further development.

It is essential background reading for researchers and practitioners in positive psychology, coaching, counselling, and social work, as well as students in various areas of psychology, counselling, education, healthcare, and related fields.

Jolanta Burke, PhD, is a chartered psychologist specialising in positive psychology and health. A graduate of Trinity College Dublin, Dr Burke worked as a programme director at the University of East London and Maynooth University before joining Royal College of Surgeons in Ireland (RCSI). She is currently a senior lecturer at the Centre for Positive Health Sciences, RCSI University of Medicine and Health Sciences. At RCSI, she is a programme director for the masters in applied positive psychology and health and a co-director of the masters in positive health coaching. She also leads a Positive Activity Research Lab, where her team explores the science behind maximising wellbeing and human flourishing. Her team secured funding from the EU, including Interreg and Erasmus+, as well as Science Foundation Ireland, Irish Research Council, Health Research Board, and Enterprise Ireland. She has authored 14 books, published over 100 peer-reviewed publications, and written for newspapers, such as *The Guardian*, *Irish Times*, and *Irish Independent*. She has over 2.5 million reads on *The Conversation* and *Psychology Today* and has been acknowledged by the *Irish Times* as one of the 30 people who make Ireland a better place. For more information, please go to www.jolantaburke.com.

The Foundation of Positive Psychology

A Compilation of Key Studies, Theory, and Practice

Jolanta Burke

Routledge
Taylor & Francis Group
LONDON AND NEW YORK

Designed cover image: Getty images via Seamni

First published 2025
by Routledge
4 Park Square, Milton Park, Abingdon, Oxon OX14 4RN

and by Routledge
605 Third Avenue, New York, NY 10158

Routledge is an imprint of the Taylor & Francis Group, an informa business

British Library Cataloguing-in-Publication Data
A catalogue record for this book is available from the British Library

Library of Congress Cataloging-in-Publication Data
Names: Burke, Jolanta, author.
Title: The foundation of positive psychology : a compilation of key studies, theory, and practice / Jolanta Burke.
Description: Abingdon, Oxon ; New York, NY : Routledge, 2025. | Includes bibliographical references and index.
Identifiers: LCCN 2024059957 (print) | LCCN 2024059958 (ebook) | ISBN 9781032870380 (hardback) | ISBN 9781032864525 (paperback) | ISBN 9781003530596 (ebook)
Subjects: LCSH: Positive psychology.
Classification: LCC BF204.6 .B85 2025 (print) | LCC BF204.6 (ebook) | DDC 150.19/88—dc23/eng/20250208
LC record available at https://lccn.loc.gov/2024059957
LC ebook record available at https://lccn.loc.gov/2024059958

ISBN: 978-1-032-87038-0 (hbk)
ISBN: 978-1-032-86452-5 (pbk)
ISBN: 978-1-003-53059-6 (ebk)

DOI: 10.4324/9781003530596

Typeset in Times New Roman
by Apex CoVantage, LLC

To my beloved Jack

Contents

About the author

Dr Jolanta Burke is a chartered psychologist specialising in the application of the science of positive psychology and positive health in daily life to improve health and wellbeing. She is an academic at the Centre for Positive Health Sciences, RCSI University of Medicine and Health Sciences, a programme director for the Masters in Applied Positive Psychology (Health), and a co-director of the Masters in Positive Health Coaching. She also leads a Positive Activity Research Lab, where her team explores the approaches maximising wellbeing and human flourishing. Her team secured funding from the EU, including Interreg, Erasmus+, as well as Science Foundation Ireland, Irish Research Council, Health Research Board, and Enterprise Ireland. She has authored 14 books and published over 100 peer-reviewed publications.

Dr Burke's research has been featured in such media as the *RTE*, *The Economic Times*, *Channel News Asia*, *CNN*, and *Fox News*. She wrote for such newspapers as *The Guardian*, *(London) Metro*, *Irish Independent*, and she is a regular contributor to *Psychology Today* and *The Conversation*, where almost 3 million people have read her articles in the last two years. She has been acknowledged by the *Irish Times* as one of the 30 people who make Ireland a better place. For more information, visit www.JolantaBurke.com.

Preface

I have been deeply immersed in positive psychology for over two decades. From an early age, I inspired to be a psychologist or psychotherapist, because I wanted to help people. Yet, shortly after completing my bachelor's degree, I gave away all my psychology textbooks and found myself at crossroads. None of the traditional topics in psychology sparked my interest well enough to pursue a master's degree. However, everything changed when I discovered positive psychology.

I remember the early days of positive psychology, when even academics were unfamiliar with it. Today, positive psychology has become mainstream, and my conversations with colleagues and strangers curious about positive psychology are different. Given that people have developed opinions about it, and they either embrace it or approach it with scepticism, I savour meaningful discussions, spending hours exploring various perspectives on its research and practice.

A pivotal moment for me came when I realised that positive psychology was my true calling. I didn't know what aspect of positive psychology I wanted to explore; I just knew I wanted it to be part of my daily life. This is why I quit my full-time, permanent, and well-paid job to pursue my dream of doing a full-time PhD in Trinity College Dublin, and spent three years reading my favourite topics. Over the years, I've had the privilege of witnessing the incredible growth of this field. It all began with a handful of researchers and evolved into a vibrant, global community with vast applications in a wide range of fields.

In Vancouver, at the International Positive Psychology Congress, an important biennial event in the field that brings together leaders and practitioners worldwide, I found myself seated at an oval table alongside positive psychology course leaders from all around the world. The committee was chaired by James Pawelski from the University of Pennsylvania and Christian van Nieuwerburgh from the RCSI University of Medicine and Health Sciences. The committee's goal was to foster collaboration among universities offering positive psychology courses worldwide. It was during these discussions that the concept for this book emerged. A key challenge we all hoped to address was the lack of consensus on the foundational studies that should underpin these courses. I wanted to create a resource that would help inform curricula worldwide by combining essential research articles in positive psychology.

To prepare for writing this book, I explored databases, such as PsyInfo, Scopus, and grey literature to identify the most cited articles in positive psychology. However, I have quickly realised that citation counts alone were not always reliable indicators of an article's influence because older articles usually accumulated more citations. Yet many recent studies are of huge importance to the field and its direction. It was important that I included them, as I wanted to make sure that this book reflected both historical and contemporary contributions to this field.

Although, positive psychology began in the USA, it has expanded globally, with many contributions made outside North America. Researchers centred around Professor Martin Seligman, to whom the establishment of the field is often attributed, have published a greater ratio of articles in the first decade of positive psychology existence. Their work appears disproportionately more influential in citation numbers than others. However, to ensure global representation, I contacted colleagues from around the world who lead positive psychology courses and programmes to gather their insights on influential studies from their regions. This allowed me to ensure that all continents were represented in this book, giving it a truly diverse and comprehensive perspective.

I also reviewed the syllabi of ten positive psychology courses when selecting key articles. This allowed me to examine the reading lists which programme and module leaders recommended for students. This analysis provided me with valuable insights as to what core readings shape the next generation of positive psychologists. Many of them recommended book chapters or books worthwhile exploring. While many influential volumes have been published in this field, I deliberately tried to avoid them and focussed on the key peer-reviewed articles to maintain academic rigorousness. At the same time, I could not resist recommending a few books that could help readers understand this field more effectively.

To further refine the selection, I consulted alumni of positive psychology programmes worldwide. I asked them to share the research articles that had most impacted their understanding of positive psychology. Their input was invaluable as they shared fantastic research articles they often refer back to, in some cases, articles they recommend to their clients. Finally, given my keen interest in positive psychology, I have added a few articles that I believe were crucial for understanding and progressing the positive psychology knowledge.

My goal in this book is not to critique research but to select the most impactful studies in positive psychology to help students and practitioners apply it. Throughout the book, I've focused on the best ways to illustrate how each concept, original research, theory, or framework can be introduced in everyday life or enrich such practices as coaching, therapy, workplace, education, and healthcare. At the same time, when needed, I have included some research limitations to ensure the practice is not mindlessly implemented without consideration.

Academic articles can be challenging to read, even for those who are passionate and knowledgeable about positive psychology. Many people enjoy science and have a great appetite for new knowledge but find dense scholarly writing hard to digest. If you relate to this, you are in luck. This book has been written with you in mind. I sought feedback from practitioners about the most effective way, in which I should format each chapter to make it relevant to them. Many of them asked for storytelling to help illustrate the key concepts. So, I have sprinkled each chapter with personal stories, anecdotes, and reflections to make the academic content of this book more accessible and engaging.

In summary, I hope you will enjoy this journey through the field of positive psychology. With tens of thousands of research articles now published in this field, it would be impossible and impractical to mention them all. Instead, I have only selected over 200 seminal papers to include in this volume. I hope you enjoy my selection. At the same time, I secretly hope that this volume will result in debates as to why some articles have been included while others have been excluded by my colleagues and me.

These key papers offer a broad and representative view of positive psychology's growth and impact. If you're new to positive psychology, I hope this book gives you a glimpse into this fascinating field and encourages you to explore it further. If you're a seasoned positive psychologist, I hope it brings back memories of the good times when you first read these articles and some additional insights. And if you're a practitioner, I hope it inspires you to use positive psychology to enhance your work and improve your clients' wellbeing. Regardless of your background and motivation for reading this book, I hope you find it valuable and that at least a few of the articles will resonate with you and prove helpful in improving your practice or personal journey.

Acknowledgements

Writing this book was an immensely rewarding experience for several reasons. Firstly, it allowed me to re-read many fascinating articles on positive psychology and reflect on how my understanding of them has evolved over time. Secondly, revisiting these articles was like a "positive reminiscence" intervention, bringing back some fond memories from my master's and PhD studies in positive psychology. Thirdly, engaging deeply with a subject, I am so passionate about allowed me to experience a further boost of interest, not to mention an avalanche of positive emotions, reinforcing my meaning and purpose associated with this exciting field. Most importantly, however, it offered me the opportunity to connect with the incredible individuals who have contributed to shaping this book. Therefore, I would like to acknowledge their insights and support.

First and foremost, I am grateful to Dr Aaron Jarden from the University of Melbourne, who pored over the book before it was even ready to be shared and offered some invaluable advice that has made this volume so much better. Thank you for all the time you spent on it and your support. I would also like to thank my research assistants from the "Positive Activity Research Lab" – Angel Harper, Branislav Kaleta, and Stephen Campbell. Angel, your meticulous proofreading of this volume was invaluable in ensuring its clarity. Thank you also to the entire team for your kindness, efficiency, and making the process of working with you so much fun – it truly means a lot!

Additionally, I am very grateful to colleagues and friends who are experts in positive psychology worldwide and who helped me shape specific sections of the book or offered their insights on the overall book content. My sincere thanks goes to Dr Andrea Giraldez-Hayes from the University of Cambridge, Prof. Christian van Nieuwerburgh and Dr Roger Bretherton from the RCSI Centre for Positive Health Sciences, Lucy Airs from the Anglia Ruskin University, Dr Pawel Fortuna from the Katolicki Universytet Lubelski, Kate Brassington and Dr Ana Nacif from the University of East London. Our discussions and the insights you have shared with me have shaped this book's content and significantly enhanced its quality and depth. I am deeply grateful for all your contributions.

Finally, I wish to express my profound gratitude to my family – Bren, Jack, and Charlie – for their unwavering love and support, especially during the final stages of writing and editing this book. Your encouragement, the endless cups of tea and snacks you brought into my office, not to mention the beautiful Jack's drawings, and warm hugs and kisses you gave me were a constant source of my strength and inspiration. Your love and support mean more to me than I can ever convey!

1 The fundamentals of positive psychology

Over the years, thousands of articles have been published explaining or critiquing positive psychology, providing valuable insights on further developing the field. In this chapter, we begin by sharing articles that define positive psychology and trace its evolution from the initial concepts to its expanded version. Next, we explore the breadth of the field by examining articles that highlight its focus, which extends widely into many other fields of research and practice. Following this, we delve into the critiques of positive psychology, analysing the main issues and recommendations for addressing them. Diversity and inclusion within the field are essential but often overlooked aspects of positive psychology. To address this, articles that explore concepts such as the Western, Educated, Industrialised, Rich, and Democratic (WEIRD) population, ethnocentrism, and multiculturalism are explored. We also discuss the key articles from positive psychology relating to how the field addresses some pressing global issues. These include climate change, bullying and the application of positive psychology with communities such as refugees and LGBTQ+. Finally, the chapter concludes with a review of the challenges with the research methods and some ethical considerations that need to be explored within the field. This comprehensive introduction offers a thorough perspective on the field, highlights its evolution over the decades, and pinpoints opportunities for enhancing its impact, output, and scientific rigour.

Introduction to positive psychology

Manifesto

In the 1990s while on family holidays in Hawaii, two psychologists, Martin Seligman from the University of Pennsylvania and Mihaly Csikszentmihalyi from Claremount Graduate University, accidentally crossed paths. Rather than lounging on the beach with cocktails in hand, they spent hours discussing the need for psychology to pivot away from discussing what is wrong with people and focus on what is right. Inspired by their conversation, they decided to take action and vowed to create a special interest group at the American Psychological Association (APA) that would explore the topics that were neglected by the psychological field, such as strengths, creativity, and optimism.

DOI: 10.4324/9781003530596-1

Soon after, Martin and Mihalyi invited Ray Fowler from the University of Alabama and, with all their families, went to a "psychodelic" Grateful Dead house in Yucatán, Gulf of Mexico, to create the field of positive psychology. Over the years, they were joined by a few other like-minded psychologists, such as Christopher Peterson, Barbara Fredrickson, Ed Diener, and others, who began to shape the contours of the field as we know it. Then in 1998, Martin Seligman became the president of the APA. In his inaugural speech, he called for others to join the conversation and explore the emerging field of positive psychology. Little did they know that what began as a small group would soon expand into the fastest-growing field in psychology. This book tells the story of how positive psychology became what it is today, through all the key studies published in academic journals.

A few years later, the first academic paper published about the new field of positive psychology was written by Martin Seligman and Mihaly Csikszentmihalyi. They outlined the need to explore the positive aspects of humanity and presented goals, rationale, and theoretical foundations of the new field. Their definition and framework helped clarify the scope of this emerging discipline. At the time, when positive psychology was largely unknown, my university friends and I dissected every word of the paper, trying to understand its meaning. The paper quickly became the top article defining the field and its scope. Over the decades, it has been cited by thousands of scholars and practitioners, making it one of the most influential articles in positive psychology to date.

The article introduces the main aims of positive psychology and positions it as a distinct field within psychology. Traditional psychology has been preoccupied with pathology, dysfunction, and treating mental illness. It neglected the study of human strengths, virtues, and optimal functioning. Positive psychology aimed to correct this imbalance by shifting focus on the positive aspects of the human experience. It redirected attention away from pathology and aimed to contribute to a more comprehensive understanding of human nature and ultimately enhance individuals' lives.

The article presents positive psychology's core aims and objectives, emphasising the importance of understanding and promoting human flourishing, psychological fulfilment, and wellbeing. As to the scope of positive psychology, Seligman and Csikszentmihalyi propose that positive psychology should address three main points:

Positive Subjective Experiences involves examining positive emotions, such as happiness, life satisfaction, and joy, to understand their role in enhancing overall wellbeing and quality of life.

Positive Individual Traits refer to studying individual strengths, virtues, and character traits that contribute to a good life. These traits can help us uncover another side of human beings that is rarely discussed in psychology. Identifying and cultivating these positive individual traits can help people improve psychological functioning and life satisfaction.

Positive Institutions and Communities emphasise the need to understand people and their contexts, such as societal and environmental factors that facilitate human flourishing, including supportive social networks, nurturing communities, educational institutions, workplaces, and other settings that influence people's wellbeing.

This transformative approach has since influenced a wide range of fields, including neuroscience, education, and cybernetics. These and other disciplines have adopted positive psychology's perspective by exploring their field's "positive" side, which has often been neglected. Consequently, this paper's impact extends well beyond psychology. Although Seligman was not the first to advocate this perspective, his voice, amplified by the emergence of the new field, played a crucial role in driving significant change, inspiring a new way of thinking and practice in psychology.

The authors articulated a research agenda for positive psychology, highlighting critical areas of enquiry such as positive subjective experiences, positive strengths, and positive institutions. This agenda has guided empirical research and theoretical developments in the positive psychology field over the past two decades. Researchers and practitioners alike often highlight the field's developments vis-à-vis this paper's recommendations. As positive psychology continues to evolve, its research agenda expands, yet foundational works like this remain essential touchstones.

For individuals not familiar with positive psychology, understanding its origins is crucial. This paper provides a comprehensive overview of the field's development, tracing its evolution and highlighting the distance researchers travelled between the year 2000 and today. It serves as a valuable resource for anyone who wishes to grasp the context behind positive psychology influence. It is also a roadmap for the practical application of positive psychology principles across diverse settings, including clinical practice, education, workplace wellbeing, community programmes, and public health initiatives. By integrating these principles into various domains, practitioners can help individuals and communities flourish, empowering them to make a positive difference in the lives of others.

Imagine living in a world where everyone focuses on what is wrong with you, defines you through all the mistakes you have made, and barely considers all the positives. No matter how resilient you are, it is bound to wear you down at some point. Some of you might start experiencing anxiety, depression, and other psychiatric conditions; others might rebel against the unfairness of this approach, yet there would be some who become shells of themselves, trying to pretend it does not bother them. Whatever your reaction to this, and how well assimilated this approach is in your daily life, you will all know at a deeper level that it is not okay, and a more balanced approach is needed. This is precisely what many people experience when introduced to the field of positive psychology – it simply makes sense.

References

Seligman, M. E. P., & Csikszentmihalyi, M. (2000). Positive psychology: An introduction. *American Psychologist*, *55*(1), 5–14. https://doi.org/10.1037/0003-066X.55.1.5

Why is it necessary?

I have a deep appreciation for old movies. In fact, I once took a course that traced the history of cinematography, starting with the Lumiére brother's early clips, including "L'Arrivée d'un train en gare de La Ciotat", which caused such panic that people screamed and ran away from the "motion picture house" thinking that the train was about to hit them. We journeyed through the Charlie Chaplin era into the present times. It was a fascinating course. But what I enjoyed most was the sentimental feelings I experienced watching the old movies. I reflected on how one person's idea could start a chain reaction that transforms the world as we know it. We have many examples from thought leaders such as Steve Jobs or Pablo Picasso. This same sense of sentimentality washes over me when reading old positive psychology articles.

I remember the early 2000s when research in positive psychology was like gold dust. We read and re-read articles slowly, savouring every word. We thought about them for ages, and word by word, they changed our perspectives as we tried to understand how to fit this new way of thinking into what we already knew. We wondered, was it new science or just a passing trend? Will it stand the test of time or not? Now, decades later, some may think these articles are redundant and outdated. Still, we need to revise them to understand the intellectual climate of the time and how it influenced subsequent research. Just like studying early cinematography deepens our appreciation for films, understanding the roots of positive psychology helps us recognise what we now take for granted.

In this article, Ken Sheldon and Laura King from the University of Missouri, USA, argued that positive psychology is essentially just psychology, but it is necessary as the traditional epistemological approaches perceive topics discussed in positive psychology with scepticism. They regard positive changes not as adaptive but as self-serving delusions, unrealistic beliefs that boost self-esteem, or biases. In other words, psychologists have been trained to spot the worst in human nature. Moreover, they perceive the Machiavellian qualities in people as their motivation to be good. For example, parents punishing their children to teach them how to behave in socially accepted ways.

Positive psychology is a paradigm shift, an invitation to view the world through a broader lens. It prompts us to ask new questions: Why are positive emotions significant? Why do most people find satisfaction in their lives despite their circumstances? Why are some individuals happier than others? These questions lead us to uncover evidence for once-obscure concepts. Armed with this knowledge, we can develop a more balanced view of human nature. It is one that doesn't just focus on flaws and Machiavellian motives but also acknowledges the good intentions and positive aspects of human character. This, I believe, is the true essence of understanding human nature.

References

Sheldon, K. M., & King, L. (2001). Why positive psychology is necessary. *American Psychologist*, *56*(3), 216–217. https://doi.org/10.1037/0003-066X.56.3.216

Cautious progress

Continuing with the cinematographic theme, have you ever seen *Sliding Doors* starring Gwyneth Paltrow? It is about parallel universes and how one seemingly small event can change the course of our lives. I have often wondered what would happen if Martin Seligman and Mihaly Csikszentmihalyi had not accidentally met in Hawaii or inspired others to develop this field, how different would psychology be today, what would the scope of positive psychology be? Without their influence as leaders, positive psychology could have been relegated to an insignificant article in an academic journal that only a few people read, and the field would have never taken off. Imagine how different the world would be without positive psychology.

Abraham Maslow, to whom *Maslow's Hierarchy of Needs* is famously attributed, first mentioned positive psychology nearly 40 years before. Yet his ideas did not gain the same traction, despite being a respected scientist and thought leader. This is something we need to consider when reflecting on the origins of positive psychology. A chance meeting, one of those "sliding doors", can change the course of humanity.

Five years after the field's inception, Shelley Gable from the University of California, USA, and Jonathan Haidt from New York University, USA, published a reflection on a rapidly emerging positive psychology field. By then, some researchers and practitioners have experienced a significant backlash. In this article, the authors assessed the field's rapid growth, explored its potential benefits, and addressed its challenges. The article serves as a "progress report" for the emerging discipline and provides a balanced perspective on the advantages and disadvantages of the field. It is aimed to reassure proponents and critics of positive psychology and instil confidence in the field's direction. At the time, many often used it to defend some of the existing criticisms.

The authors highlight several reasons that support the validity of positive psychology's existence, which are mentioned in this article. First, they argue that it brings a balance to the field of psychology. Traditional psychology focuses primarily on illness, dysfunction, and negative states, such as depression and anxiety. In contrast, positive psychology encourages researchers and practitioners to focus on the positive aspects of human experience and explore topics not ventured into before, such as curiosity. This shift leads to a more balanced perspective and a more comprehensive understanding of human beings in psychology.

The authors remind us that the psychological field has long neglected to explore specific topics, leaving us to speculate about their true nature and impact. Take joy, gratitude, or hope as an example. They are integral to our daily experiences, yet we know very little about them. This is why positive psychology tries to untangle them to understand what they are all about and how they can support us daily. One of the main advantages of positive psychology is that it draws our attention to these aspects of human experience, allowing us to recognise and appreciate the characteristics and processes we had previously overlooked. Today, because we have a better knowledge of positive emotions, we can create such films for children as *Inside Out* and help others understand the meaning and purpose of positive emotions.

Some positive psychology topics were previously mentioned by pioneers such as William James in the 19th century or Abraham Maslow in the mid-20th century or philosophers over the centuries. So, they might not be new. However, they have not been explored empirically to this extent. The contribution of the positive psychology field is not only about drawing attention to the topics relating to a good life but also about exploring their empirical foundations.

This is another benefit of positive psychology that highlights the need to prevent illness instead of focusing on the cure. The authors emphasised the critical role of positive psychology in offering a proactive approach to mental health. By exploring human strengths, positive experiences, and positive institutions, a comprehensive approach to preventative mental health can be created to benefit people and communities worldwide.

The authors highlighted the importance of positive psychology, not only in developing a solid knowledge base about positive conditions, such as wellbeing, optimism, and flourishing, but also focusing on the practical applications of this knowledge. Positive psychology helps people move beyond theory by offering strategies that can be integrated into their daily lives. It lays the groundwork for understanding the content and factors impacting practical interventions that can improve mental health and relationships and help people live good lives. These applications will help individuals and communities understand how to actively cultivate and sustain positive emotions, strengths, and behaviour, promoting a more meaningful and flourishing life.

Finally, the authors examined some of the challenges associated with positive psychology. They mentioned the scope of positive psychology and the difficulty of defining what is positive and what is not. After all, negative experiences could have a positive outcome that surpasses positive experiences in terms of developing character or meaning in life. Similarly, integrating positive psychology in the psychological field without disparaging the negativity was seen as challenging for the authors. After all, when searching for positive experiences, we could become so engrossed in our endeavour that we find it difficult to embrace all other types of experiences, perhaps even rejecting them on the way, which would be dangerous to our long-term wellbeing.

Another significant challenge the authors addressed was the need for rigorous science in studying positive aspects of human experiences. The topics discussed in positive psychology, such as happiness, awe, or joy, are often dismissed as "soft" and not rigorous. However, the authors stressed that these topics required extra effort to provide solid data. This challenge was further complicated by the difficulty in defining and measuring these topics, as it involved exploring individuals' subjective experiences.

Finally, the authors pointed out the cultural differences that must be considered when exploring topics in positive psychology. In the first five years, a significant amount of research has been conducted in the US with undergraduate students. Studying this group primarily meant that most of what we knew about positive experiences came from a small population representative. This needed to change and expand, and other socioeconomic and cultural groups needed to be included in positive psychological research.

When I read this article for the first time, I was a student studying for a Masters in Applied Positive Psychology and a practitioner. This article made me stop and think: How relevant and valid are the topics I introduce to my clients? Inspired by Gable and Haidt's article, I remember spending a day exploring the positive outcomes of negative experiences. A few years later, two books were published on this topic that added value to the importance of balance. However, when the article was published, this information wasn't as easy to find.

This article has also helped me find ways to discuss positive psychology with non-academics. It's crucial not to overpromise what positive psychology can deliver. Equally, we should not downplay the role of negative emotions in our lives, and should carefully consider the methodologies in all studies we read. Research-based practice is only valid when we examine research topics critically. For example, when sharing character strengths with clients, I realised needed to identify their benefits and limitations so that the results were not overinflated. I believe this was the most significant contribution of this article to practice back then.

References

Gable, S. L., & Haidt, J. (2005). What (and why) is positive psychology? *Review of General Psychology*, *9*(2), 103–110. https://doi.org/10.1037/1089-2680.9.2.103

PP 2.0

Career advisors from four universities in Ireland invited me to introduce them to strength-based coaching and figure out how to apply it in their practice. During the day, I asked them to role-play this new approach. The most challenging part of the role play for everyone was the process of shifting clients' attention to their strengths rather than fixing the problems they came to address. It just felt like they were ignoring their clients' needs. The shift from the problem to "let's discuss your strengths" was unnatural for those playing the role of clients. However, after a full day of practice, the career advisors felt more comfortable with this approach. A year later, when I returned to check their progress, most advisors shared that they enjoyed using strengths in their practice. They no longer felt unnatural.

This re-shifting of people's perspective from what is wrong to what is right and then focusing attention on the positive to crowd out the negative is a significant part of positive psychology practice. However, it also sparked one of the field's early criticisms: the belief that the negatives will disappear if we focus on the positives. While it is a very simplistic perspective on positive psychology, this is also why Paul Wong (Canada), a prominent figure in the field, believed it was essential to address it. To tackle this concern head-on, he introduced the concept of positive psychology 2.0, an evolution of the field that acknowledges the importance of addressing both the positive and the negative aspects of human experience.

Paul Wong emphasizes the need for clarity associated with happiness and the good life. Various terms emerged in the first decade, such as hedonic, eudaemonic, prudential, or chaironic happiness, all referring to different pathways people took to improve their wellbeing. Since then, we have expanded this terminology by introducing flourishing, which is often confused with wellbeing and similar concepts. Establishing a shared language that describes wellbeing and its various aspects is essential to understand the field.

Another suggestion is creating a positive psychology taxonomy representing a balanced approach to positive psychological concepts. He offers a few examples, such as good living conditions, which could lead to self-determination as part of the adaptive process, resulting in positive wellbeing outcomes. Similarly, poor living conditions could also lead to an adaptive process of accepting where a person is, resulting in positive wellbeing outcomes. Expanding this taxonomy across a range of processes, including both positive and negative experiences, would help us understand the field further. Additionally, the author proposes that more effort should be dedicated to exploring the four pillars of positive psychology, which he considers essential. These include virtue, meaning, resilience, and wellbeing. Given that a significant body of research already exists in this area, it is essential to focus on expanding it further.

Wong also distinguishes between meaning and happiness orientations to wellbeing, and their impact on desirable outcomes. These orientations offer different life purposes and core values; because of this, they need to be considered separately when studying wellbeing in more detail. For example, those who prefer a meaning orientation enjoy pursuing worthy ideas and are interested in nurturing the inner self – concepts like delayed gratification and perseverance. In contrast, those who prefer to orient themselves towards happiness aim to maximise their positive experiences in life, are concerned with what makes people happier, and search for more immediate gratification. The meaning orientation aligns with eudaimonic wellbeing, and happiness orientation with hedonic wellbeing. Both approaches offer value to people but need to be explored as distinct concepts.

Wong concludes that a dual-system model that integrates contrasting approaches is needed. For example, while it is important to pursue positive experiences, so is avoiding negative situations. Both the approach (seeking positive experiences) and avoidance (avoiding negative experiences) are essential in our lives and need to be acknowledged in the positive psychology field.

Overall, this article heralds the beginning of the second wave of the positive psychology movement that brings together the "ying" and the "yang" of human experience. It reminds readers that when positive psychology was created a decade earlier, it was meant to provide balance, not a one-sided focus on the positive. As such, the time for bringing the traditional and positive approaches is "now", and we should not wait for the future to do it.

References

Wong, P. T. P. (2011). Positive psychology 2.0: Towards a balanced interactive model of the good life. *Canadian Psychology/Psychologie Canadienne*, *52*(2), 69–81. https://doi.org/10.1037/a0022511

The second wave

When I worked at the University of East London, UK, I had the privilege of sharing my office with Tim Lomas and Itai Ivtzan. One afternoon, Itai and I crossed paths and had an impromptu conversation that has stayed with me since. We talked about being wise in how we use positive psychology research and the importance of expanding our horizons within positive psychology. This was an essential consideration that sparked the emergence of the second wave of positive psychology.

One of the major criticisms of positive psychology, especially in the first decade, was its focus on the positive. While Seligman and Csikszentmihalyi's foundational paper did not intend to disregard negative human experiences, it inadvertently contributed to misunderstanding the field. This focus on the positive sparked controversy, with some researchers pointing out the lack of balance in positive psychology (see the criticism section for more detail).

In response to this criticism, the concept of "second-wave positive psychology" was introduced in Europe as a new paradigm within positive psychology. It all began with a book by Itai Ivtzan, Tim Lomas, and Kate Hefferon of the University of East London, UK, and Piers Worth of the Buckinghamshire New University, UK, followed by an article written by Lomas and Ivtzan. Interestingly, two of the four authors were trained psychotherapists, and the other two came from research fields that explored the positive impact of negative states, which may be why they wanted to highlight the need for balance and the search for the positive in the negative. This blend of clinical and research expertise offered unique insights that recognised the importance of the positive and negative aspects of the human experience.

In their article, the authors argue that the second wave moved beyond the simplistic emphasis on positive traits and experience. It introduces the idea of a dynamic interplay between positive and negative aspects of life. Their stance has added more complexity and depth to the field. Not to mention, this approach is more palatable to those searching for balance in positive psychology.

The authors draw on the concept of dialectics, a tension between two opposing forces, such as optimism and pessimism, negative and positive, or light and darkness. They advocate embracing the complexity and dialectical nature of human emotions and experiences in pursuing wellbeing rather than reducing it to a simple "positive equals good" and "negative equals bad" heuristic.

The notion of Carl Jung's "shadow", the dark side of our psyche that we often find challenging to accept, is a fundamental part of the second-wave approach. Integrating "shadow" elements of human experience, such as pain, suffering, and existential angst, into the concepts of wellbeing is essential. Denying this part of ourselves or repressing it in any way can hinder our personal growth, resilience, and overall wellbeing.

Instead, we must cultivate wisdom, resilience, and personal growth by acknowledging and navigating life's challenges and adversities. Rather than seeking to eliminate negative experiences, practitioners are encouraged to help individuals develop the skills and resources to cope effectively and derive meaning from their adversity. Complex life circumstances can become a foundation for building strengths and personal growth.

Lomas and Ivtzan's article contributed to the ongoing evolution of positive psychology by introducing the concept of the second wave and the positive-negative dialectics of wellbeing. This acknowledgement has paved the way for more comprehensive explorations of wellbeing, thus opening doors to a better understanding of human experience.

For practitioners, this approach is enlightening as it does not ignore the negative while idealising perpetual happiness. I remember when I was at an EU conference on positive psychology in Amsterdam, the Netherlands, when their ideas were first presented. The room was packed, and as the discussion unfolded, people responded with a resounding *Finally!* It was ironic how positive psychologists craved talking about the "dark side" of human experience. But more than irony, it also highlighted how important it is for people to acknowledge life's challenges. It is about accepting ourselves as we are and acknowledging the need for a full range of human experiences. We can find growth not only in our successes but also in our struggles. Those struggles can sometimes help us become the people we want to become. It is all about the interplay between the light and the shadow, not about getting rid of one.

References

Lomas, T., & Ivtzan, I. (2016). Second wave positive psychology: Exploring the positive – negative dialectics of wellbeing. *Journal of Happiness Studies: An Interdisciplinary Forum on Subjective Well-Being*, *17*(4), 1753–1768. https://doi.org/10.1007/s10902-015-9668-y

The third wave

Every time I read this article, I'm reminded of Peter Gabriel's song "Washing the Water". While the lyrics differ from this article, the sentiment remains the same. Washing the Water explores the depths of human nature and what we can and cannot control in our lives. It teaches us how to turn dangerous waters into a support system when we simply let go. We travel down the river on its back as it teaches us to float. When we start sinking, it lifts and takes us home where we belong. The song is all about life as movement and travelling in and out of emotional turmoil. Similarly, in this article, the waves of positive psychology are described poetically as coming in and out, marking their existence. The third wave of positive psychology is just one of the waves we see coming in and out with the tide.

This article heralds a paradigm shift in how the field of positive psychology is perceived. Written by a team of colleagues coming mainly from an Australian university, it shifts the focus of positive psychology towards the future. At the same time, it acknowledges that those waves can work in tandem with each other. Therefore, research continues to be published under the first- or second-wave umbrella. Also, given that Tim Lomas from Harvard University, USA, the leading author of the paper, is also the co-author of the second-wave positive psychology, it demonstrates a post-Covid field progression of positive psychology that co-exists with all other waves.

Some of the tenets of this progress include the acknowledgement of the complexity of understanding wellbeing. Over the preceding decade, our comprehension of wellbeing has increased significantly. We stopped seeing it as one or two wellbeing models anymore but explored its nuances associated with factors impacting them. The third wave broadened the scope of positive psychology further by acknowledging the multifaceted nature of individual experiences and factors impacting them, such as cultural influences, social dynamics, or ecological systems. This allows us to see human beings more as they are rather than a simplified version of them.

In a way of an example, let me take you to a primary school in Ireland. When my little boy started his junior infants, one of his teachers complained that he did not talk to her and she asked me to "tell" him to start conversing with her. I found this request bizarre for many reasons, one being that he was a chatter-box at home. So, I re-shifted the teacher's focus from him (and what was wrong with him) to what happens in the classroom that does not make him feel safe to talk. Many factors relating to the social environment came out as soon as we began to discuss it. Once they were addressed, my son had no issues speaking in the class. This is just a small example of how much easier it is to blame an individual for not speaking up or minding their wellbeing, than addressing a range of other environmental influences.

Sometimes, the cause for any undesirable behaviours, associated with such concepts as individual wellbeing, lies in the complexity of people's personality, culture, or social dynamics, which are often underestimated. This wave of positive psychology recognises the dynamic systems approach that underlies the interconnectedness and continuous interaction between a range of elements within an individual and their environment that impacts their wellbeing. It highlights understanding wellbeing and other positive psychology contexts not only as silos connected by vacuum, but also acknowledges the non-linear nature of human development.

Most importantly, positive psychology has already established itself as a multidisciplinary field. From information technology, through to health, environmental sciences, and education. So, the third wave broadens its perspective towards multidisciplinary and multi-methodological approaches to research. It encourages interdisciplinary collaboration within positive psychology, drawing insights from systems theory, complexity science, sociology, and ecology. This interdisciplinary approach enriches our understanding of wellbeing and informs more holistic interventions.

The paper also offers some practical implications for researchers, practitioners, and policymakers involved in positive psychology. By broadening the scope of inquiry and incorporating complexity into their work, individuals in these roles can contribute to developing more effective interventions and policies to promote human flourishing. Overall, Lomas et al. (2021) contribute significantly to the field of positive psychology by introducing the concept of third wave positive psychology and advocating for a broader, more nuanced understanding of wellbeing that considers complexity, cultural sensitivity, and interdisciplinary collaboration.

References

Lomas, T., Waters, L., Williams, P., Oades, L. G., & Kern, M. L. (2021). Third wave positive psychology: Broadening towards complexity. *The Journal of Positive Psychology*, *16*(5), 660–674. https://doi.org/10.1080/17439760.2020.1805501

Beyond the third wave

Positive psychology continues to change, and as we explore the latest developments in the field alongside the world crises that require our attention, new waves continue to emerge. For example, at the 11th European Conference on Positive Psychology in Innsbruck, Austria, Judith Mangelsdorf from the German University of Health and Sports in Berlin discussed the emergence of the fourth wave of positive psychology called "globality". It aims to use the science of positive psychology to address the pressing global challenges such as climate change, water shortages, and other United Nations Sustainable Development Goals (SDGs). Mangelsdorf urged researchers to pivot their research agendas towards developing SDGs while recognising that more research is being conducted to address it.

However, other researchers offer an alternative scope for the fourth wave of positive psychology. For example, Tim Lomas from the University of Harvard, USA, in an article that explored the historical perspectives and the evolution of wellbeing scholarship, argues that the fourth wave that is currently emerging brings together culturally distinct concepts of wellbeing. That fusion creates a globally inclusive conceptualisation of wellbeing.

In contrast, Marie Wissing from the North-west University Potchefstroom, South Africa, called for the fourth wave that transcends positive psychology beyond the traditional boundaries of psychology. She argues that the field of positive psychology has changed to such an extent that positive psychology is no longer merely a subdiscipline of psychology. The old approaches in positive psychology focused primarily on individual wellbeing and explored it within specific contexts. However, the new post-disciplinary field that goes beyond the third wave adopts a transdisciplinary approach that considers the wellbeing of broader systems, including ecological and non-human systems. The author suggests that, subsequently, the field could use names such as "Planetary wellbeing" to incorporate the wellbeing of individuals, their immediate environment, and the entire planet. She identifies two parallel trajectories of wellbeing studies.

1. **Mainstream Positive Psychology** would explore wellbeing and processes with the established frameworks.
2. **Post-disciplinary Wellbeing Studies** would highlight balance, interconnectedness, coherence, and harmony across various systems (individual, collective,

ecological). They would also consider values, metatheoretical assumptions, and integrative theories such as Aristotelian virtue ethics.

While the researchers cannot agree as to what waves come beyond the third wave of positive psychology, one thing they have in common is that they acknowledge that we are on a cusp of the field expanding beyond anyone's imagination. Positive psychology has impacted not only the American Psychological Association or the field of psychology as usual, but it merged into other disciplines and transformed them beyond recognition.

References

Lomas, T. (2022). Making waves in the great ocean: A historical perspective on the emergence and evolution of wellbeing scholarship. *The Journal of Positive Psychology*, *17*(2), 257–270. https://doi.org/10.1080/17439760.2021.2016900

Wissing, M. P. (2022). Beyond the "Third wave of positive psychology": Challenges and opportunities for future research. *Frontiers in Psychology*, *12*, 795067. https://doi.org/10.3389/fpsyg.2021.795067

The scope of positive psychology

Expanding field

I remember the early days when I had to explain positive psychology to people. Even psychologists in related fields had limited knowledge about it. They often asked me, "What's the point of it?", and I used to quote single database searches demonstrating the imbalance in how we conceptualise wellbeing, such as the difference between research on depression and happiness or mental health versus mental illness. However, one key aspect missing in this conversation was a more comprehensive evidence of the spread of positive psychology research across various fields, a gap that Reuben Rusk and Lea Waters from the University of Melbourne, Australia, addressed in this article.

Having explored over 1.7 million articles in the fields of psychology, psychiatry, neuroscience, management, business, public health, and sports science, the researchers identified over 18,000 articles that fit into the remit of positive psychology. They used a technique that included two approaches. One was a co-word analysis, which is the analysis of the occurrence of some of the keywords in a text alongside the relationships and interactions between similar topics, and the other one was a bibliographic coupling, which happens when two documents cite a joint third document. This method produced findings about the extent of positive psychology compared over the years, from 1992 until 2011.

The results were striking. Just over a decade after the official launch of positive psychology, its impact was more significant than articles in some of the more established fields. Also, within a range of fields impacted by positive psychology, the growth of this new perspective on human beings was astounding. For example, in 1996, barely 1.25% of management articles were within the positive psychology remit. By 2011, they increased eightfold to 10.98%. Similarly, in applied psychology, barely 2.68 articles explored the applications of positive psychological concepts, whereas, in 2011, the positive articles increased by 13.95%. Similar trends were shown in social psychology, business, education, and social sciences.

Despite its significant expansion in many research fields, positive psychology lagged in other areas. For example, in neuroscience, significantly more articles were published about dementia and other brain disorders than about exploring the healthy brain. Similarly, public health, psychiatry, and developmental research saw minimal growth in articles. This analysis was conducted a long time ago, so hopefully, these fields have seen a spurt in development. Still, the impact of these findings continues to serve as a foundational basis for further expansion of the field.

As a practitioner applying positive psychology in education and the workplace, I found that this paper was a compelling example of how little we knew about what was right with people, their experiences, and the outcomes of their actions. While it's easy to focus on negative outcomes of our experiences, if we were to continue doing it, we would not be able to tap into what Carl Rogers described as self-discovery and the development of the whole person.

In essence, this article highlights the progress of the field of positive psychology in research and practice. However, it is also a call for action to continue exploring more positive aspects of human experience. The more we understand the optimal human functioning and positive aspects of our lives, the more we can support people in living their best possible lives.

References

Rusk, R. D., & Waters, L. E. (2013). Tracing the size, reach, impact, and breadth of positive psychology. *The Journal of Positive Psychology*, *8*(3), 207–221. https://doi.org/10.1080/17439760.2013.777766

Universities united

In 2023, something important happened in Vancouver, Canada. Programme leaders of all major universities, offering degrees in positive psychology worldwide, got together to make a collective pledge to make a lasting impact on our current, past, and future students of positive psychology. We committed to developing course content that complement each other so that instead of competing, we would work together. One of the key topics we discussed was the curriculum for positive psychology courses. As we talked, I was reminded of several important papers on this subject, including the one presented next.

Kenneth Hart and Thomas Sasso from the University of Windsor in Canada have mapped the themes that emerged in the first decade of positive psychology research. They explored the most common definitions, which viewed positive psychology as a study of:

- Strengths and positive traits
- The phenomenon of happiness and wellbeing
- The process of growth and fulfilment
- Involving the good life and life worth living
- Thriving and flourishing
- Optimal human functioning

They have also offered the five themes found in eight US positive psychology course syllabi, which included:

1. Happiness, positive emotions, and subjective wellbeing
2. Interpersonal relationships, forgiveness, and gratitude
3. Virtues and character strengths
4. Resilience
5. Hope, self-efficacy, and perceived control

This article was interesting as it reflected what academics believed should be included in a positive psychology curriculum at the time. It prompted a conversation that continues over a decade later. Since then, several books have been published on how to deliver positive psychology content in an engaging way and which topics should be included in positive psychology programmes worldwide. Hopefully, the "Universities United" group will do fantastic work to improve everyone's educational experience. In the meantime, we continue to learn from articles such as Hart and Sasso, which offer valuable insights into the content of positive psychology courses.

References

Hart, K. E., & Sasso, T. (2011). Mapping the contours of contemporary positive psychology. *Canadian Psychology/Psychologie Canadienne*, *52*(2), 82–92. https://doi.org/10.1037/a0023118

Is positive psychology American?

After a busy day at the International Congress of Positive Psychology in Montreal (Canada), I sat down for a drink with a colleague from the UK to catch up after not seeing her in person for a year. Soon, we were joined by a Canadian colleague asking how we enjoyed the conference, and then colleagues from the US and Mexico joined us to say "hi". Before the night ended, I realised that I had chatted with colleagues from 6 continents in 3 hours while I was chilling out after the conference, and was amazed at how international positive psychology has become.

For years, positive psychology has been seen as a North American phenomenon that expanded worldwide. Critics have often argued that the rest of the world was learning about wellbeing from American ideals rooted in misconstrued notions of success and happiness. As a result, the field has sometimes been dismissed as superficial, unrealistic, and disconnected from genuine daily life experiences. This raises the question of how significantly American researchers versus academics from the rest of the world have influenced the positive psychology field's development. The article by Kim and colleagues (2018) explored the answer to this question.

This study included all articles published from the inception of positive psychology until 2014. It included 863 articles in its review from the initial search of over 2,000. It explored each article's prevalence, characteristics, research topic, and delved into the sample of research participants, what continent they were from, the region, and the country. Given that positive psychology originated in the US, a significant number of articles were published in the US. However, the prevalence of non-US articles was higher, with 52% of papers published by non-US researchers.

The highest publication rate was seen in the UK, followed by the US, Australia, Germany, China, Spain, Israel, South Africa, the Netherlands, Switzerland, Italy, India, Sweden, Japan, Norway, and many other countries. The publications extended across various continents, such as Africa, Asia, and South America. Thus, this article showed that our knowledge of positive psychology is no longer predominantly informed by the US research.

The authors have also identified that while all researchers had some generic interests, such as wellbeing, life satisfaction, and gratitude, there were differences in topic interests across continents. For example, in Asia, researchers were keen on emotional intelligence, resilience, and employability. In Africa, topics related to trauma, coping, and recovery were paid more attention. In the Americas, papers on motivation, moral excellence, and compassion were published. In Europe, papers on engagement, anxiety, and flow were published. In Oceania, interests were leaned more towards coaching, positive youth development, and positive relationships. In the US, topics such as achievement, courage, and organisational commitment were covered. These differentiating interests are interesting reflections on the challenges that each continent might be experiencing.

In addition to the topics, authors, and regions, the researchers in this article have also explored methodological differences in how positive psychology has been researched worldwide. Not surprisingly, it has shown that most research was quantitative, correlational, and focused on individual-level analysis. Specifically, US researchers conducted studies focused on individuals, whereas Asian researchers were more interested in collectivism and group-based research studies. African researchers have presented many qualitative studies, whereas those from Oceania introduced a significant portion of mixed methods research.

Overall, this academic paper is an excellent indication of the expansion of positive psychology worldwide. What is important to note is that due to the inclusion and exclusion criteria applied, it is based on just over 863 articles. While it might not reflect the broader research, seeing this level of positive psychology expansion worldwide is very promising.

References

Kim, H., Doiron, K., Warren, M. A., & Donaldson, S. I. (2018). The international landscape of positive psychology research: A systematic review. *International Journal of Wellbeing*, *8*(1), 50–70. https://doi.org/10.5502/ijw.v8i1.651

A bibliometric analysis

My mum is great at making bigos, a Polish national dish. One day, I made it myself, and it tasted different. It was partially because I didn't follow the recipe, and partially because the ingredients I used were Irish. In cooking, what you put in the pot matters. Including and excluding ingredients will change the dish's taste and enjoyment of food. The same applies to any bibliographic studies. The inclusion and exclusion criteria in any systematic review make a difference in the results.

Previously, we discussed a bibliographic review led by Heejin Kim from Army Medical University, China, which included 863 articles in the review. The Wang and colleague's review, however, included 4,378 articles, a significantly higher number, due to the differences in their methodology. As such, some of their results differed from Kim's paper. For example, they differ about researchers' contributions to positive psychology in various regions. Nonetheless, it confirms that while approximately 40% of articles on positive psychology have been published in the US, the vast majority of research in the field is published outside, such as the UK, Australia, the People's Republic of China, Canada, Spain, the Netherlands, South Africa, Germany, and Israel. All these are the top 10 countries from which the most influential research on positive psychology has been published, highlighting the global nature of this field.

The most cited author in positive psychology is Martin Seligman, which is not surprising given that he founded the positive psychology field. However, regarding the contribution of several publications in the field, Willibald Ruch from the University of Zurich, Switzerland, has produced most of the research articles. They were followed by Jeff Huffman and Christopher Celano from Harvard Medical School, USA, Rene Proyer from Martin-Luther-University Halle-Wittenberg, Germany, Barbara Fredrickson from the University of North Carolina, USA, and Tim Lomas from Harvard University, USA. Therefore, this article provides some of the details about the most prolific researchers in the field and highlights many other continents that are not adequately represented.

Surprisingly, however, Pennsylvania University, where Martin Seligman used to work, is not the most cited institution. Instead, Harvard University is leading with over 100 publications. This is followed by the University of Michigan, then the University of Pennsylvania and the University of Melbourne, which are featured as the most influential universities contributing to positive psychology knowledge.

Finally, the article provides tons of other interesting information about the most influential journals, specific references that are worth exploring, and other topics.

The article is a great way to keep up with the developments in the field and explore new thought leaders in this area. It also highlights the need for ongoing analysis in the field, as it is crucial for understanding the ever-evolving landscape of positive psychology and for uncovering new.

References

Wang, F., Guo, J., & Yang, G. (2023). Study on positive psychology from 1999 to 2021: A bibliometric analysis. *Frontiers in Psychology*, *14*, 1101157. https://doi.org/10.3389/fpsyg.2023.1101157

Critiques of positive psychology

Walk before you run

When positive psychology was first established, Martin Seligman was a man on a mission. At 56, with barely a decade before his retirement, he was determined to develop a field and create lasting impact. His extensive network of academics gave him a decisive advantage, enabling a flurry of activities that happened remarkably quickly. He persuaded Christopher Peterson to take a sabbatical to develop the anti-DSM (Diagnostic and Statistical Manual of Mental Disorders), that is, Values in Action (Character Strengths). He established a Centre for Positive Psychology at the University of Pennsylvania, a hub for collecting positive psychology data from millions worldwide. His first book on happiness became a bestseller, and he secured grants from the Templeton Foundation to support positive psychology research. All this unfolded in the first five years, leading to a whirlwind of activity happening rapidly. This has also become one of the criticisms of positive psychology.

Richard Lazarus, who was Professor Emeritus at the time from the University of California, USA, was one of the first critics of the field and claimed that it started running before it could walk. He mentioned in his article that a handbook of positive psychology was edited before the field was well established, even though the book was a bow towards past psychological research that could fit into the concept of positive psychology. More importantly, he found that positive psychology oversimplified the human experience. He pointed to its neglect of negative emotions and underplaying the importance of stress, suffering, and coping, which are essential aspects of human experience and support us in experiencing the full range of psychological functioning. He argued that the artificial dichotomy of dividing psychology as negative and positive was not helpful, as the experiences are interdependent and should not be studied separately.

Lazarus's critique of positive psychology's focus on happiness is fundamental. The field's emphasis on happiness, a notion developed by the Western world, is not universally shared. By exploring these topics, Lazarus highlighted that Western biases are being disseminated, which may not necessarily add value to others. This critique demonstrated the need for a more culturally inclusive and sensitive approach to positive psychology.

Another critical issue that Lazarus raised was the research methodology used to quantify complex human experiences such as happiness. He questioned their rigour and the lack of longitudinal data that helped researchers understand how positive and negative emotions and experiences have evolved. This understanding is a luxury and a necessity in pursuing a comprehensive understanding of human psychology.

I remember my first year as a PhD scholar when I was stopped in a corridor of the Trinity College Dublin in Ireland by a psychology professor. He asked me to tell him about my Ph.D. I was bright-eyed and bushy-tailed, as positive psychology was a new science and I looked forward to contributing to it. So, I enthusiastically began explaining the topic of my study and what I hoped to achieve over the next three years. The professor listened attentively and asked many questions. The final question he asked me stopped me in my tracks: "Positive psychology seem to offer many benefits, but how do you know it does not harm people?" This question stayed with me for a long time. I spent the rest of my academic career reminding myself of it and doing my best to practise caution when encouraging the application of positive psychology.

Over the years, I have worked with students studying for their dissertations and creating wellbeing interventions or programmes. Sometimes, they resulted in positive outcomes; other times, we saw no difference in experimental groups compared to control groups, and there were also times when we saw a reduction in some aspects of wellbeing in those who engaged in wellbeing interventions. Our responsibility as researchers and practitioners is to exercise caution when reading and acting upon these results. It is crucial to remember people's individual differences and ensure we are not causing harm. This is what Lazarus asked indirectly when writing this article. He cautioned against assumptions and encouraged rigorous research exploration before recommending actions.

As we continue to develop the field of positive psychology research and practice, we must remain mindful of Lazarus's criticisms of walking before we run. Recent systematic reviews highlight the need for more replicable studies within positive psychology and the lack of studies confirming some of the theories all use. Caution is advisable to ensure we do not harm people.

References

Lazarus, R. S. (2003). Target article: Does the positive psychology movement have legs? *Psychological Inquiry*, *14*(2), 93–109. https://doi.org/10.1207/S15327965PLI1402_02

The tyranny of positive thinking

Toxic positivity can be incredibly draining, especially when it is imposed upon you. Years ago, I had a leader who refused to let us "complain", insisting that our negativity brought everyone's spirits down. We were expected always to remain positive, no matter the circumstances. This approach led to low staff morale, dwarfed team development, and took a personal toll on many of us. Ironically, I complained more about working with this leader than ever. The tyranny of positive thinking was exhausting and harmful – this is one of the challenges of positive psychology mentioned by Barbara Held from Bowdoin College in Brunswick, USA, in her article.

Held rehashes similar arguments for critiquing positive psychology as others, which refer to the overemphasis on positive traits and experiences. But one interesting contribution she added to her criticism is the concept of the tyranny of positive thinking. She posited that by emphasising the positive, the negative experiences, states, emotions, or traits were being disregarded. Valuing positive experiences too much could lead to unrealistic and harmful effects, such as those I have mentioned above in my past work experience. This tyranny of positive thinking is about individuals feeling obliged to maintain a positive outlook, not because they feel like this, or are ready to embrace the silver lining, but because it is seen as the right thing to do. It's crucial to strike a balance between positive and negative experiences, as a lack of authenticity in their experiences can further exasperate their stress and result in mental health issues. This balance is not just a theoretical concept, but a practical necessity for maintaining mental wellbeing. It is important to note, as over the years I have heard many people mentioning it as a criticism, yet no positive psychologist I have ever known would encourage this relentless pursuit.

Held's main argument was that too much emphasis was placed in positive psychology on distinguishing positive and negative, or good and bad. For example, she mentioned how positive psychologists disregarded and vilified negative emotions and negative emotional experience in support of positive emotions. She quoted texts from a range of positive psychologists who claimed the adverse impact of negative experiences and the need to explore the contribution of positive experiences. This dichotomous perspective of early positive psychologists could have stemmed from the field trying to differentiate themselves from others. Subsequent developments in the field, such as the second wave of positive psychology, which focused on a more balanced approach to positive and negative experiences, have attempted to put this right. However, Barbara Held remained unconvinced.

Over a decade later, she wrote another article, arguing that despite many researchers' efforts, original dichotomy introduced in the late 1990s persists in the field. She considered the self-proclaimed division between positive and negative an epistemological issue. She explained that "a priori" refers to knowledge not based on experience or empirical evidence. As such we do not require experiencing anything to know that the knowledge is true. On the other hand, "a posteriori" knowledge is based on our experience of the world, or evidence we gain in research to justify our knowledge. For example, a priori knowledge was knowing that a one-year-old child is smaller than an adult. We do not need to see the child to know they are smaller. On the other hand, posteriori knowledge is about knowing that this child can speak 10 words or have red hair or an agreeable personality. We have experienced this by observing a child, hence we have posteriori knowledge of it.

Similarly, Barbara Held argued that positive psychologists make assumptions about concepts being positive or negative a priori, even though they do not have the evidenced knowledge of them: hence whether or not something is positive or negative should be determined postpriori. For example, how can you know if the experience of "pride" is positive or negative until you research the topic thoroughly. Only then you will realise that, in some cases, authentic pride can have a lot of beneficial outcomes, whereas hubristic pride is associated with adverse outcomes. According to Held, labelling a concept as positive or negative before conducting empirical research is unwise. Equally, many emotions considered by psychologists as negative, such as sadness or anger, may have a range of adaptive functions they serve. From this perspective, their outcomes might be deemed "positive" by positive psychologists. This is what led Held to question the essence of the decisions made by positive psychologists as to whether a concept is positive or negative.

This critical perspective on positive psychology is very useful as it helps the field of positive psychology develop. It advocates for more rigorous scientific approach, urging us to explore concepts thoroughly before making decisions about their functionality. This emphasis on rigorous science is not just a call for academic integrity, but a reminder of the ethical obligations we have towards our clients and patients. It also questions the use of the term "positive" within positive psychology, which many original researchers have expressed concern about, wishing the term "positive" would not be used to describe what the field is about, as it misinterprets the field and creates confusion. That said, from the practical perspective, it is always useful to ask yourself *What is the function of what I am experiencing? Is it beneficial to me or not? Does it support me?* Reflecting on these questions allows us to fully embrace our experiences, regardless of their nature.

References

Held, B. S. (2004). The negative side of positive psychology. *Journal of Humanistic Psychology*, *44*(1), 9–46. https://doi.org/10.1177/0022167803259645

Held, B. S. (2018). Positive psychology's a priori problem. *Journal of Humanistic Psychology*, *58*(3), 313–342. https://doi-org.elib.tcd.ie/10.1177/0022167817739409

The systematic review of critiques of positive psychology

Critical thinking is one of the most challenging skills to develop, especially for students completing psychological degrees. Many join programmes as they enjoy studying positive psychology topics, either out of personal interest or due to having people close to them who struggle with wellbeing. Regardless of their motivation, students often accept the knowledge presented in lectures at face value and tend not to practise critical thinking. To help them develop their ability for objective research evaluation, we often encourage them to examine the pros and cons of everything they learn and identify gaps in their knowledge. Exploring the limitations plays a crucial role in developing the field further. This is why a systematic review of such critiques is a great starting point for deeper engagement in positive psychology.

Llewellyn van Zyl from the University of Eindhoven, the Netherlands, and colleagues (2024) explored over 10,000 articles, from which they selected 32 of them detailing 117 unique criticisms and critiques of positive psychology. They grouped them into 21 categories and created six overarching themes. Let's explore each of these themes individually.

1. Positive psychology **lacks proper theorising and conceptual thinking**. The field is not grounded in a metatheory based on philosophical principles, meaning that the way virtues and positivity were conceptualised is inadequate. Furthermore, the concepts are seen as confusing, with different terms being used to describe the same ideas: for example, unclear difference between terms "flourishing" and "wellbeing". Also, there is a clear lack of theoretical underpinnings of positive psychology interventions.
2. **Issues with measurement and methodology** – there is an overemphasis on positivist approaches, assuming that if there is no empirical evidence of something, then the concept does not exist. Furthermore, the research designs are poor, along with measurements of constructs, which are inadequate.
3. Positive psychology **is a pseudoscience with poor replication and lacking evidence** – the challenge of replication of studies exists across the entire psychological field, but it also applies to positive psychology. This criticism related to false claims about the benefits of some concepts and researchers practising a confirmation bias, meaning that they seek out and interpret research in a way that confirms their beliefs, even if there is no empirical evidence for some of these claims.
4. Positive psychology **lacks novelty and self-isolates from mainstream psychology** – critiques around the usefulness of the field and lack of creation of any new models and paradigms. In particular, this criticism relates to positive psychologists using well-established psychological frameworks, such as Cognitive Behavioural Therapy methods, to amplify the impact of positive psychology interventions. Also, the lack of integration with the remaining psychological fields is mentioned, whereby positive psychologists seem to view other fields of psychology as negative. This creates barriers between fields and discourages collaborations.
5. Positive psychology **is a decontextualised Neoliberalist ideology that causes harm** – much of the research is conducted with the WEIRD population (from the Western, Educated, Industrialised, Rich, and Democratic); therefore, the findings are not representative of the diverse population. They also critique its Neoliberalist ideology, which is focused on self-fulfilment, perceived control, or setting up personal goals. Some claim that positive psychology causes more harm than good when normal states and behaviour, for example, grieving is pathologised, and there is significant emphasis on optimism, happiness, and similar wellbeing concepts raising unrealistic expectations. Furthermore, it highlights that often big issues, such as racism, transgender rights, and feminism, are ignored in positive psychology, so it does not add adequate value to what is important in the world.

6. Positive psychology **is often viewed as a capitalistic venture** – it is seen as a field that creates and perpetuates the pursuit of happiness, often feeding the wellbeing industry for individuals to pay for services to live a good life.

Reading these criticisms can be disheartening for some. However, many of them came from a place of concern and dissonance that some academics and practitioners experienced when reading positive psychology texts and reflecting on their personal values and existing knowledge. Some critiques are more valid than others and should be addressed by researchers. From the application viewpoint, it is essential to consider these criticisms and keep an open and balanced mind when working with clients, many of whom may feel the same way. Also, it is crucial to consider the limitations of the research and not make claims of the generalisation of findings if such evidence does not exist. Just because something was effective for a small group of university students does not mean it would work for all clients. By embracing these insights, we can approach the application of positive psychology with greater humility and responsibility in daily life.

References

van Zyl, L. E., Gaffaney, J., van der Vaart, L., Dik, B. J., & Donaldson, S. I. (2024). The critiques and criticisms of positive psychology: A systematic review. *The Journal of Positive Psychology*, *19*(2), 206–235. https://doi-org.elib.tcd.ie/10.1080/17439760.2023.2178956

The complexity of systems

I have recently watched a keynote address delivered by Geoffrey Hinton, endearingly named as the grandfather of Artificial Intelligence (AI). He claimed that AI is dangerous and will soon make human intelligence irrelevant, the same way as the great revolution made human strength irrelevant. This notion of AI's potential danger is not dissimilar to the complexities that exist in the practice of positive psychology, as highlighted by Margaret Kern from the University of Melbourne and colleagues. Both AI and positive psychology involve understanding complex systems and their implications. Hinton illustrated the danger of AI with an example showing that when working with three neurons, we can easily examine their action and reaction and draw conclusions as to why they behave the way they do. However, whenever they are mixed up, they begin to impact each other on such a scale that it is impossible to clearly pinpoint their cause and effect.

Similarly, Kern and colleagues' article highlighted the complexities involved in the practice of positive psychology. It encouraged the researchers to explore these intricacies to understand the mechanisms for their effectiveness better. They provided an example of a child who was bullied and, as a result, began misbehaving at school. In response, the teacher spent more time with them, unintentionally neglecting the needs of others. This led to other students' resentment and exasperating bullying. This example illustrated how every action triggers a reaction, making events interconnected and hard to isolate from each other. Understanding these complexities is crucial for improving the practice and effectiveness of positive psychology.

The authors have created a model of "systems-informed positive psychology". This approach considers the interconnectedness of various elements within a system and how they influence each other. It comprises a shared purpose of systems' elements facilitating and cultivating the wellbeing co-evolution and positive functions. It explores the systems principles upon which it is based, including boundaries that determine what is included in the research enquiry or practice, and the varied perspectives that people have on their experiences of the system. It considers the system evolving itself and the need for the system to constantly adapt and the new concepts coming up as a result of this adaptation. Finally, the self-organisation aspect of the system refers to the system's ability to make sense of the parts of each element and come together as one. These system principles are based on the notion that each element of the system interacts with other elements, creating a new reality.

In addition to the principles, the assumptions and commitments guide the system's evolution. The authors have identified three main assumptions relating to epistemology (the theory of knowledge), politics, and ethics. They have made assumptions on behalf of the field and argued that they guide the research and practice of positive psychology. Differences may be noted between individuals or organisations engaging in positive psychology practice. However, the overall argument of the assumptions about positive psychology comes from researchers' and practitioners' generic approaches.

The authors believe that system-informed positive psychology has significant implications for practice. They mention nine such benefits. These include the practices that make people aware of how systems work – for example, reflections on exploring various perspectives that can facilitate the development of diversity appreciation. Also, practitioners need to explore how systems impact them and their systems. This needs to be conducted at a greater level than immediate groups. For example, when working with clients in a workplace, the interventions that individuals practise will be influenced by their workplace team, organisational values, and other social groups in their lives, such as friends or community. These are just a few examples of how the systems must be considered.

In summary, the whole is much greater than its parts. Therefore, the system within positive psychology can be perceived as a strength within social networks that can support and amplify wellbeing rather than a nuisance that makes interventions too complicated to use. Just as systemic interactions can lead to unintended negative consequences, they can create meaningful and positive change. While navigating these complexities may be challenging, it is crucial to consider them when applying positive psychology in daily life.

References

Kern, M. L., Williams, P., Spong, C., Colla, R., Sharma, K., Downie, A., Taylor, J. A., Sharp, S., Siokou, C., & Oades, L. G. (2019). Systems informed positive psychology. *The*

Journal of Positive Psychology, *15*(6), 705–715. https://doi-org.elib.tcd.ie/10.1080/17439760.2019.1639799

Diversity and inclusion in positive psychology

How WEIRD are positive psychology interventions?

When I worked at the University of East London, I had the privilege of engaging with students worldwide. I will never forget this one particular online seminar on wellbeing. During a discussion, one of the students from Zimbabwe commented that the positive psychological concept of wellbeing differs significantly from how it is understood in her country. Curious, I invited her to share with us her perspective on wellbeing. This sparked a lively discussion during which we explored diverse wellbeing views with students from China, New Zealand, and other places. This was one of the most engaging seminars I had the pleasure of facilitating, and it made me realise how elitist and narrowly focused positive psychology can be if it is not carefully contextualised.

Tom Hendriks, a psychology professor at the Anton de Kom University of Suriname in Suriname, led a team (2018) that conducted a bibliometric analysis of randomised controlled trials on the science of wellbeing. They examined whether the positive psychology research reached beyond the WEIRD populations, an acronym for White, Educated, Industrialised, Rich, and Democratic population. They explored research from 1998 until 2017 and found studies from merely 24 countries. Their analysis showed that 78.2% of randomised controlled trials, with over 34,000 participants, were from WEIRD populations. This means that when applying some of the findings from positive psychology and working with multicultural groups, the findings might not be relevant to them. Their findings highlight the urgent need to expand on positive psychological research across more diverse populations.

Since 2012, there has been a noticeable increase in articles that extends beyond the WEIRD populations, and this trend is expected to continue. The authors propose that further research is necessary to culturally adapt positive psychology interventions and key concepts. It is crucial that we continue to tweak and test these interventions using methods best suited for each population. Expanding research on existing interventions beyond WEIRD populations will provide valuable insights into their effectiveness across diverse cultural contexts. This is an important consideration for practitioners, given the multicultural world we live in.

References

Hendriks, T., Warren, M. A., Schotanus-Dijkstra, M., Hassankhan, A., Graafsma, T., Bohlmeijer, E., & de Jong, J. (2018). How WEIRD are positive psychology interventions? A bibliometric analysis of randomized controlled trials on the science of well-being. *The Journal of Positive Psychology*, *14*(4), 489–501. https://doi.org/10.1080/17439760.2018.1484941

Ethnocentrism and the ideology of individualism

I am European – my genetic tests show I am over 97% Slavic. I was raised in an individualistic ideology, so positive psychology research speaks to me loud and clear. From a young age, I was taught the values of self-determination and personal responsibility. I believed that if I worked hard and studied, I could make my dreams come true. Coming from a post-Soviet culture in which our liberties have been suppressed for decades, I strongly believe in the idea that individuals have fundamental rights, such as freedom of speech or the right to privacy. Individuals also make a difference in the community, so they must choose their actions wisely.

At the same time, one of my friend's family was culturally mixed, with one parent from Europe and one from Asia. Therefore, he was exposed to a collectivist culture apart from the individualistic culture during his childhood, which have shaped his values and behaviour. I always learn so much when chatting with him about his worldviews, as he is somewhere on a scale between the collectivist need for harmony and an individual's authentic pursuits. At times, our choices differ, influenced by the cultural values ingrained in us since childhood. This is why it is important to remember that our early experiences and ongoing life journey shape how we see the world.

According to Christopher and Hickinbottom (2008), positive psychology is deeply rooted in a Western ideology of ethnocentric individualism, a perspective that can have significant negative consequences. This approach inadvertently promotes the idea of an individual isolated from others, thereby undermining social connections and collective wellbeing. It disregards social contexts, potentially leading to individuals' isolation. The emphasis on personal success and the responsibility placed on individuals to achieve it could backfire when they are unable to meet these "ideal" goals. Individualism can also exacerbate social inequality, as it often overlooks factors such as poverty, discrimination, or unequal access to resources, which play a significant role in achieving success. Subsequently, individuals are often considered without the contextual factors that impact them.

This article is an exciting read that can help us reflect on the impact of some positive psychology messages shared with others. The ideology of individualism can have a significantly negative impact on people. Hence, cultural backgrounds need to be taken into consideration by practitioners. Positive psychology should be reframed to embrace a broader, culturally inclusive understanding of wellbeing that incorporates individual and collective wellbeing. We need to become less ethnocentric and more attuned to diverse cultural values. This is particularly important when working with diverse communities. Wellbeing is not a one-size-fits-all approach. Instead, it is shaped by individual and collective pursuits and values. Thus, we must consider our assumptions behind the approaches we use for enhancing wellbeing to adopt a more holistic, culturally sensitive perspective.

References

Christopher, J. C., & Hickinbottom, S. (2008). Positive psychology, ethnocentrism, and the disguised ideology of individualism. *Theory & Psychology*, *18*(5), 563–589. https://doi.org/10.1177/0959354308093396

Beyond the WEIRD population

Robert Biswas-Diener is widely known as the Indiana Jones of positive psychology. He loves travelling, and especially in the early stage of his career, he has conducted some unique studies with individuals from different cultures and fed this information into the field of positive psychology to enrich its perspective. One such study was conducted with 83 residents of Calcutta (Biswas-Diener & Diener, 2001). Some of them lived in slum housing, while others were sex workers or lived on the street. They were interviewed and completed the assessment of life satisfaction. While their wellbeing was lower than that of more affluent participants, their life satisfaction was not as low as expected. Despite their financial situation, they were satisfied with themselves – for example, their morality or physical appearance. They also had a robust social connection, which added to their satisfaction; these included close connections with romantic partners, family, and friends. In summary, this study showed that the Western perception of people living in poverty being unhappy does not hold in this case.

Another study led by Robert Biswas Diener (2005) was conducted with Kenyan Maasai, the United States Amish, and the Greenlandic Inughuit and showed many differences between cultures regarding wellbeing. On average, all the cultures reported moderate levels of wellbeing (life satisfaction and emotional balance). However, despite having fewer material possessions and resources, the Maasai displayed higher regard for their cultural identity, boosting their wellbeing. Cultural norms have also influenced how participants reported emotions, such as pride. The Amish emphasised humility, whereas the Inughuit downplayed their achievement and reported lower price levels. Thus, even though their wellbeing was similar, each culture had its pathway for reaching a state of wellbeing.

These studies highlight the importance of expanding wellbeing research in the multicultural context. Biswas-Diener's work with diverse cultural groups demonstrates that cultural factors impact how individuals experience and report wellbeing. Learning about the pathways they take to gain or maintain their wellbeing is a concept worthy of exploration. Wellbeing is not necessarily a universal experience that means the same thing to everyone. It is essential to conduct further research across diverse cultural settings to develop a more comprehensive understanding of wellbeing. Such studies will enrich the field of positive psychology by exploring alternative pathways to wellbeing and challenging assumptions based on Western-centric models.

References

Biswas-Diener, R., & Diener, E. (2001). Making the best of a bad situation: Satisfaction in the slums of Calcutta. *Social Indicators Research*, *55*(3), 329. https://doi-org.elib.tcd.ie/10.1023/A:1010905029386

Biswas-Diener, R., Vittersø, J., & Diener, E. (2005). Most people are pretty happy, but there is cultural variation: The Inughuit, The Amish, and The Maasai. *Journal of Happiness Studies*, *6*(3), 205–226. https://doi-org.elib.tcd.ie/10.1007/s10902-005-5683-8

Multiculturalism in positive psychology education

A cohort of positive psychologists argue that positive psychology is universal and, thus, can be used across cultures. For example, several articles have been published over the years demonstrating the universality of character strengths or happiness as a multicultural value. Others argue that while some concepts may be universal, how they are expressed differs. For example, in an individualistic culture, wellbeing interventions may be directed towards the self, whereas in a collective culture, they could be directed towards a group to improve the community cohesion. Yet some see apparent differences in how various cultures view positive psychology concepts.

The integration of multiculturalism in the field of positive psychology, particularly through education, is of paramount importance. By introducing multicultural concepts early in their studies, scholars can develop a broader perspective on wellbeing and associated topics. This was exactly the focus of an article written by Jeniffer Pedrotti from CalPoly, USA, which provides positive psychology scholars with practical strategies for acknowledging and incorporating multiculturalism in their research and practice.

First, the author argues that it is helpful to introduce the concept of multiculturalism at the beginning of the course so that students will have it in the back of their minds as they learn about positive psychology. This way, when they read about forgiveness, they will ask themselves what forgiveness looks like in other cultures, not only from the Western perspective. For example, in an individualistic culture, people are often focused on self-reflection and its impact on the self, whereas in a collectivist culture, forgiveness is interdependent with a focus on the impact on others. When reading academic papers, they will be more inclined to check the participants' cultural backgrounds to consider their perspectives. Even more importantly, if they are from a different culture, they will be more likely to consider the differences between what they read vis-à-vis their view of the world. For example, spirituality may be more important in their culture than others, as this reflection may be a foundation for how they practise wellbeing. Making students sensitive to the multicultural perspective can help them incorporate those differences into their knowledge and practice more efficiently.

Even though we often think of race when considering multiculturalism, the concept is significantly broader than this. For example, Hays (2008) created an ADDRESSING framework that explores the multifaceted approaches from cultural perspectives. This is an acronym which stands for Age, Disability (acquired), Disability (developmental), Religion, Ethnicity, Sexual orientation, Socio-economic status, Indigenous heritage, Nation of origin, and Gender. These differentiating factors may impact how we perceive wellbeing. We may reflect on the strengths of each one of these perspectives that can add value to the multicultural approach.

Developing critical thinking skills is a key objective of positive psychology education. This includes the ability to identify and challenge existing worldviews, particularly those related to positive psychology concepts or measures that may not be universally applicable. It is crucial to approach these one-dimensional perspectives with caution and a willingness to consider alternative viewpoints that are more in line with multicultural thinking.

According to Pedrotti (2011), another way to foster inclusivity in positive psychology classrooms is by exploring culturally relevant strengths. In some cultures, specific strengths are valued more than others. By becoming aware of these distinctions, we can reach closer to the various cultural perspectives by practising these strengths with this cultural perspective in mind. This can help us develop a deeper understanding of what it means to, for example, be more spiritual to be closer to an African tribe's way of thinking or practise thinking in collectivism to be closer to the Asian cultural views. This approach, with its emphasis on multicultural thinking, not only enhances wellbeing but also empowers us to foster inclusivity, promoting empathy and open-mindedness.

References

Hays, P. A. (2008). *Addressing cultural competencies in practice: Assessment, diagnosis, and therapy* (2nd ed.). American Psychological Association.

Pedrotti, J. T. (2011). Broadening perspectives: Strategies to infuse multiculturalism into a positive psychology course. *The Journal of Positive Psychology*, *6*(6), 506–513. https://doi.org/10.1080/17439760.2011.634817

Pursuit of happiness across cultures

After *Outliers* was published, Malcolm Gladwell's 10,000-hour theory became a major topic of conversation. In his book, he cited research suggesting that some prodigies had reached an average of 10,000 hours of practice by age 20. This oversimplified interpretation of research sparked a heated debate, with many researchers trying to debunk this theory. Subsequently, Gladwell published a follow-up book in which he updated his thinking about it. However, given that the original book came out around the same time as Carol Dweck's growth mindset research, which emphasized the benefits of believing that individual's abilities are not innate, but can be improved through effort, readers were getting a consistent message from different sources reinforcing the idea that by putting effort into something, regardless of your talent, you can become an expert.

When I first read Gladwell's book, I was puzzled by it. How did they test it? – I wondered. The most puzzling fact for me about the role of the predisposition to something in developing expertise. Predisposition is an individual's inherent tendency towards a particular activity, behaviour, state, or outcome. For example, my geophysical coordination is terrible, and I often bump into objects. While I love dancing freestyle, I struggle to follow steps and learn routines. I wondered if, regardless of my predisposition to dancing, or lack thereof, I could become an expert if I put in 10,000 hours. I was doubtful about that, but at the same time, I wanted to believe it in the context of positive psychology research.

I figured that if I put more hours into studying and thinking about positive psychology, I might someday become an expert and perhaps even write a book about it.

The idea excited me. I shared this with my cousin, for whom the 10,000 hours had the opposite effect. She loved photography, but the idea of putting 10,000 hours into it to become an expert got her so demotivated she quit her hobby for a few months. So, we both received the same information, filtered it through our attitudes and beliefs, and came up with the opposite outcomes. This is what the article led by Brett Ford from the University of Toronto, Canada, is all about, except they discuss the impact of the pursuit of happiness on people with a different cultural background.

Building on the research led by Iris Mauss et al. (2011, 2012) from the University of California, USA, which showed that the pursuit of happiness can be detrimental to wellbeing, a study was conducted across the US, Germany, Russia, and East Asia. The researchers confirmed that while the pursuit of happiness in individualistic cultures resulted in decreased wellbeing, it had the opposite effect when applied in collectivist culture. This research highlighted the need for replicating studies across various cultures to understand the impact of positive psychology research on wellbeing.

Furthermore, the results showed openness to pursuing socially engaged ways in collectivist cultures. These included interventions that encouraged to connect with others or had social interaction at the centre of this intervention. In an individualistic culture, however, such motivation was insignificant. So, it is not only about the pursuit of happiness that has different impact on wellbeing, but our culture influences the type of interventions we are interested in pursuing to improve our wellbeing.

These cultural distinctions are crucial when designing research or applying positive psychology in real life. All the studies we read, or evidence-based advice we are given, are filtered through our systems of beliefs, values, attitudes, and habitual behaviour. Just as the idea of 10,000 hours motivated one person and demotivated another, so are the chances of experiencing different outcomes when we practice the same interventions. The effect of interventions varies even more across cultures.

This article highlights the urgent need in positive psychology to embrace approaches to wellbeing from various cultures. It is equally important to evaluate the impact of interventions developed in one culture on people in another. Treating positive psychology interventions as universal would be unwise. What is important is that we follow the famous Latin phrase "Primum non nocere", translated into English as "First, do no harm", when recommending any positive psychological tools. Remembering this when applying research in practice will prevent us from negatively impacting others.

References

Ford, B. Q., Dmitrieva, J. O., Heller, D., Chentsova-Dutton, Y., Grossmann, I., Tamir, M., Uchida, Y., Koopmann-Holm, B., Floerke, V. A., Uhrig, M., Bokhan, T., & Mauss, I. B. (2015). Culture shapes whether the pursuit of happiness predicts higher or lower well-being. *Journal of Experimental Psychology. General*, *144*(6), 1053–1062. https://doi.org.elib.tcd.ie/10.1037/xge0000108

Mauss, I. B., Savino, N. S., Anderson, C. L., Weisbuch, M., Tamir, M., & Laudenslager, M. L. (2012). The pursuit of happiness can be lonely. *Emotion (Washington, D.C.)*, *12*(5), 908–912. https://doi.org/10.1037/a0025299

Mauss, I. B., Tamir, M., Anderson, C. L., & Savino, N. S. (2011). Can seeking happiness make people happy? Paradoxical effects of valuing happiness. *Emotion (Washington, D.C.)*, *11*(4), 807. https://doi.org/10.1037/a0022010

Wellbeing worldwide

How similar are hedonic and eudaimonic approaches to wellbeing? While both concepts stem from the translation of philosophy into psychological sciences, the ongoing debate on their similarities and differences persists. The article by Disabato and colleagues (2016), stands out for its unique approach. It delves into these differences using a large, multicultural sample, a distinctive feature that sets it apart from others' research in the field.

Their study was conducted with over 7,000 participants from seven regions around the world: Oceania (e.g. New Zealand, Australia), Anglo nations and Northern Europe (e.g. Ireland, the UK, the US), Former USSR and Eastern Europe (e.g. Hungary, Russia), Southern Europe (e.g. Germany, Greece, Spain), Latin America (e.g. Mexico, Columbia), East and South Asia (e.g. China, India), and Southeast Asia (e.g. Philippines, Malaysia). The researchers found that the way each one of these nations scored on the assessments of eudaimonic wellbeing was similar, thus demonstrating no specific differences between nations. The only difference was that some nations' correlation between the two concepts was slightly different.

I can see the two sides of the argument about multicultural wellbeing. While certain universal concepts of wellbeing may be shared across cultures – regardless of where we live, our identity, or our background – our values often differ. Subsequently, the importance of some of the components of wellbeing may vary from person to person. For example, what one person or society values may not be necessarily be a value to another and vice versa. This is why it is crucial to consider the components of wellbeing in the context of how they play out vis-à-vis societal values.

Also, how we express those universal components matters. For example, for some, spirituality could be closely associated with their religious beliefs; for others, it could be detached from structured religion. In this case, both individuals might score highly on the spirituality scale, but their expression of spirituality could be different. That said, how spirituality or other concepts in wellbeing are measured could also impact whether someone is deemed spiritual. Even though the surveys showed no significant differences between the countries, language differences may exist.

For example, I have been recently discussing a translation of a depression scale with one of my PhD scholars, Laura Elsner, who is conducting research based on longitudinal data in Lichtenstein. The translation of the word "happy" that was used in the German scale was "freundlich" as opposed to "glücklich" – both words with similar meanings yet distinct features. The skill of a translator and the validation process help people understand positive psychology concepts. At the same time, the nuances of our understanding will continue to make studying positive psychology within a diverse community much more exciting.

References

Disabato, D. J., Goodman, F. R., Kashdan, T. B., Short, J. L., & Jarden, A. (2016). Different types of well-being? A cross-cultural examination of hedonic and eudaimonic well-being. *Psychological Assessment*, *28*(5), 471–482. https://doi.org/10.1037/pas0000209

Big issues in positive psychology

Covid-19

The Covid-19 pandemic was one of the most shocking experiences of our generation. I will never forget the uncertainty caused by the virus and all its variants, the trauma of seeing millions of people dying each day, the unpredictability of deaths, the inability to meet our family and friends, the loneliness of some people, and the vulnerability of those who were unwell and unable to look after themselves. I will remember how our freedoms were restricted, how our children were brought up looking at masked-up teachers, how schools and workplaces were closed down for many months, how the millions of people were losing their jobs, how the business they worked so hard to grow was affected, and their lives were gone as they knew them. But apart from the trauma and hardship, it was also a time of profound hope and unwavering solidarity, a time of kindness and love that gave us optimism for the future.

Lea Waters, from the University of Melbourne, has delved into the research that sheds light on the pandemic's positive psychology angle. Her work and that of her colleagues have provided valuable insights into the resilience and hope that have emerged during this challenging time. The authors concluded that positive traits and experiences, such as life meaning, effective coping, self-compassion, courage, gratitude, character strengths, positive emotions, positive interpersonal experiences, and high-quality connections, have buffered people against hardship. This positive psychology has not only protected them against further adversity during Covid-19 but also instilled a sense of hope and optimism for the future.

It's essential to recognise that it was not just the circumstances, but our own positive qualities, that bolstered and built mental health during Covid-19. Individuals who used effective coping skills, compassion, or their character strengths have built their resources further and have grown personally. This highlights the role of each individual in fostering resilience and hope, making the pandemic not just a hard time, but also a time of personal growth and optimism for some.

References

Waters, L., Algoe, S. B., Dutton, J., Emmons, R., Fredrickson, B. L., Heaphy, E., Moskowitz, J. T., Neff, K., Niemiec, R., Pury, C., & Steger, M. (2021). Positive psychology in a pandemic: Buffering, bolstering, and building mental health. *The Journal of Positive Psychology*, *17*(3), 303–323. https://doi.org/10.1080/17439760.2021.1871945

Climate change

As I write these words in the tranquillity of my home, the world outside is imploding. Nearly half of the global population is grappling with poverty. The relentless march of global warming is unleashing unprecedented natural disasters, claiming the lives of hundreds of thousands annually. Wars are spreading like wildfire, robbing adults and children of their right to life. What is worse, over 3 million lives are lost each year to drugs and other substances. The most distressing part is that these crises show no signs of abating as they worsen each year.

When the war in Ukraine began, I felt a strong urge to write an article for *the Conversation,* an online platform where academics share research in an accessible way, to give all the displaced Ukrainians hope. I thought about it for days, my days turned into weeks, and I could not find the words. No words or research seemed adequate to share without sounding patronising and demanding. This is when I realised the limitations of positive psychology and the potential harm of toxic positivity while some people are in the throes of the worst trauma of their lives.

Michael Steger (2024) from Colorado State University did what I could not. His focus on the climate and environmental crisis is a cry for us not to be mere spectators but to use our knowledge to support meaningful action. He begins his article by posing an important question: Has the world truly improved since the birth of positive psychology in 1998? Then, he asks another question: How can we amplify this impact? This shift in perspective enlightened a pathway towards what he calls regenerative positive psychology, which could inspire meaningful change that extends beyond an individual.

The author mentions a range of crises people experience, such as income inequality, gender inequality, or diminishing trust. However, the one area he focuses on is climate change, with high CO_2 emissions, fossil carbon emissions, rising global temperatures, outdoor air pollution deaths, deforestation, and many other significant issues. He argues that positive psychology research is so focused on an individual that it does not consider the context, such as climate change. This individualistic perspective makes people consider only their lot while ignoring the imploding world around them. It also makes them use the resources around them for their benefit without considering how they deplete them. This is why he calls for researchers to instigate change.

Steger introduces the concept of regenerative positive psychology that takes the attention away from destroying resources and systems that sustain life and instead focuses on increasing the capacities of these systems. He presents three pillars of this approach:

1. He encourages positive psychologists to explore not only the wellbeing of individuals and their social or organisational context but also the wellbeing of all living systems that support them in sustaining life.
2. He encourages positive psychologists to begin research and education to develop resources that address the social, political, and environmental systems that benefit the planet and other systems.
3. He encourages positive psychologists to develop research, education, and interventions that help people improve the collective wellbeing that supports the entire system.

By focusing on helping the planet and the greater causes and spending less time focusing on ourselves, we could not only shift the wellbeing of individuals but also make the planet a better place.

In my recent book (Burke et al., 2024), co-authored with colleagues who specialise in environmental psychology and other sciences, we explored practical ways in which positive psychology can be used to improve the environment.

We examined recent studies that provide preliminary evidence of how happiness increases our chances of doing well for the environment. Additionally, we have explored the opposite, how looking after the environment can boost many aspects of our wellbeing. Thus, while the combination of climate change and positive psychology is new, it offers exciting alternative pathways for boosting wellbeing.

References

Burke, J., Clarke, D., O'Keeffe, J., & Corrigan, S. (2024). *Positive psychology and biodiversity conservation: Health, wellbeing and pro-environmental action*. Routledge.

Steger, M. F. (2024). Regenerative positive psychology: A call to reorient wellbeing science to meet the realities of our world. *The Journal of Positive Psychology*, 1–24. https://doi.org/10.1080/17439760.2024.2365259

Bullying

According to the World Health Organisation (WHO), suicide is the third leading cause of death among adolescents. When bullied, young people are nine times more likely to consider suicide or attempt it. This alarming statistic highlights the urgent need for proactive measures to prevent bullying and safeguard our youth, urging us to act swiftly and decisively. The widespread use of social media by young people may not only contribute to bullying but also exacerbate mental health issues, highlighting the importance of prevention.

To address this big issue, Jonathan Haidt from New York University, USA, has recently published a book about the "Anxious Generation", a term he uses to describe the current generation of young people who are experiencing unprecedented levels of anxiety and depression. He quotes statistics on the detrimental impact of social media and access to digital devices on young people's health, with cyberbullying being a significant contributor to this trend. Haidt emphasises the crucial role of governments and parents in taking combined action to reduce the prevalence of anxiety and depression by removing phones from young people's lives.

While Jonathan Haidt's suggestion of banning social media among youth is one way to resolve societal issues, we call for developing young people's character strengths to protect them against bullying. My colleague Conor Mc Guckin from Trinity College Dublin and I have conducted research with almost 3,000 young people aged 12–20 and found that a range of character strengths, such as love, forgiveness, or kindness, were associated with non-aggressive behaviours online and offline. We hoped that discovering such strengths could help us figure out how to help young people develop these strengths to create a forcefield around themselves, shielding them from aggression.

To our surprise, we have found one character strength in particular that all non-aggressive children had in common. Non-aggressive children were defined as those who did not use violence (bullying) nor were the recipients of violence (targets of bullying), be it online or in person. That one strength they all had in common was prudence. Prudence is a trait that helps young people make wise choices. It slows down the process between an action and its reaction. It allows them to consider the consequences of their behaviour and make careful choices. Prudent children do not take unnecessary risks as they avoid doing anything they might regret later. This lack of impulsivity shields them from becoming either the victims of bullying or the bullies, a fascinating finding in our research.

We were very encouraged by these results, and given the prevalence of cyberbullying, we have recently received funding from the Irish Teachers' Council to explore this topic further. My colleague Joan Finley from the University of Limerick and I have developed a 4-week Prudence programme for young people in post-primary schools. Young people learn how to slow down their decision-making and consider consequences. The programme explains what prudence is (driven by what is the right thing to do) and how it differs from self-control (the ability to regulate our urges regardless of whether we consider them moral). This programme aims to improve their strength of prudence and wellbeing and, most importantly, equip them with the skills and mindset to avoid engaging in or being affected by cyberbullying. We cannot wait for the results of our experiment, which should be available in a few months.

References

Burke, J., & Mc Guckin, C. (2022). Bullying and character development: An examination of character strengths associated with bullying and cyberbullying in post-primary schools in Ireland. *Journal of Character Education*, *18*(1), 51–67.

Prejudice

I am Polish, yet I have lived in Ireland most of my life. I find Irish people incredibly open, inclusive, and welcoming. In all my years of living here, I have never been subject to discrimination – until recently. Around the time when Europe was swept by the right-wing ideology with its anti-immigration movement, for a brief moment, I saw violence on the streets of Dublin. Incited by the crowds, people who had been silent for years began to find their voices, and they not only shared their views, but shouted them out loud. Once the floodgates opened, it all came out indiscriminately.

Around that time, while driving out of a car park, I saw a driver pulling out right in front of me. I beeped to let him know I was there and slammed on my brakes to avoid a collision. I let him out before me. When we met again at the barrier, he opened a window and began yelling at me. I explained that I beeped at him to warn him – it was not an act of aggression. When he heard my accent, he swore at me and told me to return to my home country.

In all my years of living abroad, this was the first time someone said something like this to me. I was so astounded by his reaction that I laughed out loud – it was almost a reflex to cope with the shock of prejudice. He sat silent, not knowing what to say – it was not the reaction he had expected from me. After all, prejudice is not a laughing matter.

In an article led by Christopher Sanders et al. (2023) from the University of Missouri, USA, the researchers discussed ways in which positive psychology can assist in tackling the significant issues of discrimination, stereotyping, and prejudice. They draw on the research showing that the targets of prejudice often show lower levels of wellbeing and health. Being a minority often predicts chronic health problems and non-communicable diseases, such as cancer, stroke, or diabetes. This is why it is crucial to figure out ways to use some of our positive characteristics to "disrupt" the discrimination process.

Harbouring prejudice is not good for us. It is primarily associated with lower levels of life satisfaction. In contrast, qualities like openness, creativity, kindness, gratitude, and compassion – opposites of discrimination – are associated with greater happiness. Even though longitudinal studies on this topic are scarce, the current evidence points to the need for us to explore ways to support people in recognising their prejudice and turning away from it so that they can improve their own wellbeing and live a good life.

Finally, the authors call for developing positive psychology interventions that help marginalised people cope more effectively with prejudice. More importantly, they encourage the development of interventions that would reduce oppression. For example, one such intervention is practising gratitude towards an outgroup member, such as a person with a different skin colour, cultural background, sex orientation, or age (Rambaud et al., 2021), which can improve wellbeing and diminish discriminatory attitudes. Another intervention is mindfulness, such as loving-kindness meditation, which encourages spreading love towards outgroups.

Positive psychology offers an opportunity to enhance the wellbeing of both the oppressed and those who perpetuate oppression. It also has the potential to address crucial issues such as prejudice, stereotyping, and most importantly, social divisions. Even though more research in this area is needed, if these interventions are implemented early in life, they can contribute to making the world a better place.

References

Rambaud, S., Collange, J., Tavani, J. L., & Zenasni, F. (2021). Positive intergroup interdependence, prejudice, outgroup stereotype and helping behaviors: The role of group-based gratitude. *International Review of Social Psychology*, *34*(open in a new window)(1(open in a new window)), 10. http://doi.org.elib.tcd.ie/10.5334/irsp.433

Sanders, C. A., Rose, H., Booker, J. A., & King, L. A. (2023). Claiming the role of positive psychology in the fight against prejudice. *Journal of Positive Psychology*, *18*(1), 61–74. https://doi-org.elib.tcd.ie/10.1080/17439760.2021.2012342

Refugees

The war in Ukraine began in 2022, displacing nearly 7 million people to date. In response, European governments swiftly amended their laws to welcome and support Ukrainian refugees. As they integrated into new communities, most of them were met with care and compassion. Psychological services have opened their doors to Ukrainian families offering their support. Programmes have been created to support their wellbeing, and positive psychology has sometimes been used as the foundation for its curriculum.

At our Centre for Positive Health Sciences, we tried to find home for displaced academics from Ukraine and supported their applications to transfer their research to our university. Each faculty member reached out to their community to engage in food collection and parcels for families and children. Yet I couldn't help but wonder: Were we doing this for them or for ourselves? After all, taking action to help, no matter how small, feels better than feeling helpless and doing nothing.

Of all the articles published about refugees in the context of positive psychology, one published by Shaheen Mohamed and Miles Thomas from the University of East London, UK, was the most cited. It explores the psychological wellbeing of children who live as refugees in the UK. They included refugees from such countries as Afghanistan, Albania, Congo, Ethiopia, Pakistan, Somalia, and Uganda, as well as their parents and school staff. Currently, in the UK alone, there are almost 150,000 refugees, asylum seekers, and stateless persons. To add to it, almost 5% of school children in the Greater London Area hold a refugee status, meaning they were forced to leave their home country due to war or violence that has threatened the safety of their family and community. The trauma associated with their circumstances so early in their lives is incomprehensible.

The study adopted a "what is working well" approach. Among the findings, researchers shared that children have felt safe and secure within education. They became part of a community which helped them feel they belonged. Despite the challenges of losing their family network, and in some cases feeling lonely and experiencing bullying, they eventually made friends. This resilience and the friendships they formed were crucial for coping with their changed circumstances. Social support from refugee agencies played an important role in their lives, and schools have given them stability in their lives of uncertainty.

This is just one of a few articles published that explore positive psychology aspects of refugees' lives. Given the world's unrest, and a constantly increasing number of refugees in many countries, there is an urgent need for more research. By expanding our understanding of the psychological impact of displacement and the role of positive psychology in refugee support, we can develop more effective interventions and policies to help these vulnerable populations.

References

Mohamed, S., & Thomas, M. (2017). The mental health and psychological well-being of refugee children and young people: An exploration of risk, resilience and protective factors. *Educational Psychology in Practice*, *33*(3), 249–263. https://doi.org/10.1080/02667363.2017.1300769

LGBTQ+

Thirty years ago, I met a boy who was the most fun ever. We had become best friends and spent our twenties enjoying the good times. I was there by his side when he came out. I was there keeping him company at the family functions. I was there comforting his mum when she worried that her gay son would not find a life partner and spend his life alone. I was by his side when he met his first boyfriend and then again when he met the love of his life. I was there by his side when he married his husband. His mum's prediction of a disastrous life never came true. He has now been happily married for over a decade and surrounded by lots of love, kindness, and friendship from everyone. Yet I still remember the challenging beginning of his journey, and the uncertainty of what the future might bring for him when living in Catholic Ireland. Being a minority is never easy. This is why it is important for positive psychology to open the door wider for the LGBTQ+ community research and practice, to celebrate their resilience and optimism.

Daniela Domínguez from Our Lady of the Lake University, USA (2015), led a paper presenting a framework that addressed the LGBTQ+ community's needs and the impact of systemic factors in positive psychology. Most of the positive psychological research explores the wellbeing of heterosexuals. Yet non-heterosexual individuals and families cope daily with the additional pressure of heterosexism and sexual prejudice. Therefore, researchers and practitioners must consider this when exploring concepts in positive psychology. This approach is particularly important for practitioners, as it equips them to identify and amplify the systemic strengths that can support non-heterosexual families. Understanding the systemic relationship between the LGBTQ community and the sociocultural and political context is a crucial foundation for making changes that support these families, highlighting the urgent need for a holistic approach to positive psychology.

The LGBTQ-Relationally-Based-Positive-Psychology framework explores ways in which non-heterosexual families protect their relationships and children from hardship while at the same time coping with stress and adversity imposed by the system. The framework amalgamates Walsh's family resilience model (Walsh, 1996), insights from non-heterosexual families, and positive psychology. The additional stressors that families need to deal with, such as prejudice, ripple down throughout the entire family and could impact their self-identity and self-worth. The framework is developed for therapists and aims to get what is best from positive psychology to support non-heterosexual couples.

Systemic strengths, such as resilience, adaptability, and community support, play a crucial role in supporting non-heterosexual families. This includes building optimism to enhance resilience in these families. Often, non-heterosexual couples are froth with insecurities about being parents. Optimistic thinking can help them change their self-talk when dealing with such issues as children being bullied for having LGBTQ+ parents.

Also, exploring ways in which non-heterosexual families can build supporting relationships outside their families. For example, through healthy relationships with heterosexual couples, between parents and children, and between the couple and the close and extended social network within their community. This also includes exploring the system within which the LGBTQ+ family lives, which can include societal attitudes, legal frameworks, and community resources, and ways in which these factors could be used to support them.

The authors explore positive emotions and their broadening and building effect within a family. Also, there is a shift from being deficit-based to strength-based when exploring a family that does not have heterosexual parents. The ability to change these perceptions and use positive psychology science to support all families regardless of their sexual orientation is of utmost importance.

References

Domínguez, D. G., Bobele, M., Coppock, J., & Peña, E. (2015). LGBTQ relationally based positive psychology: An inclusive and systemic framework. *Psychological Services*, *12*(2), 177–185. https://doi-org.elib.tcd.ie/10.1037/a0038824

Walsh, F. (1996). The concept of family resilience: Crisis and challenge. *Family Process*, *35*, 261–281. http://dx.doi.org/10.1111/j.1545-5300.1996.00261.x

Research methods and ethics in positive psychology

Ethics in positive psychology practice

Happyology is everywhere – on social media and in motivational posters. Positive psychology research is shared without context. It thrives in environments where findings are exaggerated and research limitations are ignored, making it the opposite of ethical positive psychology practice. To address this, the field must develop ethical standards. Led by Aaron Jarden et al. (2021) from the University of Melbourne, Australia, a team of researchers have developed ethical guidelines for positive psychology practice. Once implemented, these guidelines can transform the field, bringing about a more ethical and responsible approach to applying positive psychology in daily life.

The process of creating these guidelines began in 2016 with a call from researchers to professionalise positive psychology. It was based on a mixed bottom-up and top-down approach to ethical guidelines development. This inclusive process comprised a review of the current guidelines across several professional organisations, as well as insights from a workshop, discussions, and consultation with professionals, shaping the structure and content of the guidelines.

The developed guidelines are not static and are currently at their second iteration. They are based on agreed-upon values, strengths, and principles and are expected to continue to evolve. They are also not prescriptive, meaning that positive psychology practitioners are not expected to practise them as stated. Instead, they are designed to guide their practice while tapping into their own strengths, and their own values to ensure the best results for their clients.

The authors encourage practitioners to ask themselves three questions before applying positive psychology interventions to their clients. First, consider whether the interventions are appropriate for the client in the context of their situation. Second, it's the practitioner's role to consider to what extent the interventions match the clients' needs, empowering them to make the best decisions for their clients. Third, consider evaluating the effectiveness of an intervention so that the client can see the progress. Then, each guideline is explained in more detail to help practitioners reflect upon their practice.

The guidelines are not merely theoretical; they explore the key factors that need to be considered in the context of client work. Some guidelines are broad and can apply to any client work involving psychological interventions. These include guidelines such as practising wisdom, or the importance of prioritising self-care.

Other guidelines are specific for positive psychology practitioners, such as watching out for overusing strengths or assessing clients' current level of wellbeing. They provide practical insights into the practice of positive psychology, equipping you to work with clients effectively and in a more research-informed way.

One of the most valuable sections of the guidelines are the appendices, which delve into ethical dilemmas and provide step-by-step strategies for addressing them. They include a self-evaluation guide, which is helpful for self-reflection and discussion with practice supervisors. Most importantly, the guidelines are just the first part of the process for professionalising positive psychology. The next steps involve setting up a code of practice and an organisation that oversees and manages the process.

Given the interdisciplinarity of positive psychology, not all professionals who practise it come from the social sciences field, especially the psychological background, which typically provides individuals with an ethical framework for working with clients. This "ethical guideline" and "the code of practice" approach will give all positive psychology practitioners an equal opportunity to engage in optimal practice, levelling the playing field regardless of their background. At the same time, it will offer clients reassurance that the support they are offered adheres to recognised quality standards in positive psychology practice.

References

Jarden, A., Rashid, T., Roache, A., & Lomas, T. (2021). Ethical guidelines for positive psychology practice (version 2.0: English). *International Journal of Wellbeing*, *9*(3), 1–30. https://doi.org/10.5502/ijw.v9i3.921

Research methods in positive psychology

A few years ago, my colleague and friend Majella Dempsey from Maynooth University, Ireland, joined me in writing two research methods books about Capstone Projects. We did it because there was no such book we could recommend to students, so we decided to research this topic and publish it with Routledge. The books have challenged traditional research conventions. We aimed to make research methods more accessible for students without making them too simplistic. We were very nervous about sending the books for peer review.

One of the reviewers was Professor Keith Morrison, a co-author of what we consider one of the most influential research methods textbooks ever written (Cohen et al., 2018), so when he initially replied that he was busy but still asked for a copy, we sent it off. We took the weekend to relax with our families. To our surprise, on Monday morning, we found an email from him – he had not only read the book over the weekend but loved it. He mentioned that he had intended to skim through it but became so engrossed that he couldn't put it down, even calling it a "page-turner". His feedback meant the world to us. For us, research methods aren't just important – they're also a lot of fun. For positive psychology, getting the research methods right is crucial.

One common criticism of positive psychology is its perceived lack of research rigour. To address this, an analysis of 250 research articles was conducted

(Helwig et al., 2020), which compared research methods in positive psychology versus well-established educational psychology. The findings confirmed that positive psychology research was of good methodological quality. However, compared to educational psychology, it relied more on self-reported measures and less on experimental and laboratory research. This difference could be due to the nature of both fields of research. The focus of the educational psychology field is learning. Learning-related research can be easily conducted in a laboratory, whereas designing a study in a laboratory to assess wellbeing is more challenging and perhaps less useful. The differences between the two fields are, therefore, understandable.

Curiously, positive psychology used fewer experimental methods than educational psychology. It may be associated with the field's growth, whereby educational psychology is more established. It is a natural progression first to explore relationships between concepts and then identify causation, which requires experimental method designs. Perhaps positive psychology, a relatively new science, still conceptualises the field, thus showing fewer experimental studies.

The authors recommend increasing the proportion of longitudinal studies, as positive psychology research relies heavily on cross-sectional study designs. This approach limits the insights into intraindividual differences. They also recommend that positive psychology researchers use more laboratory studies where variables can be isolated and studied closely. Additionally, the study found that most positive psychology research samples were drawn from student populations. The authors advocated for more diverse participant groups to enhance the field's validity and applicability.

Another gap identified in this article related to the participants' ethnicity and recruitment methods, which is essential to ensure that high-quality data collection methods are used. A small percentage of published research in the field reported on them. Understanding this will ensure that the research findings are both accurate and generalisable. Not including diverse populations could undermine the validity of findings. While all this is useful for researchers, it is also important information for practitioners to consider when they read research papers, especially those working with diverse populations.

References

Cohen, L., Manion, L., & Morrison, K. (2018). *Research methods in education* (8th ed.). Routledge. https://doi.org/10.4324/9781315456539

Helwig, N., Yatsevich, D., Vetter, A. C., Wuttke, A. M., & Schmitz, B. (2020). A comparative review of current research methods in positive psychology. *European Journal of Applied Positive Psychology*, *4*(2), 1–30.

Epistemological fruit salad

To address the World Health Organisation's (WHO) call to improve workplace health and wellbeing, a large financial organisation based in Ireland took matters into their own hands when it introduced a wellbeing department and a series of validated scales that assessed their employees' wellbeing. These scales were meant to provide their team with targeted training to address their needs. However, after receiving the results, they didn't know what to do with them, so they called me for a consultation.

"We have a group of languishing employees who scored low on their psychological, emotional, and social wellbeing", they said. "Now, what kind of training do we need to help them?", they asked. My answer was: "I don't know". I could have given them ideas for a generic training that improves all three areas. The challenge was that we only had quantitative data about their employees without context, so I asked to speak with some of their languishing employees. After all, the complexity of wellbeing is too important to ignore.

Two individuals in particular stayed on my mind. The first one had experienced significant trauma in their life and, a year earlier, attempted suicide. This became a wake-up call for them to improve their wellbeing, and since then, they have engaged in regular therapy, reconnected with family and friends, and have been motivated to get their health and wellbeing back on track. The other employee did not know where to start as they were surprised by the results. Two people scored the same on their workplace wellbeing assessment, yet with diametrically different needs. This context is often missing when we conduct research using the typical quantitative approaches in positive psychology; this is why we need a mixed-method research approach.

Kristen Hamling from the Auckland University of Technology, New Zealand, and colleagues wrote an article encouraging researchers to expand on their methodological approaches and paradigms when designing research. We all view the world differently because our life experiences are different. Therefore, we make many assumptions about the reality of the social world (ontology) and how we acquire knowledge (epistemology). A research paradigm is our philosophical assumption that guides our thinking and action when designing and conducting research.

The predominant paradigm in positive psychological research is the same as in psychological research in general, that is, positivism or post-positivism, which is a belief that reality exists independently of us; hence, as researchers, we need to find ways to access it objectively. The difference between positivism and post-positivism is the confidence level in accessing knowledge, whereas, in post-positivism, that knowledge is tentative. This paradigm uses objective methodologies such as quantitative research.

In this article, Hamling and colleagues (2020) called for expanding on the methodologies in positive psychology to understand the context. They provide three examples of studies that demonstrate the application of mixed methods in wellbeing research. The first one is a quantitative analysis followed by grounded theory interviews and analysis. This approach combines the statistical analysis of quantitative data with the in-depth understanding provided by qualitative interviews. The second one was a prototype analysis, which is a sequence of qualitative and quantitative approaches applied in a loop. This iterative process allows for the refinement of the research design based on the findings from each method. The final methodology was a case study involving qualitative assessments followed by participants completing a quantitative survey assessing their wellbeing. This approach allows for a deep exploration of individual experiences while also providing a broader understanding of the population's wellbeing.

These three examples demonstrate the benefit of combining research methods and how they can enrich the findings. Hamling and her colleagues argue that researchers should embrace mixed methods designs that incorporate qualitative data that enrich the context of the quantitative findings. This potential for enrichment is the core value of mixed methods in research.

Similarly, when working with clients, it is important to remember that each person's wellbeing is shaped by their life circumstances, experiences, and beliefs. Without this context, it is hard to understand, appreciate, but most importantly act upon the findings. This context is not just a detail, but a crucial aspect that creates a fuller and richer picture of wellbeing.

References

Hamling, K., Jarden, R., Jarden, A., & Synard, J. (2020). Epistemological fruit salad: Broadening methodology in positive psychology research to develop contextualised interventions and understandings of well-being. *The Journal of Positive Psychology*, *15*(5), 670–674. https://doi.org/10.1080/17439760.2020.1789708

Strength of evidence behind happiness strategies

It happened in North America. I was about to leave, pick up my bags from the hotel, head to the airport, and go home to Europe after attending an excellent conference when I ran into colleagues, who encouraged me to stay. I walked back into the auditorium for one of the final presentations I had planned to skip to avoid missing my flight home. "I guess a few minutes won't hurt", I thought, taking a seat in the last row to let me slip out early without causing a stir. But the talk was so interesting that I stayed until the end. That presentation was by Elizabeth Dunn, who discussed the evidence behind the happiness intervention designs.

Dunigan Folk and Elizabeth Dunn from the University of British Columbia published an article exploring studies that assessed the impact of expressing gratitude, enhancing sociability, exercising, practising mindfulness/meditation, and increasing nature exposure. All these strategies were found to be most common in the media for enhancing happiness. They explored these studies to identify whether they produced "high-quality" evidence, focusing specifically on their research design and reporting. One aspect they considered was the "research power", which refers to the ability of a study to detect true effect, and the other was "pre-registration", a practice where researchers declare their research questions, methods, and analysis plans before conducting the study. These two components, or lack thereof, can contribute to false-positive results that often don't hold at replication. For instance, you might find that an intervention improves wellbeing. Still, when another study with a different sample size and location replicates the study, the results show no impact of the intervention on wellbeing. This is why the research needs to be designed carefully to avoid it.

Research can increase statistical power in many ways. For example, by increasing the sample size of a study, we can ensure that no covariates are added or that only the selected results are reported. To prevent this, researchers are encouraged to pre-register their studies, whereby they identify straightforward research questions, methodology, and approach to analysis. Thus, the studies analysed in this article were analysed for their statistical power and pre-registration.

The results showed that most studies reporting on strategies for happiness have not met the power and pre-registration criteria. For example, in meditation research, of 195 studies, 186 did not meet the criteria. In gratitude studies, of 89 studies, only 2 were sufficiently powered and met the pre-registration criteria, while a further 24 were powered but not registered, and the majority of 63 did not meet the criteria. These are just two examples of five, with similar results. The bottom line is that most studies reporting the impact of common happiness strategies cannot be fully trusted. This means that practitioners should approach these studies with caution and consider their limitations when applying them to their practice.

References

Folk, D., & Dunn, E. (2023). A systematic review of the strength of evidence for the most commonly recommended happiness strategies in mainstream media. *Nature Human Behaviour*, *7*(10), 1697–1707. https://doi.org/10.1038/s41562-023-01651-4

RE-AIM evaluation of positive psychology interventions

I remember sitting in a coffee shop near Maynooth University, Ireland, with a fellow psychologist, discussing wellbeing interventions and how they can be assessed for effectiveness. My colleague preferred atypical approaches to assessing the effectiveness of interventions, such as design-based research, action research, and qualitative research designs exploring the impact of research. My colleague's perspective differed from the typical approach to assessing interventions as recommended by Archie Cochrane. He was an epidemiologist, and in 1972, he suggested that treatments and interventions should follow a logical sequence of phases, and social sciences, such as the field of positive psychology, have widely adopted his approach.

According to Cochrane, the efficacy of an intervention must be first established in highly controlled conditions. For example, in a laboratory or by testing an intervention within strict conditions. The next step is an effectiveness trial to see if it causes harm or helps people in real-life situations. This process step also explores the conditions under which the intervention implementation is effective. They examine the impact of an intervention in the short, medium, or long term and the effect sizes to identify its actual impact, not only whether or not differences exist between variables. Various approaches exist to ensure interventions' effectiveness. One of them is a RE-AIM approach.

Lucy Hone (2015) from New Zealand and the team explored over 300 studies. They selected 40 positive psychology articles in the final review to assess their adherence to the RE-AIM approach for exploring the impact of positive psychology interventions. Here are their results.

The R stands for *Reach* and relates to the methods used to recruit participants, whether or not the inclusion and exclusion criteria were selected, whether sample size and participation rate were reported, or whether participant characteristics were recorded. The studies analysed in this research scored 64% of 100%, meaning they were good but not excellent at reaching out to the appropriate participants.

The E stands for *Efficacy and Effectiveness*, which refer to factors such as the measures used in research and results, including negative results reported. They were reported at 73%, which was rather good. However, the internet-to-treat analysis relates to including participants in the analysis regardless of whether

Table 1.1 Strategies for deep reading academic paper.

Strategies for deep reading	*Practical considerations*
Reading purpose	Reflect on why you are reading this specific article. What is your objective for doing it? Consider at least one question you would like answered by the end of reading the article.
Context	Learn about the author, their general views. Are they representative of mainstream thinking, or are they radical? What experiences have they had that could have influenced their writing? What were their previous articles about?
Author's main ideas	What does the author intend to do with this article? What is their purpose of writing it? Are they trying to challenge the current views about the topic, or have they identified a research gap or a variable that needs further exploration? What are the author's main arguments?
Explore assumptions	You must be aware of some of the assumptions associated with the field of research you are reading about. They are the concepts, debates, and principles that the author takes for granted and needs to understand to engage with their argument fully. This is a problematic aspect of deep reading, and it becomes easier the more we read.
Critically evaluate the research findings	It is crucial to evaluate the author's research design. How did they collect their data? What sampling technique did they use? How are they presenting their data? What kind of reasoning are they using? Are there gaps in the information provided?
Critically evaluate the author/s arguments	This section is about assessing the validity of the author's arguments. Not all authors follow logic. Ideas proposed by the author need to be questioned. How compelling is the author's rationale in arguing a stance? Did the author provide convincing examples to make their argument stick? Can you think of contra-arguments?
Explore the consequences of author's arguments	How can the author's findings, their stance be implemented in practice? How can each one of the author's views affect the practitioners? How does the author's conclusion compare with other findings or other authors?

Source: Adapted from Burke and Dempsey (2022)

they completed it. This analysis was completed by only 20% of positive psychology studies.

The A stands for *Adoption* and refers to the description of the circumstances surrounding the adoption of interventions, such as the location, who delivered the intervention, the expertise of those who delivered it, or the adoption rate of an intervention. Adoption was scored at 84%.

The I stands for *Implementation* and is concerned reporting about the type of intervention, its intensity, the extent to which a protocol was followed, and its cost. This component was reported in 100% of studies.

The M stands for *Maintenance* and is about reporting on the changed behaviour at least 6 months after the intervention, the current status of the programme implemented, and how much it would cost to maintain it long term. Maintenance reached the most miniature score at 16%.

This study helped identify the standard of intervention research design that needs to be followed. By improving the quality of research, we can improve the quality of positive psychology interventions. This in turn will have impact on the wellbeing improvement, which is currently merely small to moderate for most interventions. For practitioners, this article highlights the need to practise critical thinking when reading academic papers. Taking on board research just because it was published is just not enough.

To ease this process, Table 1.1 provides some examples of questions that you can ask yourself when reading academic papers.

References

Burke, J., & Dempsey, M. (2022). *Undertaking capstone and final year projects in psychology: Practical guide for students*. Routledge.

Hone, L. C., Jarden, A., & Schofield, G. M. (2015). An evaluation of positive psychology intervention effectiveness trials using the re-aim framework: A practice-friendly review. *The Journal of Positive Psychology*, *10*(4), 303–322. https://doi.org/10.1080/17439760.2014.965267

2 The primer to wellbeing

Positive psychology is the field of optimal functioning. While it does not solely focus on wellbeing, wellbeing and the good life are inevitably the most prevalent topics within positive psychology. This chapter will explore the main wellbeing models that underpin positive psychology. It will start with the original models of subjective and psychological wellbeing and progress through the contemporary flourishing frameworks and the recently introduced psychological richness model. We will then explore the main components of the models through key articles relating to such concepts as positive affect, accomplishment, optimism, meaning in life, or self-acceptance. Then, additional components of wellbeing will be discussed, such as hope, authenticity, or self-compassion. While they are not officially part of any of the leading models of wellbeing, they provide alternative pathways for improving wellbeing. Next, we will address some of the critiques of the wellbeing models in positive psychology and identify key areas where improvement is required to refine both research and application. Finally, while most wellbeing models emphasise the development of resources that contribute to the good life, they do not explicitly focus on how people cope with adversities. In the final section of this chapter, we will examine key papers relating to wellbeing in the context of adversity. Specifically, we will explore how individuals can cope with challenges in a way that can facilitate their wellbeing. Overall, this comprehensive chapter will provide a detailed overview of current approaches to wellbeing in positive psychology, including the tension between wellbeing and illbeing. It will also highlight ways in which wellbeing should be rethought and redesigned to best address the needs of the modern world, inspiring the readers with the potential for innovation.

The main wellbeing models

Subjective wellbeing

Ed Diener, aka Dr Happiness, coined the concept of subjective wellbeing when he published his first article in 1984. He has always been fascinated with happiness research, even during the times when it was looked down on. The model of Subjective Wellbeing was the first one that emerged to describe wellbeing. It was aligned

DOI: 10.4324/9781003530596-2

with the philosophical stance of hedonism, a concept that has been a part of human thought for centuries, which described the pursuit of pleasure.

The model was created following a literature review on the topic in 1967. It comprised three elements: two affective and one cognitive (Diener, 1984, 2000). The affective elements were experiences of higher levels of positive emotions and lower levels of negative emotions, while the cognitive aspect related to life satisfaction. Life satisfaction is a relatively complex process of establishing where we hope to be now and how we compare to it. If our lives are better than expected, our life satisfaction is higher. If it is worse than we expected, it becomes lower. Even though cognitive processes are involved, life satisfaction can depend on our experiences of positive emotions or moods. When in a good mood, we are more likely to score higher on the life satisfaction scale.

Many of the large-scale measures of wellbeing have been based on the Subjective Wellbeing model as it is one of the most straightforward assessments of wellbeing. However, it has also been heavily criticised by Carol Ryff, who didn't see subjective wellbeing as wellbeing but as happiness. While not universally accepted, this criticism has sparked a healthy debate in psychology. Nowadays, the affective part of the Subjective Wellbeing model is absorbed by the flourishing models in positive psychology. Nonetheless, a significant body of research continues to explore the correlations of subjective wellbeing with various concepts in psychology and other processes. The contribution of Ed Diener to the science of positive psychology and, in particular, wellbeing cannot be overstated – no wonder he was seen as the Jedi Master of Happiness Studies. Further research has often incorporated many of his findings.

References

Diener, E. (1984). Subjective well-being. *Psychological Bulletin*, *95*(3), 542–575. https://doi.org/10.1037/0033-2909.95.3.542

Diener, E. (2000). Subjective well-being: The science of happiness and a proposal for a national index. *American Psychologist*, *55*(1), 34–43. https://doi.org/10.1037/0003-066X.55.1.34

Psychological wellbeing

Nestled within the ancient city walls of Lublin's old town in Poland, I met with Carol Ryff on the steps of the Cathedral, where we had a chance to chat before a conference where we were both scheduled to speak. After a warm greeting, we headed to a nearby restaurant serving delicious local food, which I thoroughly enjoyed discussing and tasting, given my Polish heritage. As we sat in the bustling square, sipping fruit tea and a melange of Polish pierogi, soups, and salads, our discussion inevitably turned towards the Psychological Wellbeing model – a model that has changed the direction of wellbeing research after decades of discussing happiness and hedonism as a basis of what it means to be well. I asked Carol what inspired her to create it. Her response was simple: The Subjective Wellbeing model didn't feel right. So, she decided to search the existing literature and draw from the fathers of psychology to see what else matters in life, what we know improves our wellbeing. Carol Ryff's model resonated with many when it came out.

Following from a number of original studies, Carol Ryff published her first position article in 1989, in which she critiqued the hedonistic approach to wellbeing and explored alternative perspectives. She examined the broader definitions of hedonism and eudaimonia and discussed differences between happiness and psychological wellbeing. She provided the basis of her model which integrated mental health, clinical, and life span development theories. This paper set the foundation for her future research and introduced the Psychological Wellbeing model.

Then, in the following paper (Ryff, 1989; Ryff & Keyes, 1995), she provided additional empirical evidence for her theoretical model. Both articles are worthy of exploring to understand the foundations of the Psychological Wellbeing model.

The model comprises six components:

1. **Self-acceptance** relates to having a positive attitude towards oneself. A person acknowledges and appreciates many aspects of themselves. This includes accepting good and bad qualities about oneself and feeling largely positive about the past. This is the most frequently mentioned aspect of oneself in the past literature relating to wellbeing. It is also a main characteristic of people who enjoy high levels of positive psychological functioning.
2. **Positive relations** with others are about having warm and trusting relationships with others, whether in their immediate or extended circle. It is associated with experiencing deep empathy for others, expressing affection towards others, and being able to experience intimacy. A person who has positive relations with others tends to care for other people and understands the concept of give and take in a relationship; thus, they can make compromises to maintain meaningful relationships.
3. **Autonomy** relates to the ability of an individual to think for themselves and live according to their standards, free from societal fears, norms, and beliefs. This is part of a natural ageing process whereby, later in life, individuals become more resistant to and free from social norms. However, for some people, this process occurs earlier in life. An autonomous person lives their lives on their own terms and does not need an approval from others to feel good. They don't feel pressured to behave in certain ways as they resist societal pressures and are instead guided by what they believe is right.
4. **Environmental mastery** is the ability of an individual to select or negotiate the environment suitable for nurturing their health. It is an ability to manage various activities in their lives effectively; for example, it could be school pressures or the daily hassles of a family life. It is a person's choice as to whether the environment suits their physical and mental health. If not, it is an ability to walk away or negotiate changes with the environment. Knowledge of one's needs and values is crucial to manage the environment effectively. A person who has mastered the ability to manage their environment takes advantage of the

opportunities in their lives. Overall, environmental mastery is about individuals feeling like they have control over the world surrounding them and exercising this control.

5. **Purpose in life** is a sense of direction in life. It relates to having goals and intentions that make one's life meaningful. Our purpose in life evolves throughout our lifespan. It keeps changing depending on what becomes meaningful to us. It is essential to feel that life is meaningful and that we already contributed to it. When life lacks direction and we have no outlook, it becomes meaningless, negatively impacting wellbeing.
6. **Personal growth** is a feeling of continuously developing, growing, and expanding their perspective. It is not necessarily about formal education but rather a feeling that an individual is growing and journeys towards realising their potential. It is about expanding on self-knowledge and becoming more effective at what they do. It involves being interested in life and developing new attitudes and behaviours. This component of wellbeing is about self-actualisation. As life challenges change throughout our lifespan, we keep learning new skills and growing our knowledge to tackle them. That "becoming" is a hallmark of personal growth.

Those six components of Psychological Wellbeing are the foundations of eudaemonic wellbeing translated into psychological science. In the positive psychological models of flourishing discussed later, the model is also a basis for going beyond hedonistic psychology into the world of meaning. As such, this model has changed the way we view wellbeing.

References

Ryff, C. D. (1989). Happiness is everything, or is it? Explorations on the meaning of psychological well-being. *Journal of Personality and Social Psychology*, *57*(6), 1069–1081. https://doi.org/10.1037/0022-3514.57.6.1069

Ryff, C. D., & Keyes, C. L. M. (1995). The structure of psychological well-being revisited. *Journal of Personality and Social Psychology*, *69*(4), 719–727. https://doi.org/10.1037/0022-3514.69.4.719

Mental Health Continuum

Two decades ago, I went through a series of adverse events within just a few years, which ultimately led me to experience depression. For months, I felt as if I was free-falling. One death of someone close to me happened after another, and I had little control over this – I only had to deal with all the consequences. During this time, I began to question the meaning of life, and soon, it felt like my days were stripped of joy, meaning, and purpose. I remember going to my general practitioner and asking if she could help me figure out what was happening. Her recommendation was to get a hobby and exercise more. At the time, it seemed like the most ridiculous advice. I was going through an existential crisis, and I could not see how going for a run and knitting could help me. When my symptoms worsened, I went to my doctor again, and at this point, she finally diagnosed me with depression. This was a turning point. I remember feeling a relief. Finally, I knew what was happening. With the proper support, I could bounce back and regain control of my life. Until then, it just felt like I was not well, but I wasn't unwell either. It was a strange state of "blah", which I later learnt to be languishing.

Corey Keyes, Emory University, USA, is a sociologist interested in the concept of wellbeing. After reading WHO's definition of health, he was stoked by the fact that even though "Health is a state of complete physical, mental and social wellbeing and not merely the absence of disease or infirmity", we knew very little about what it means to be healthy, without seeing it as not being unhealthy. Drawing from the main theories of wellbeing, Subjective Wellbeing, Psychological Wellbeing, and Social Wellbeing which he created, he developed a Mental Health Continuum model that explored the subcategories of mental health. Within this, he found that some people were languishing, just as I was before being diagnosed with depression. This state is associated with a lack of purpose, aimlessness, feeling empty, and being stuck in a rut. Longitudinal studies indicate that those who are languishing are at significant risk of developing mental health issues. Being stuck in this state is in some ways worse than having a diagnosis of mental health, as we don't have enough symptoms of the disorder, yet we are not well either.

Past languishing, a state of moderate health indicates we are generally well, but every now and then, we experience emotionally or psychologically wobbly moments. Finally, there is the state of flourishing, which means we mostly experience optimal levels of emotional, social, and psychological functioning.

One of the most appealing aspects of Keyes's model is its validity and reliability. It incorporates well-established and validated models of wellbeing, providing a comprehensive framework for understanding mental health. Decades of research, including longitudinal studies, have provided solid evidence about what it means to be well. Thus, data is easily comparable. This wealth of knowledge, combined with the model's comprehensive approach, makes it an invaluable tool for researchers and practitioners. It offers a solid insight into what it means to be well, making it a model worth exploring in psychology. This is why, I have often used this model as a basis to discuss clients' mental health.

References

Keyes, C. L. M. (2002). The mental health continuum: From languishing to flourishing in life. *Journal of Health and Social Behavior*, *43*(2), 207–222. https://doi.org/10.2307/3090197

Flourishing in Europe

Wellbeing models come with many limitations. For example, we assume that the higher the individuals' score on a wellbeing scale, the better their lives. However, with so many different models of wellbeing, scoring highly on one scale doesn't guarantee high scores on others. As a result, wellbeing outcomes are not universal and don't necessarily correlate with a universally "better" life. It's crucial to remember that Aristotelian moderation needs to be applied to wellbeing. Excessively high wellbeing scores can be detrimental to our health, much like excessively high scores in experiencing positive emotions, which can lead to risk-taking or erratic behaviour. This is why we need a balanced approach to wellbeing.

One particular limitation of wellbeing models that I've found concerning is the hierarchy of wellbeing components. Are there any wellbeing components that are more important than others? I value having the freedom to embrace individual differences. Since models usually prescribe and weigh the components equally, we risk assuming everyone has the same values. I like having the freedom to be unique, and when we have models with the same components that carry the same value, we make an assumption that we are all the same. This is one of the reasons why I appreciated Felicia Huppert's approach.

Late Felicia Huppert,[1] a renowned psychologist from the University of Cambridge, has significantly advanced our understanding of flourishing. Her unique framework, which distinguishes between core and optional elements, is different from the traditional models for prescribed wellbeing. This is a key aspect of her valuable contribution.

Huppert's framework, which includes core elements such as positive emotions, engagement, interest, meaning, and purpose, also acknowledges the role of individual values in wellbeing. This recognition is a departure from models that assume a universal set of values, and it aligns with my belief in the importance of individual differences.

One of the most appealing aspects of Huppert's model is its flexibility. Unlike other frameworks that aim for participants to experience high scores across all areas, this model considers individuals to be flourishing if they do well in just three out of six domains. It allows for individuals to have personal choice in deciding what matters most to them. It recognises individual differences in personality and preferences. This adaptability makes it particularly valuable in wellbeing practice, reducing the pressure to conform to a rigid model that may not align with one's values.

References

Huppert, F. A., & So, T. T. C. (2013). Flourishing across Europe: Application of a new conceptual framework for defining well-being. *Social Indicators Research*, *110*(3), 837–861. https://doi.org/10.1007/s11205-011-9966-7

The wellbeing model

In 2002, Martin Seligman's book *Authentic Happiness* stirred up interest in positive psychology. Around that time, I remember going on a trip with friends, and his book was one of my holiday reads. As soon as I finished it, I passed it on to a friend, who devoured it in a day. Over 20 years later, she still talks about it as the most transformative reading that completely changed her perspective on happiness. I imagine my friend is one of many people who feel this way.

Since then, Seligman has evolved his theories, offering updated thinking about the topic. In his 2011 book *Flourish*, he shifted the focus from happiness as a life goal to "flourishing". He introduced The Wellbeing Model, a practical guide comprising five inherently motivating elements. The more one pursues these wellbeing elements, the more likely they are to flourish. The elements are as follows:

- **Positive emotions** – flourishing people experience higher levels of positive emotions. These include joy, pleasure, love, compassion, gratitude, and many others.
- **Engagement** – they are fully engaged in activities that interest them. They experience flow, which causes them to lose the sense of who they are and where they are. All they think of is the task at hand.
- **Relationships** – they have supportive relationships with other people. They feel loved by others, and others care about them. These relationships can extend from close ones to interactions with friends, colleagues, neighbours, or the greater community.
- **Meaning** – their lives are meaningful. They experience a sense of worth and value in their lives and continue to strive towards something greater than themselves.
- **Accomplishment** – they have a sense of accomplishment, achievement, or competency. They may be working hard on their goals and are good at accomplishing many of them.

The model was developed by Martin Seligman, but it was further enhanced by Julie Butler and Margaret Kern (2016) from the University of Melbourne, Australia, who created a multidimensional scale measuring the Wellbeing model. Their work has been instrumental in the widespread adoption of the model.

References

Butler, J., & Kern, M. L. (2016). The PERMA-Profiler: A brief multidimensional measure of flourishing. *International Journal of Wellbeing*, *6*(3), 1–48. https://doi.org/10.5502/ijw.v6i3.526

Seligman, M. E. P. (2011). *Flourish. A new understanding of happiness and wellbeing: The practical guide to using positive psychology to make you happier and healthier*. Nicholas Brealey Publishing.

Psychological richness

I have a friend whom I have known for over a decade. She loves to travel. When she was single, she just could not sit still. Every time I visited London, she was somewhere else, exploring, learning, challenging herself, and growing. She loved to have fun, but even more importantly, she tried to consider the meaning of her adventures. Later in life, when she got married and had children, her love for pursuing something that went beyond happiness and meaning continued. As we often tried to pinpoint her wellbeing's source, we couldn't quite put a finger on it. One day, when I heard Shigehiro Oishi speaking at one of the positive psychology conferences about psychological richness, all I could think about was my friend. "This is it! This is her source of wellbeing" I thought.

Shigehiro Oishi (2022), from the University of Chicago, USA, has been delving into the area of wellbeing since 1995. His early collaboration with Ed Diener led to several publications on subjective wellbeing. However, his most significant contribution came approximately three decades into his research pursuits when he created a ground-breaking theory of an alternative source of wellbeing. This theory, unlike the traditional hedonic and eudaimonic approaches, focused on psychological richness, a concept that revolutionised our understanding of wellbeing.

Psychological richness is a life brimming with curiosity, diversity, fascination, and evolving perspectives. While it shares connections with the other two main concepts of wellbeing, that is, subjective and psychological wellbeing, it also stands apart from them in several ways. For instance, subjective wellbeing often hinges on the circumstances and conditions we find ourselves in. This is why individuals with higher socio-economic status often report higher levels of life satisfaction and associate it with positive emotions. They have the financial means, status, and basic needs met. However, many people without disposable income to lead a happy life still live a fulfilling life. One reason for this is that their lives may be meaningful. Life meaning is linked to active engagement and commitment to significant social issues, such as helping those in need. However, psychological richness is different from these approaches.

Psychological richness is about living a life that doesn't necessarily need to be happy or meaningful but rather a life that offers many paradigm shifts. Those who find this pathway fulfilling relish the novelty of experiences and are drawn to exploring new things while they throw themselves into challenging situations. They appreciate when life challenges them with a different perspective they had not considered before. The character traits that drive them are curiosity, zest for life, and spontaneity. However, the results of their pursuits are not thoughtless actions but wise steps towards what matters.

This is why this type of life is what my friend enjoys the most. Monotony has bored her to tears, so today, despite having children, she continues to explore the world and spontaneously throws herself into the unknown to challenge herself and experience this paradigm shift that makes her feel like she is constantly growing. For my friend, travel is the primary source of living a psychologically rich life. However, others may experience similar paradigm shifts when engaging with education, expanding their social network beyond what initially felt comfortable, or rebelling against social conformity just for its sake. Whatever the behaviour, its primary aim is to create a pathway that makes their lives worth living.

References

Oishi, S., & Westgate, E. C. (2022). A psychologically rich life: Beyond happiness and meaning. *Psychological Review*, *129*(4), 790–811. https://doi-org.elib.tcd.ie/10.1037/rev0000317

The flourishing models' review

In my spare time, I am a scout leader in a local Beavers' group. Recently, we took children to the forest and asked them to use nature to create their safe place. The children's creativity was nothing short of inspiring as they scavenged for their sticks, stones, grass, and moss nearby, building their sanctuaries in the wild. When they finished their creations, we were amazed by how this simple instruction "create your safe place" led to diverse interpretations. Three children built a forest den; another child created a bow and arrows; another one debarked a wood slice and made it into a magical symbol that warded off evil; a group of boys and girls created a playground where they felt safe, and some have jumped into a hammock for safety. Every child created a safe space that appealed to them, but each safe place meant something very different to each person. In positive psychology, we are dealing with the same dilemma in understanding flourishing.

One key article led by Lucy Hone et al. (2015) aimed to explore the intricate web of flourishing models. At the time, flourishing was a buzzword, a novel concept that had inspired the positive psychology research community. The article synthesised the four primary conceptualisations of flourishing, dissecting their similarities and unique features. The models they examined were the Mental Health Continuum (Keyes, 2002), Flourishing (Huppert & So, 2013), PERMA (Seligman, 2011), and Flourishing (Diener, 2009).

What all these models had in common was that they all understood flourishing as multidimensional. Also, similar components they identified were engagement and meaning in life or purpose. However, the models varied in terms of other component inclusions. For example, the majority mentioned self-regard, self-acceptance, self-esteem, competence, accomplishment, and positive affect, and they had additional components that were included in only one framework. This variation stemmed from different foundations upon which each model was based, distinct goals behind their creation, or whether the models were developed using a bottom-up or top-down approach. Unsurprisingly, these differences led to varied outcomes.

For example, when over 10,000 participants were surveyed across all four frameworks, the prevalence of flourishing differed – according to the Huppert and So conceptualisation, approximately a quarter of participants flourished psychologically. According to Keyes and Diener's conceptualisations, approximately 40% of participants flourished. However, according to Seligman's research, almost half of the participants flourished. Depending on the measures and frameworks used to assess wellbeing, the interpretation of how well participants did varied significantly.

This research highlighted some of the challenges that exist in wellbeing models. Given that we disagree on what wellbeing is all about, just like beavers in the scout group, even though we are talking about the same human wellbeing and their experience, what we mean by it differs. Hone and colleagues measured different dimensions of wellbeing, and the scales they used for assessing the presence of flourishing differed too; for example, for some, wellbeing experiences were measured over a month; for others, during the past week, yet others made statements relating to their lives in general. This is why when, as practitioners, we read academic papers, it is crucial to explore what framework of wellbeing they use, as they are not all the same.

References

Diener, E. (2009). *Assessing well-being: The collected works of Ed Diener*. Social Indicators Research Series, vol. 39. Springer.

Hone, L. C., Jarden, A., Duncan, S., & Schofield, G. M. (2015). Flourishing in New Zealand workers: Associations with lifestyle behaviors, physical health, psychosocial, and work-related indicators. *Journal of Occupational and Environmental Medicine*, *57*(9), 973–983. https://doi.org/10.1097/JOM.0000000000000508

Huppert, F. A., & So, T. T. C. (2013). Flourishing across Europe: Application of a new conceptual framework for defining well-being. *Social Indicators Research*, *110*(3), 837–861. https://doi.org/10.1007/s11205-011-9966-7

Rethinking flourishing

Astronauts consistently share similar experiences when they leave the Earth and view it from far above. Initially, they search for their hometown. Point at it and cheer. Then, as they continue to orbit the Earth, they see their country and the continent as their home. Finally, upon the umpteenth time they orbit, their home becomes the planet Earth. As such any socially or politically constructed differences between people cease to exist, as we all become one. This change in perspectives is not uncommon. When we break down silos, our vision expands, and we can notice the details we have not seen before. This is also what happens when we begin to explore flourishing from beyond the positive psychology perspective.

Even though flourishing is synonymous with positive psychology, non-psychologists view it from their fields' perspectives and offer slightly different definitions. Being stuck in one way of thinking can limit our perspective and curb our and the field's growth. As such, considering a helicopter view could be more beneficial for developing flourishing research. It would also avoid the constant battle between researchers trying to argue for their perspective, and more importantly, it could aid the application of flourishing across fields. This is why the article written by Willen et al. (2022) from the University of Connecticut, USA, with its valuable insights and essential considerations, is a significant contribution to positive psychology research.

In this article, the authors explore the benefits of flourishing that extend beyond psychology. For example, they consider the impact of the research on healthcare and how it can inform the famous WHO (1946) definition of health as being "a state of complete physical, mental and social well-being and not merely the absence of disease or infirmity". More importantly, however, it offers an interdisciplinary perspective on flourishing, which can help unite the fields.

Let's begin with the confusing definition of flourishing. The definition of flourishing is not only different when presented by a range of psychologists working within the positive psychology field, but it is often used synonymously with such concepts as resilience, optimal functioning, or wellbeing. This confusion stems from the theoretical framework researchers use when exploring it. For example, the Mental Health Continuum (Keyes, 2002) conceptualisation derives from exploring WHO's positive health and focuses on high, moderate, and low functioning. Therefore, flourishing individuals are seen as being high-functioning. In contrast, the PERMA, otherwise known as The Wellbeing theory, draws from the difference between happiness and wellbeing, in which case those who experience high levels of wellbeing are seen as flourishing. These are two examples of how a different theoretical framework may confuse what we understand as flourishing.

Willen and colleagues presented nine definitions of flourishing that exist in the literature. Five stemming from positive psychology and the remaining four from bioethics, disability studies, critical legal theory, anthropology, and public health. Within the positive psychology definitions, researchers saw it as a complete mental health or a state in which all aspects of person's life are good. Some have considered flourishing as a state of eudaemonia; others as an amalgamation between eudaemonic and hedonic wellbeing. Therefore, even psychologists within the positive psychology field did not agree on the definition and scope of flourishing.

Beyond positive psychology, researchers explored flourishing akin to a flower growing fast. It is viewed as creating an environment for people that will nourish them and allow them to develop. This could include being part of a society that facilitates growth, as opposed to perpetuating inequality and giving further advantage to those already privileged. Therefore, researchers from outside the field of positive psychology call upon creating an environment of rights, equality, dignity, and respect for each person to facilitate their development of capabilities and pathways for self-development and create positive self-identity that will help society flourish. Finally, they see it as a dynamic process of striving for congruence between personal values, vision, commitments, and family and community needs, considering the social, political, and economic structures within which individuals live.

The value that other fields of research add to the conceptualisation of flourishing extends beyond an individual, family, community, and society we live in. It also explores the concept of privilege and access to resources that help people flourish. Imagine two people aiming to strive to improve their flourishing levels. One has a good education, an excellent job providing a lot of disposable income, and family support. Another one has a family living overseas, struggles to make ends meet, and works two jobs to ensure their family's basic needs are addressed. The chances for both these people and their families to flourish psychologically are unequal. All this needs to be considered when applying any flourishing models to wellbeing or striving to have 51% of flourishing people by 2051, as per Martin Seligman's mission.

Furthermore, the environment needs to be considered. We all live in politically different regions with varied social supports. Government policies, societal trust, community cohesion, and other important factors impact the wellbeing of people living there. Therefore, they can never be disregarded when discussing the potential of flourishing. All these environmental structures are foundations for human flourishing. It is not only up to an individual to be happy. To flourish like a flower, one must be rooted in soil rich with equality, nurtured by respect, and sheltered by a community that values all. We need to consider all this when practising positive psychology.

References

Willen, S. S., Williamson, A. F., Walsh, C. C., Hyman, M., & Tootle, W. (2022). Rethinking flourishing: Critical insights and qualitative perspectives from the U.S. Midwest. *SSM – Mental Health*, *2*, 100057. https://doi.org/10.1016/j.ssmmh.2021.100057

The main components of wellbeing

Positive affect

Broaden and build theory

What is good about positive emotions? This is a question that researchers have overlooked for decades. However, the narrative changed when Alice Isen, a professor of psychology and marketing, began studying the impact of positive emotions on decision-making and their ability to improve cognitive processing. Following her work, Barbara Fredrickson expanded on this research and developed a theory that became a cornerstone of positive psychological research. When conducting background research on this book, I discovered that her article introducing this theory was the most cited in positive psychology – an extraordinary achievement.

The theory states that there are three main functions of positive emotions. Firstly, they broaden our perspective, meaning that physiologically, we are more likely to see what is in our peripheral vision. On a psychological level, positive emotions open the door to our creativity, allow us to see solutions to a problem and consider options not accessible to us when experiencing negative emotions. On the other hand, negative emotions narrow the focus to help us come up with responses to challenges quickly. After all, having too many options when experiencing negativity can lead to indecision, which would be less effective in a tricky situation.

Let me offer you an example of a broadening and narrowing of the mind associated with the experiences of emotions. I was once driving my car. It was Friday afternoon, and I was thinking about what my friends and I would do over the weekend. I was smiling, singing to a tune on the radio and feeling happy. Then suddenly, a car in front of me slammed on its brakes, and I immediately slammed on mine. However, instead of stopping, my car began to aquaplane. I remember that in that short moment, my options had narrowed down from what I could do over the weekend to a simple dichotomous decision: Will I hit the car head-on or turn left and hit the railings? Amid the crash, I knew instinctively that turning right and hitting the oncoming traffic would be the worst option, so it did not appear in my head. I chose to hit the car head-on. Thankfully, everyone was ok. However, the trauma of this situation made me realise the functional power of emotions: negative emotions help us narrow our options to survive and positive help us open up our minds when trying to come up with options for a good weekend. This is precisely what Barbara Fredrickson pointed out in her model as a broadening effect of positive emotions.

The second function of positive emotions is to build our resources. When we regularly experience positive emotions, they have an accumulative positive effect on our lives. For example, those who reported high levels of hope before 9/11 tended to report even higher levels of hope afterwards. Thus, experiencing positive emotions becomes a magnet for attracting and multiplying them in the future. This, in turn, helps us build other resources. For example, people who experience positive emotions may be more optimistic or resilient than those experiencing a lot of negative emotions. Positive emotions also increase our cognitive resources, helping us problem-solve and boost our physiological health via improvements in cardiovascular health. As such, they build our psychological, emotional, physiological, and cognitive resources.

Finally, another function of positive emotions is to undo the effect of negative emotions. When we are going through a challenging event, having moments of positive emotions can help us recover from the harmful effects of negativity. For example, in an experiment about worry, the researchers asked participants to watch a movie that evoked many negative emotions. Those who completed an activity that boosted their positive emotions shortly after the movie experienced significantly less worry 24 hours later than those who watched the upsetting movie but did not undo its harmful effect. Therefore, the undoing of negative emotions serves an important adaptive function.

This theory and subsequent research is a fundamental perspective on the function of positive emotions. It allows practitioners to use positive emotions not only as sources of happiness but also as tools for moderating activities in our daily lives. For example, whenever I speak with someone who shares something upsetting, I do not let them leave until we undo the negative emotions. So, I ask them a question that changes their emotional state to more positive. When I see someone grieving and feeling guilty about experiencing joy, I encourage them to give themselves at least a short break each day to experience positive emotions. Whether it's spending time in nature, nurturing hopeful thoughts, or enjoying a bubble bath, these small acts can serve as a reset for the soul, helping them reconnect with positive emotions.

References

Fredrickson, B. L. (2001). The role of positive emotions in positive psychology: The broaden-and-build theory of positive emotions. *American Psychologist*, *56*(3), 218–226.

Fredrickson, B. L. (2004). The broaden-and-build theory of positive emotions. *Philosophical Transactions of the Royal Society of London. Series B: Biological Sciences*, *359*(1449), 1367–1378. https://doi.org/10.1098/rstb.2004.1512. PMID: 15347528; PMCID: PMC1693418.

WHO (1946). *Constitution of the World Health Organization*. Basic Documents, Geneva: World Health Organization.

Positivity ratios

I remember the day when I learnt about positivity ratios – I found this research fascinating. Before Barbara Fredrickson introduced the 3:1 ratio for wellbeing and the 5:1 ratio for flourishing, I read about a similar ratio in business literature and research about thriving romantic relationships. As a psychology student, I once experimented with myself, assessing my positivity daily for a month. I found that it did not make sense to me. On days when I had a high positivity ratio, I didn't necessarily feel fulfilled or content; it was just that my balance of positive versus negative emotions was biased towards the positive making me more giggly. Also, during my PhD, I spent a good few years working with people with anxiety and depression. When together we tried to find a way on how to introduce the 3:1 ratio in their daily lives, we found it a challenge and often settled for aiming to experience more positive than negative emotions. So, perhaps the ratio was not as useful as it seemed.

When Nicolas Brown, a student of Masters in Applied Positive Psychology at the University of East London, UK, first encountered the concept of the positivity ratio, he was intrigued. With his critical mind, he delved deeper into a paper by Fredrickson and Losada (2005), which introduced the "Losada Ratio". This ratio suggests that a balance of three positive emotions for every negative emotion is associated with moderate wellbeing, whereby experiencing five positive to one negative emotions is linked to flourishing. The authors argue that understanding these dynamics can enhance personal and societal flourishing.

However, Nicolas Brown was not convinced. He approached two professors, one of mathematics, Alan Sokol, and the other of psychology, Harris L. Friedman, to explore the research behind the ratio. They wrote a paper (Brown et al., 2013), in which they claimed that the algorithm used to assess the Losada ratio, which involved a complex mathematical model to quantify emotional experiences, was defective. Subsequently, the results of this research were invalid. Following this, Barbara Fredrickson distanced herself from the Losada ratio, but urged people not to throw the baby out with the bathwater. While the exact ratio might not be correct, experiencing more positive than negative emotions is essential for health and wellbeing.

In practical terms, these research publications show that a focus on experiencing more moments of positivity continues to be true. When working with clients or minding our wellbeing, when we are having a bad day with a lot of extra experiences of negativity, it is useful to balance it out by doing something extra that boosts our positivity. Positive psychology interventions, such as practising gratitude or engaging in activities that bring joy (e.g. reading a book, watching your favourite TV programme, playing with children, chatting with friends, or going for a run), might prove helpful as we reflect on what we are grateful for on the day, or explore how we have used humour throughout the day and what we can do to perceive our circumstances in more humorous ways.

References

Brown, N. J. L., Sokal, A. D., & Friedman, H. L. (2013). The complex dynamics of wishful thinking: The critical positivity ratio. *American Psychologist*, *68*(9), 801–813. https://doi.org/10.1037/a0032850

Fredrickson, B. L. (2013). Updated thinking on positivity ratios. *The American Psychologist, 68*(9), 814–822. https://doi.org/10.1037/a0033584. Epub 2013 July 15. PMID: 23855895.
Fredrickson, B. L., & Losada, M. F. (2005). Positive affect and the complex dynamics of human flourishing. *The American Psychologist, 60*(7), 678–686. https://doi.org/10.1037/0003-066X.60.7.678
Friedman, H. L., & Brown, N. J. L. (2018). Implications of debunking the "critical positivity ratio" for humanistic psychology: Introduction to special issue. *Journal of Humanistic Psychology*. https://doi.org/10.1177/0022167818762227

Emotional ecosystem

Over two decades ago, I went to the Vue cinema in Dublin to see Jonathan Glazer's *Birth*. In one scene, Nicole Kidman watches a Wagner opera as the camera records her face for several minutes. What was unique about this moment that stayed with me until today was the range of emotions registered on her face. I have never seen it in any movie before or after. Professor Emeritus Paul Ekman, the researcher who specialises in this field, must have had a field day when watching her performance. The diversity of emotions Nicole showed and we experienced when watching her is called the Emodiversity.

Emodiversity describes both the variety and the abundance of emotional experiences. When we are capable of experiencing such a range of complex emotions, we are more likely to live rich and authentic lives, filled with depth, understanding, and resilience. The study led by Jordi Quoidbach et al. (2014) from the Universitat Pompeu Fabra in Barcelona, Spain, was conducted with 37,000 participants and showed that emodiversity could improve not only our mental health (lower levels of depression) but also our physical health, leading to fewer doctor visits. These results were above and beyond experiencing positive and negative emotions.

While positive psychology often advocates for the cultivation of positive emotions, it's crucial to remember that all emotional experiences are equally important. Recognising and accepting all emotions, whether they are positive, negative, or somewhere in between, is a key factor in our overall wellbeing. Embracing the full spectrum of our emotional life, regardless of how small, unpleasant, or undesirable, is a powerful contributor to our emotional health. This understanding empowers us to navigate our emotional landscape with wisdom and grace.

References

Quoidbach, J., Gruber, J., Mikolajczak, M., Kogan, A., Kotsou, I., & Norton, M. I. (2014). Emodiversity and the emotional ecosystem. *Journal of Experimental Psychology. General, 143*(6), 2057–2066. https://doi.org/10.1037/a0038025

Taxonomy of positive emotions

Charles Darwin is famous for developing an "evolutionary taxonomy", a system for classifying organisms into groups based on their evolutionary relationship. For example, he identified 18 species of passerine birds known as Galapagos Finches, whose beaks adapted to serve various functions over generations. His taxonomy helped us understand what birds belong to which group and how they are related to each other. Similarly, in positive psychology, researchers Dacher Keltner and Alan Cowan from the University of California, Berkeley, created a taxonomy of positive emotions that helps us understand emotions better. Their approach involved classifying emotions in the context of an emotion-related experience, expression of emotions, and physiology.

Having a taxonomy of positive emotions is beneficial in many ways. Firstly, it helps us focus the research on specific emotions and explore their meaning, advantages, and disadvantages in specific contexts. This knowledge allows us to improve our measurement of them and our knowledge of nuances. More importantly, this, in turn, will help us design interventions that would expand on emotional intelligence, improve wellbeing, and support people's lives in various contexts, thereby significantly impacting the field of psychology.

To create such a taxonomy, the researchers first explored the existing literature and drew from unique studies and theories in this area. Then, they used a computational approach that measured participants' full-bodied expressions of emotions, including spontaneous and vocal expressions. This allowed for the creation of a map of semantic space, which explored a variety of emotions, how they are distributed in the population, and ways in which they could be conceptualised.

Through this technique, 11 emotions have emerged: love, compassion, desire, amusement, pride, triumph, awe, interest, joy, relief, and contentment. They were created using mostly Western samples; therefore, additional research is required to explore this in various cultural contexts. This ongoing research not only keeps the audience involved but also makes them feel part of a larger community. Practitioners can use this taxonomy to explore their own emotions and those of their clients. By applying the taxonomy, they can better identify and understand emotional needs which will, in turn, allow them to select more precise interventions. This approach could enable practitioners to address emotional concerns more effectively, drawing on relevant research tailored to each specific emotion.

References

Keltner, D., & Cowen, A. (2021). A taxonomy of positive emotions. *Current Opinion in Behavioral Sciences*, *39*, 216–221. https://doi.org/10.1016/j.cobeha.2021.04.013

Accomplishment

Grit

One of the most intelligent people on Earth is a man with an IQ in the region of 195–220. To get into Mensa, the largest and oldest IQ society, a person must be in the top 2% of the most intelligent people on Earth, which is currently over 130. However, despite his high IQ, he has not been very successful in life, which some attribute to his low social development. Coming from a poor background, he was abused by his step-father and bullied at school, and despite receiving perfect scores on his SATs, he has never completed university, and found it challenging to hold down a job. When you review this man's life and try to explain his lack of apparent success, what springs to mind is GRIT or their lack of.

GRIT is a phenomenon explored by a former maths teacher and now an academic, Angela Duckworth. When teaching maths, she noted that rarely the students with a higher aptitude for maths at the beginning of the year did well at the end of the year. It is because GRIT goes beyond the IQ or even beyond any talent one may have. GRIT is the ability to sustain perseverance and passion over extended periods. The initial interest we get in doing something exciting is one thing, but keeping the interest going is a challenge.

In this main paper introducing the concept of GRIT, Angela Duckworth presented studies from around 5,074 participants from various backgrounds (Duckworth et al., 2007). She found that GRIT was associated with success; however, it had little to do with people's intelligence or talent. Instead, it was an ability to work hard over a long period of time, regardless of adversities, failures, or any plateaus they experienced during the process.

GRIT comprises two components, one of which indicates consistency of interest, that is, the passion that kept them going. This relates to maintaining the same goal instead of changing it. It is about not being distracted by new pursuits and not changing interests. Instead, it is about maintaining interest and focusing on one thing they are interested in. The other one comprises the perseverance or the effort individuals put into it. This part is about individuals achieving their goals regardless of setbacks, working diligently, and finishing what they began.

Educators have embraced GRIT, with some schools aiming to become GRITTY schools by helping students develop their passion and perseverance. However, a systematic review of a decade of research showed only a weak to moderate correlation of GRIT with other variables (Christopoulou et al., 2018). More importantly, a meta-analysis of GRIT research (Credé et al., 2017), including almost 67,000 individuals, showed that while GRIT was only moderately associated with higher performance, it was strongly correlated with a personality trait of conscientiousness, which relates to doing our work dutifully and thoroughly. Furthermore, this review found that what drove the GRIT's results was, in fact, perseverance. Thus, the exciting aspect of the model was not as relevant.

It is important to note that this research is essential for several reasons. Firstly, it has been conducted with a large number of people, and it is important that both the benefits of the research and its limitations are known before it is recommended. More importantly, however, one crucial point it explored was the need to look beyond the IQ as the reason for people's success. Learnt perseverance behaviours could be very beneficial to explore about accomplishment.

References

Christopoulou, M., Lakioti, A., Pezirkianidis, C., Karakasidou, E., & Stalikas, A. (2018). The role of grit in education: A systematic review. *Psychology*, *9*, 2951–2971. https://doi.org/10.4236/psych.2018.915171

Credé, M., Tynan, M. C., & Harms, P. D. (2017). Much ado about grit: A meta-analytic synthesis of the grit literature. *Journal of Personality and Social Psychology*, *113*(3), 492–511. https://doi.org/10.1037/pspp0000102

Duckworth, A. L., Peterson, C., Matthews, M. D., & Kelly, D. R. (2007). Grit: Perseverance and passion for long-term goals. *Journal of Personality and Social Psychology*, *92*(6), 1087–1101. https://doi-org.elib.tcd.ie/10.1037/0022-3514.92.6.1087

Personal goals

I love music. When I was 15, I dreamed of working for the Polish Radio "Trojka". In the 1980s and 1990s, it was the coolest radio station, with a top 50 hit list broadcast on Friday nights. Back then, teenagers gathered around their radios, listening intently to the latest hits, recording songs on cassette tapes to re-play them during the week – missing the show was not an option and when the tape got stuck in the record-player, it was a disaster. My friends and I often organised Friday night parties, where we listened, danced to the music, and giggled at all the DJ jokes. I absolutely loved this show, and I wanted to contribute to it meaningfully.

Determined, I set up a goal for myself and attempted to break into the station several times, without luck. Finally, I managed to speak directly with the DJ himself. In a brief conversation, I convinced him that we should work together, and to my excitement, he agreed. I stayed with the station for four years, during which I was offered unique development opportunities. I interpreted live interviews with famous artists, attended "Music and Media" conferences where I got to meet DJs from around the world, wrote a monthly music column for a teenage magazine, and, most importantly, I got to be a DJ for a year. Despite the fun I have had, a few years into it I realised that it was not what I wanted to do in my life. The goals I have set up for myself have allowed me to connect with people I have never thought or imagined possible. My work brought me immense happiness and helped me shape my identity. Most importantly, these four years of my life gave me the confidence to pursue any dream I had for the future.

Personal goals are a powerful driver for wellbeing. Ken Sheldon and colleagues designed a six-month experiment encouraging people to set and pursue personal goals. These goals aim to satisfy their basic psychological needs, which include relatedness, competence, and autonomy (see the section on Self-Determination theory for more details). As such, goals like building a social network, pursuing education, or getting a part-time job to gain independence may have been included. Participants were encouraged to identify their goals and reflect on how they aligned with those needs. Results of this study showed that those who sustained their efforts to achieve their goals have, over time, improved their wellbeing. This study also highlighted the need to maintain progress when pursuing personal goals. It is that progress that keeps us going.

These findings offer significant value to practitioners, demonstrating that improving wellbeing is not tied to the specific wellbeing models. We don't need to teach people about positive psychology to help them improve their wellbeing. Instead, the mere re-shifting of their attention towards intrinsically motivating goals can transform their wellbeing and make their lives more worthwhile.

References

Sheldon, K. M., Abad, N., Ferguson, Y., Gunz, A., Houser-Marko, L., Nichols, C. P., & Lyubomirsky, S. (2010). Persistent pursuit of need-satisfying goals leads to increased happiness: A 6-month experimental longitudinal study. *Motivation & Emotion*, *34*(1), 39–48. https://doi-org.elib.tcd.ie/10.1007/s11031-009-9153-1

Optimism

When I ask my students to differentiate between optimism and hope, it never fails to spark a lively debate. Some view optimism as synonymous with hope; others mix the definitions of optimism (the belief that all will work out) and hope (having agency and a pathway to make things work). However, the consensus is clear that the debate is crucial for our exploration and better understanding to help us live a good life.

This paper by Gillham and colleagues (2001) explores one of the most influential theories of optimism. There are currently two main approaches to it. The first one views optimism as a trait (Dispositional Optimism), and the second one considers it a thinking style that can change (Explanatory Style). The changeable nature of the explanatory styles made them an attractive way to help people develop.

Explanatory styles refer to how we explain positive and negative events in our lives. Taking negative events as an example, the optimistic explanatory style refers to thinking that negative events are not due to our stable characteristics about ourselves. For example, if a person fails their driver's licence test, a pessimist would blame their intelligence or inherent lack of ability to do any tests or drive. On the other hand, an optimist would be more likely to consider the circumstances surrounding their failure, such as not getting enough sleep the previous night, the examiner being too strict, or not putting enough hours of driving beforehand. Another example could be a job interview. A pessimist might attribute a failed interview to their lack of skills or inability to present themselves. At the same time, an optimist might see it as a learning opportunity and focus on the aspects they can improve for the next interview. Therefore, an optimist would be more likely to dust themselves off and try again. It is much harder to do it when you think you are a pessimistic thinker and see your traits and personal characteristics as less malleable about yourself.

Furthermore, an optimist would consider their setback temporary, whereas a pessimist would see it as a problem that will never change. Finally, an optimist can compartmentalise the issue and see that while they may not have successfully gotten a driver's licence, they would reflect on other aspects of their lives going well, such as living in an area with ample public transport or having friends who can support them in the times of trouble. Pessimistic thinkers would catastrophise and see their lives ruined when a bad thing happened to them. So, optimism and pessimism, according to this theory, are matters of choice and different thinking styles rather than innate qualities.

The first time I came across explanatory styles, I completed a test showing that I was primarily pessimistic. This surprised me, but inspired by research claiming that explanatory styles can change, I began working hard to change my pessimistic thinking into optimism. Years later, I attempted the assessment again, and to my delight, it seemed to have worked. My thinking changed to be more optimistic. In fact, I remember the days when I was aware of how my thinking was altering from pessimistic to optimistic. My automatic reaction to a negative situation was pessimistic, then after a few minutes, shortened to a few seconds as years passed by, the optimistic thoughts slowly began to kick in, and it felt as if I had a person inside my head convincing me that everything will work out well. While every now and then pessimistic thinking wins the battle of attention, I trust optimism will very soon follow. The benefits of this change were immense. I found myself more resilient in the face of challenges, more open to new opportunities, and overall, happier in my daily life. So, this simple process described in this paper has worked well for me.

References

Gillham, J. E., Shatté, A. J., Reivich, K. J., & Seligman, M. E. P. (2001). Optimism, pessimism, and explanatory style. In E. C. Chang (Ed.), *Optimism & pessimism: Implications for theory, research, and practice* (pp. 53–75). American Psychological Association. https://doi.org/10.1037/10385-003

Optimism bias

When people say that opposites attract, they could be right. My mum has always been an eternal optimist, thinking everything would work out well. In contrast, my late father was a self-proclaimed pessimist, always finding a downside to everything. As a child, I was in the middle trying to figure out which picture they painted, optimistic or pessimistic, was more likely to happen. I admit that while it was a little confusing when I was younger, I found it entertaining as a teenager. Optimism bias is the difference between what we expect from life and its outcome. If the reality is worse than expected the bias is optimistic, if it is better than expected it is pessimistic.

For example, when my parents and I once went to the circus in the middle of a freezing Polish winter, swept by Siberian winds, my father tried to convince us it was not a good idea. The weather was too severe, we would freeze and catch a cold, bad things would happen to us, so it was better to stay home. On the other hand, my mum said that the weather didn't matter; we would wrap up well and have fun, and it would all work out well. On the way to the circus, I slipped on the icy path and fell down, knocking down my mum and then my dad. And there we were, all lying down on ice, trying to get up but slipping back down, with very sore bums, and laughing our heads off. Even though both my dad's and my mum's predictions came true – that comical moment has become a memory I will treasure forever.

Neuropsychologist from the University College London (UK) and MIT (USA) Tali Sharot's theory of Optimism Bias suggests that over 70% of people overestimate positive outcomes in the future. We predict that we are more likely to experience positive events in the future, such as better job opportunities, maintaining health, or getting birthday presents we like than we actually do. At the same time, we underestimate the likelihood of bad things happening to us, such as accidents, divorces, or chronic disease. "These bad things are more likely to happen to others" – we say – "not us". Interestingly, this bias persists, even if we are presented with facts that contradict our initial views. For example, optimistic individuals who predicted a 10% likelihood of being diagnosed with cancer do not update their thinking even after learning that their actual probability of having cancer is 30%. Conversely, pessimists who initially thought they had a 40% likelihood of getting a cancer diagnosis updated their views and dropped their likelihood to 30%. This discrepancy demonstrates how our minds trick us when faced with negative information.

The important question is whether it is helpful for us to hold on to these optimistic views. If not for my mum, we would have stayed at home each time it was snowing, which was often in my hometown. Optimism encourages us to seek out opportunities to turn our dreams into reality. And interestingly, this optimism bias, while not always adaptive, has significant evolutionary benefits. It has helped us survive and sometimes even thrive. So, it is something that is worthwhile embracing.

References

Sharot, T. (2011). The optimism bias. *Current Biology, 21*(23), R941–R945. https://doi.org/10.1016/j.cub.2011.10.030

Defensive pessimism

A while back, I experienced a cancer scare that left me anxiously waiting for appointments and biopsy results for many weeks. It was an upsetting time for me, my family, and my friends, even though I recognised that others had much tougher times, enduring diagnosis and long-term treatment. During this time, some of my friends gave me well-meaning advice to relax and not think about it, which I could not do. Instead, I preferred grabbing the devil by its horns, confronting the uncertainties, and planning for the worst-case scenario. By the time my results came back clear, I had mapped out a comprehensive plan for every eventuality and felt ready to face it, no matter what came my way. Upon reflection, during my cancer scare, I engaged my defensive pessimism strategy to help me cope with it.

Julie Norem from Wellesley College, USA and Nancy Cantor from Rutgers University-Newark, USA (1986) introduced the concept of defensive pessimism. It describes a coping strategy people use in risky situations. Instead of focusing on the best possible outcome, they lower their expectations and use the anxiety they experience as a motivator to keep going. This approach allows them to mentally prepare for what will come and protect themselves if things go wrong. It is like building a raft just in case, instead of doing nothing and hoping that a boat will soon arrive.

Think of it as a spectrum between the worst-case and best-case scenarios. Optimistic people tend to expect the best from life when in a risky situation. They may briefly consider a negative outcome but spend most of their energy exploring positive possibilities that make them feel good. On the other hand, defensive pessimists will be more inclined to stay closer to the worst-case scenario so that they can prepare all their resources to cope with it in case they need to. "It is better to be prepared" is their motto.

Interestingly, denying defensive pessimists an opportunity to reflect on the worst-case scenario makes them more anxious. In contrast, optimists prefer to avoid contemplating the worst-case scenario; when forced to do so, they feel more anxious. While the wellbeing outcomes for both optimists and defensive pessimists are similar, their process of dealing with adversity is different.

These findings are, therefore, very useful for practitioners. They highlight that optimistic thinking is only sometimes beneficial. Pushing defensive pessimists into a positive mindset without allowing them to prepare could increase their anxiety. Equally, pushing optimism into the worst-case scenario could be anxiety-provoking. Practitioners must be aware of their preferred approach and not force others into their preferred way of thinking. Also, bearing in mind that for some, support could mean that we allow them the time and space for catastrophising and planning for the worst-case scenario – this is how they find comfort in a difficult situation.

References

Norem, J. K., & Cantor, N. (1986). Defensive pessimism: Harnessing anxiety as motivation. *Journal of Personality and Social Psychology*, *51*(6), 1208–1217. https://doi.org/10.1037/0022-3514.51.6.1208

Life meaning and purpose

Life is pretty meaningful

On 15 May 1972, Alabama Governor George Wallace survived an assassination attempt. The diary of the assassin, who was a very disturbed man, read that he planned the act of violence as a desire to be seen, a desire for his life to matter. Mother Teresa, Mahatma Gandhi, and Martin Luther King, Jr. are on the opposite end of this spectrum. They lived a truly meaningful life that mattered for the right reasons. Their actions, beliefs, and words have changed how people thought and acted – they have changed the course of history. Lives like theirs were undoubtedly meaningful, but what about our lives, the ordinary lives we live? Could they be meaningful, too? The researchers Samantha Heintzelman and Laura King explored this in their article.

Despite various definitions of a meaningful life, the authors describe it as a life that has a purpose and matters to people. They review research suggesting that most people perceive their lives as meaningful. We don't need to be Mother Teresa to do it. This challenges the notion that meaningful lives are special, exceptional ways of living. They link it to eudaimonic wellbeing, which focuses on a virtuous, meaningful life experienced by most people. Extensive national surveys consistently showed that life is meaningful for most people. Therefore, we do not need to engage in extraordinary activities to make our lives meaningful. What most of us do every day suffices.

The authors also explore the literature relating to the sources of meaningful life and the first one they mention are social connections. When people are lonely, socially excluded, or ignored, their overall wellbeing and their meaning in life suffer. This applies to constant exclusion as well as temporary one. Associated with it is mood. When in a positive mood, or experiencing positive emotions, our meaning in life is rated as higher than when we are in a negative mood. So, our mood and social connection colour the extent to which our life is meaningful.

Most importantly, however, a significant source of a meaningful life is a life that makes sense. In a series of studies, the researchers created clear patterns of pictures that made sense as they depicted changing seasons. When participants completed an assessment of their meaning in life, they showed higher levels of it compared to participants whose pictures were shown randomly. The results of this study indicate that even small changes in our environment that either make or do not make sense to us impact our perception of meaningfulness in life.

This paper has many implications for practitioners. When supporting individuals searching for meaning or trying to articulate it for the first time, it is tempting to disregard their ordinary lives. Yet research indicates that these ordinary lives are inherently meaningful. This is why practitioners should emphasise this when discussing meaning with clients. After all, meaning is subjective rather than universally objective.

Also, given the research findings showing how a fleeting emotional state influences our perceptions of meaning, it is vital to bear this in mind when discussing life meaning. When individuals are confused or uncertain about their life course, when their daily life does not make sense, a discussion about meaning may add to their confusion. Helping them make sense of the chaos and open the door to deeper insights about their lives can provide the clarity they need to discuss the meaningfulness of their lives – the timing of our discussion matters.

References

Heintzelman, S. J., & King, L. A. (2014). Life is pretty meaningful. *American Psychologist*, *69*(6), 561–574. https://doi.org/10.1037/a0035049

In search of meaning

My grandmother was 18 when the Second World War (WW2) began. Shortly after, she joined the underground army and fought for the freedom of Poland and the city of Warsaw she loved so much. She became a courier, passing secret messages between battalions as they prepared to defend their city. She trained as a nurse, tending to the wounded on the front lines. One of her most heroic acts was saving a group of people who were being marched into a concentration camp. Every other night, she threw food parcels over the Ghetto wall to feed the starving. She knew that if she were caught, her death would be inevitable, but that didn't stop her. At the time, my grandfather, who was madly in love with her, and her entire family begged her to stay home, get married, and wait until the war ended. But my grandmother chose to risk her life fighting for freedom with her battalion. What is remarkable is that, as a grandmother, she was never a risk-taker. She was one of the wisest and most prudent people I have ever known. When I asked her why she had done it, she said it made her life meaningful. It gave her life purpose.

Having meaning is a powerful drive to do anything in life. On the other hand, searching for meaning is a very different state of mind. Michael Steger (2008), from Colorado State University, USA, led a team to explore what happens when people search for meaning. The study found that while people search for meaning, they experience more anxiety and dissatisfaction with their past and tend to ruminate more. At the same time, they become more curious, open, and engaged with their experiences. This, in turn, is beneficial for them when searching for their meaning. The duality of this process, marked by being torn between an unsatisfactory past and an uncertain future, contributes to their lower overall wellbeing.

For my grandmother, meaning emerged as soon as the war began. She found her purpose in the fight for freedom, and it guided her actions from the beginning of the war, during the Warsaw Uprising, when all her closest friends perished in a single day, and in the aftermath when she helped rebuild the city of Warsaw, brick by brick. In contrast, my grandfather struggled to find meaning during the war atrocities. It wasn't until many years after the war had ended that he began to understand his own purpose in life, as a husband and a father.

References

Steger, M. F., Kashdan, T. B., Sullivan, B. A., & Lorentz, D. (2008). Understanding the search for meaning in life: Personality, cognitive style, and the dynamic between seeking and experiencing meaning. *Journal of Personality*, *76*(2), 199–228. https://doi.org.elib.tcd.ie/10.1111/j.1467-6494.2007.00484.x

Global meaning-making

One of my friends thinks big. He is an editor of one of the daily newspapers and rarely worries about the small stuff. He rarely misses sleep over arguments with colleagues, health issues, or other personal matters. He was once made redundant and has rarely mentioned it as an issue. He said it was part of life; jobs come and go, so he took the redundancy as an opportunity to travel. While he doesn't sweat the small things, he gets upset about the big issues.

He commonly loses a night's sleep over the European state of the economy, the war in Ukraine, or the United Nation's Paris Climate Agreement. These are the matters that churn in his head, and he finds them difficult to adapt to. This mindset could be associated with his job as an editor, but I'm sure many others who are not journalists feel the same way.

Even though it might not be to the same degree, many of us are affected by the current affairs. Our meaning-making comprises global meaning and situational meaning (Park, 2022). This is a universal process that we all go through. Global meaning is made from beliefs, values, and goals that help us understand how the world works. Situational meaning relates to specific situations. When we attempt to make new meaning of something, we do it best by reducing the discrepancy between our global beliefs and our experience of a situation.

For example, take a terrorist attack. We may feel we live in a safe country, and it is safe for us to go to a concert, Christmas market, or work. In other words, our global belief is that attacks may happen in other countries or cities, but not in our own and not in these circumstances. But then, when a terrorist attack occurs, it causes us distress, and all our beliefs are questioned. This is how our assumptions of safety are shattered.

To return to status quo, we need to make meaning by reappraising the event as less threatening so that we can let go of our fears and go on living our lives. We can do it by reflecting on how the attack led to the government setting stricter guidelines on protecting citizens. This may be more thorough security checks. This changed meaning allows us to see value in the ordeal of an attack, reaffirms our values of compassion and perhaps safety, and impacts our new global beliefs and self-identity.

This global meaning-making model emphasises the process we take to come to terms with upsetting events. More importantly, it clarifies the pivotal role that global meaning plays in this process, empowering us to take control of our reactions and cope with distress.

The process could also apply to a personal situation. For example, your mother's scans have shown a lump on her ovaries. She went to a doctor and was scheduled to have an ultrasound to explore it 3 months later. Is this in line with your global beliefs of how soon a cancer scan should take place after detecting a lump? If you believe the wait time is reasonable and trust that doctors would have expedited the process if they deemed it urgent, you may feel little or no distress. However, if you believe it is inconsistent with your expectations of how long she should wait for a scan, it may cause you distress. To reduce it, you will need to make meaning by reappraising it. Perhaps you will see the healthcare system as overwhelmed and unable to cope with the demand, so your new goal will be to contact a private service to do it promptly. In this case, your changed belief about the system could be that it is inefficient. This is how we can tweak our global beliefs to serve us better.

For my friend journalist, this reappraisal of global thinking is a fundamental part of his daily life to help him cope with the twists and turns associated with current affairs. For many other people, it is a process hidden from their consciousness, making the global meaning so much harder to comprehend. Whatever the starting point is, the end result is the same – a changed belief about both the situation and the way the world works could help us make sense of it better. It is important to note that this change could impact us in many different ways, but it also holds the potential for positive transformation.

References

Park, C. L. (2022). Meaning making following trauma. *Frontiers in Psychology*, *13*, 844891. https://doi.org/10.3389/fpsyg.2022.844891

Relationships

Capitalisation

My cousin has been married to her college sweetheart for three decades. Their relationship is amazing, despite their ups and downs, as every couple experiences. One evening, over a glass of wine, we started to discuss what mattered to them. Two things have stuck with me after this conversation. One is how they never go to sleep after an argument without reconciling. Either of them always offers an olive branch, and the other accepts it immediately. The second thing is how they celebrate each other's successes. When my cousin took a photograph which went viral online, her husband got a bottle of bubbly and spent the whole night looking at her photograph, discussing the composition, light, and all other aspects of the picture. When he invented his first machine and sold it to a factory, they celebrated for the whole weekend, daydreaming about the future. These are examples of big things they cheer each other on, but even small achievements seem like big celebrations. This is what the capitalisation model is all about.

Shelley Gable from the University of California and Harry Reis from the University of Rochester describe four distinct ways people can react to others' good news:

1. With support and enthusiasm, for example, the way my cousin and her husband react to the good news, giving a person time to talk about it, asking questions, cheering them on (active-constructive)
2. With support but little enthusiasm, for example, being pleased for the person but not going beyond "well done". It is a quieter and more understated support (passive-constructive)
3. Being dismissive and critical, that is, pointing out all the negatives in the good news; for example, if the good news is about promotion at work, pointing out that it would mean working more hours (active-destructive)
4. Ignoring the event, for example, pretending like the good news never happened, is not essential (passive-destructive)

Only active-constructive responding leads to deep connections and thriving relationships. All other reactions tend to breed resentment or may even lead to relationship conflict. This model has now been tested with couples, showing that it leads to increased intimacy, a critical factor in healthy relationships. Interestingly, further studies have demonstrated that the support for adverse events is more complex, nuanced, and less predictable, meaning that the same approach to supporting people works differently for individuals. However, capitalising on positive events consistently shows positive results in building relationships.

This model is crucial for practitioners. Firstly, it is useful when developing relationships with their clients. It offers strategies for evaluating how much we capitalise on our clients' positive events. Secondly, it is a great foundation for helping clients understand what they can do to improve relationships with others. Instead of focusing on how they argue with people, we can shift our focus to a less contentious topic of how to improve relationships by changing their reactions to the good news in all aspects of their lives. This is a safer topic for individuals to experiment on, as the opportunities for capitalising on positive events are more frequent than experimenting with changed reactions to adverse events. Finally, this model invites us to hold up a mirror and offer opportunities to put it in front of us and see how much of what we do capitalises on those positive events and how many opportunities for connection and joy we miss out in our daily interactions. It also inspires us to make small changes that strengthen our relationships with others.

References

Gable, S. L., & Reis, H. T. (2010). Good news! Capitalizing on positive events in an interpersonal context. *Advances in Experimental Social Psychology*, *42*, 195–257. https://doi.org/10.1016/S0065-2601(10)42004-3

Positivity resonance

A few years ago, I stood at a bus stop nearby the Liffey river near O'Connell Street in Dublin. The chilly air made me press against the wall with my arms wrapped tightly around my body to keep warm. Three other people were waiting at the bus stop, some doomscrolling through their phones or pacing to keep warm. Suddenly, a woman rummaging through her bag accidently sent a pile of paper tumbling out. They all caught by the wind began to scatter widely. Without hesitation, everyone at the bus stop came to the rescue. We ran around the street, darting after the swirling pages, grabbed them midair, and chased after the papers falling on the ground. Passers-by joined us on our mission to retrieve all the pages. The traffic stopped; the drivers were cheering us on pointing out to the flying pages, especially those dangerously close to the river. Amid all the commotion, I realised that we were all smiling or laughing out loud. Once the mission was complete everyone huddled together, a bunch of strangers talking over each other like friends and sharing the joyful and very unexpected experience. At that moment, I felt an amazing connection with people whose names I will never know – a connection known as positivity resonance.

Positivity resonance is a high-quality interpersonal connection experienced by romantic partners, friends, work colleagues, or strangers (Major et al., 2018). The three components of this connection are (1) shared positive affect, (2) mutual care and concern, and (3) synchronicity at behavioural and biological levels. This is exactly what that moment on the street in Dublin felt like – a momentary explosion of sparks among a group of strangers who began to care about something or someone and shared a lot of joy doing it.

To date, growing research shows the positive impact of such connections on wellbeing at the psychological and cellular levels. Researchers have also developed interventions to create positivity resonance. So, we don't need to leave it to chance and wait around bus stops to experience similar events. Instead, we can recreate these moments ourselves. Practitioners' awareness of such a concept makes it more likely for us to experience it. It is about noticing those moments of connection and acknowledging when they happen. While we are in the middle of these moments, it is about keeping them going to experience more connection and joy, which helps us live a good life.

References

Major, B. C., Le Nguyen, K. D., Lundberg, K. B., & Fredrickson, B. L. (2018). Well-being correlates of perceived positivity resonance: Evidence from trait and episode-level assessments. *Personality & Social Psychology Bulletin*, *44*(12), 1631–1647. https://doi.org/10.1177/0146167218771324

Flow

Autotelic personality

I once had lunch with a group of professional musicians from a national symphony orchestra, when one of them asked me to share a curious positive psychology fact that might resonate with them. I immediately thought of "flow", which is a state of becoming so absorbed in a task that we lose ourselves in what we do, lose the track of time, place, and who we are. During a flow experience, our entire focus is on the task at hand. For musicians, I thought, that task would be making music. What is wonderful about a flow process is that after we come out of flow, we experience a boost of wellbeing, which is so addictive that it makes us crave more flow.

Interestingly, everyone around the table related to it. They nodded their heads enthusiastically and shared stories about their flow experiences, such as working through the night and not realising that the dawn was coming. Or, playing a concert in front of an audience and their time flying so fast that a 3-hour concert felt like minutes. They have all been there, except for one person. He said that while he really enjoyed playing music, he rarely experienced flow. A few years later, I met him on a university campus walking with a purpose. He said he quit his job in the orchestra and was now rushing to his lectures, pursuing a different career. I often wondered if our conversation that day at lunch had influenced his decision. I hope it didn't, but I also hope that in his new job he finds more opportunities to experience flow.

Some of us are lucky to experience flow every day. Others only encounter it occasionally or not at all. For those who do, the secret often lies in how they approach their tasks. Flow is a nexus between the task being challenging and our capabilities to address this challenge. When the task is too hard and surpasses our skills, it may trigger anxiety. If it is too easy and does not stretch our abilities, it leads to boredom. The experience of flow occurs when the challenge and skills are just right. We can cultivate our flow experiences by adjusting our tasks to match our skillset.

Apart from balancing challenge and skills, some of us are fortunate to have an autotelic personality that makes us more likely to get into the state of flow. This is what the late Mihaly Csikszentmihalyi, the psychologist who pioneered the concept of flow, explored in one of his final articles led by Dwight Tse from Claremont Graduate University, USA. They shared the attributes of individuals with an autotelic personality, which included natural curiosity about the world, persistence in pursuing our interests, low centredness, intrinsic motivation that drives our interest, enjoyment of challenges, transformation of boredom into this highly alert state, and being able to control our attention. These attributes led to "flow proneness", increasing the likelihood of experiencing flow regularly.

This study also examined how autotelic personality impacts wellbeing. The researchers found an indirect effect of autotelic personality on wellbeing, via their daily flow experiences. This means that individuals with the propensity to flow engage in regular flow experiences, and they, in turn, help them sustain their wellbeing.

For practitioners, these findings highlight the importance of creating conditions that support their clients' flow experiences. This is particularly crucial for individuals who may not have an autotelic personality. Practitioners can support them in developing flow by cultivating traits, such as curiosity or persistence, or by exploring and designing environments that help them balance a bit of a challenge with their skills. Whether in educational, workplace, or therapeutic settings, flow can provide a valuable pathway towards enhanced wellbeing.

References

Tse, D. C. K., Nakamura, J., & Csikszentmihalyi, M. (2020). Living well by "flowing' well: The indirect effect of autotelic personality on well-being through flow experience. *The Journal of Positive Psychology*, *16*(3), 310–321. https://doi.org/10.1080/17439760.2020.1716055

Self-acceptance

I have an obsession with prioritising things. I like to know the relationships between concepts, their structure, and which one is central and makes the most difference in the mix. This is why I had to ask Carol Ryff about her model of Psychological Wellbeing, which comprises six components: (1) environmental mastery, (2) autonomy, (3) personal growth, (4) relationships, (5) self-acceptance, and (6) purpose and meaning. From all her research over the last 40 years, I asked which of the six components is the most important. She reflected on it and said: self-acceptance. Yet self-acceptance does not even appear in the *Encyclopedia of Positive Psychology*, nor is it mentioned in the *Handbook of Positive Psychology*. Curiously, it is ignored in the positive psychology literature despite being part of one of the key wellbeing models.

Carl Rogers has published much valuable work about the importance of self-acceptance. He claimed that unless we give ourselves unconditional regard and fully accept all that is good, bad, and ugly about ourselves, we are not able to grow or reach a state of self-actualisation. Self-acceptance is, therefore, a necessary route to optimal human functioning. Let us take as an example a friend who spent all her adolescence beating herself up, thinking that something was seriously wrong with her. Until one day when her therapist suggested she should do an attention-deficit hyperactivity disorder (ADHD) assessment. It transpired that the confusion she felt was due to an undiagnosed condition. Once she became aware of it, it changed her life. She began to embrace herself, and it helped her explain why she felt and behaved in the way she did. The diagnosis opened the door to her self-acceptance. It was a transformational moment for her.

Self-acceptance is also a fundamental part of all the research on self-compassion, Rational Emotive Behaviour Therapy, Acceptance and Commitment Therapy, and many other approaches that put us first. Apart from these therapies, research on self-acceptance within positive psychology is scarce. It is explored mainly with clinical populations as a pathway for recovery. That scarcity exists even though it is a significant part of the Psychological Wellbeing model and consequently of a Mental Health Continuum model, a model that incorporates self-acceptance as a key component and provides a comprehensive understanding of mental health.

Of the articles that exist, I selected one that has one of the highest citations and explores self-acceptance as the concept of positive psychology. An article led by Danilo Garcia from the University of Gothenburg (Sweden) explored which aspects of psychological wellbeing are associated with harmonious living. Harmony in life, in the context of psychological wellbeing, refers to a state of balance, peace, and agreement within oneself and with the environment. It requires us to consider our subjective assessment of our global view of harmony and then reflect on where our life is in its context – specifically, whether or not our life involves balance, whether we fit in or feel attuned with our life.

From this perspective, Garcia et al.'s research demonstrates that harmony in life is closely tied to self-acceptance and environmental mastery – see the review of PWB model (Ryff & Singer, 2008) for details. This suggests that for our lives to be harmonious, we must accept all aspects of ourselves, including our past actions and decisions. Self-acceptance is about refraining from self-judgement and taking responsibility for our actions, regardless of how we perceive them in hindsight. This study not only underscores the importance of self-acceptance in wellbeing but also highlights it as a pathway to living in harmony with ourselves and our environment.

References

Garcia, D., Al Nima, A., & Kjell, O. N. (2014). The affective profiles, psychological well-being, and harmony: Environmental mastery and self-acceptance predict the sense of a harmonious life. *PeerJ*, *2*, e259. https://doi.org/10.7717/peerj.259

Ryff, C. D., & Singer, B. H. (2008). Know thyself and become what you are: A eudaimonic approach to psychological well-being. *Journal of Happiness Studies*, *9*(1), 13–39. https://doi-org.elib.tcd.ie/10.1007/s10902-006-9019-0

Personal growth

Personal growth

It is fascinating to witness the transformative power of therapy on individuals. Their new way of thinking and the vocabulary they use to describe the world around them are different and inspirational. It's as if the journey of personal growth elevates them to a new level of self-awareness, enabling them to perceive nuances they hadn't noticed before and then eloquently articulate their thoughts and feelings relating to their daily experiences and needs. While all experiences shape us to some extent, therapy influences our personal growth significantly.

What does it mean to grow? This is the question that Christine Robitschek from Texas Tech University, USA, sought to answer when she delved into the concept of Personal Growth Initiative (PGI) and its updated version, PGI-2. PGI defines an individual's capacity to orient themselves towards an environment or use their personal resources for self-development. PGI relates to our pro-active and intentional engagement in personal growth, a trait that either drives us towards a journey of growth or not. It is an amalgamation of beliefs, attitudes, and values that encourage people to change. What differentiates it from beliefs that drive it is the action people take to grow. Research suggests that higher levels of PGI are linked to improved coping skills when facing life's challenges and greater psychological wellbeing. This approach is particularly beneficial in counselling, coaching, or any context explicitly emphasising self-development.

PGI comprises four key components:

1. **Readiness for change** – this is a crucial component of PGI. It reflects our willingness to recognise our needs in relation to personal development, the need for change, and be open to taking steps towards it. This readiness is not just a passive state, but an active decision to embrace change, which is often the catalyst for our personal growth.
2. **Planfulness** – this is our ability to plan for change. It involves setting up goals for personal development. To do it, we practise a range of complex skills, such as strategic thinking, and an ability to develop a detailed plan for self-growth.

3. **Using resources** – this is the ability to draw from external resources at our disposal. For example, we can recognise mentors who can help us grow, ways to tap into the systems around us, or any educational materials that can support our growth. This component of personal growth is about proactively using these resources rather than waiting for others to suggest them.
4. **Intentional behaviour** – this is our ability to take proactive action to further develop ourselves. It is about being consistent with setting goals and aiming to reach them.

Practitioners can easily use this model as a guide to personal development, be it as a self-measure of PGI or a structure for discussion with a client. We can explore how much each person values personal development, what their strengths are in relation to each of its four components, and what actions they could take to move from one state to another to ensure personal growth.

References

Robitschek, C. (1998). Personal growth initiative: The construct and its measure. *Measurement and Evaluation in Counseling and Development*, *30*(4), 183–198. https://doi.org/10.1080/07481756.1998.12068941

Personal growth process model

Most people have heard of person-centred or client-centred therapy. It describes therapy focused on the client's experience rather than the therapist's interpretation (e.g. Freudian psychoanalytic approach). At the foundation of this approach lies a belief that clients can self-heal and experience personal growth. To facilitate it, the therapist needs to offer clients empathy and unconditional positive regard. While many of us are familiar with this concept to some extent, as most therapists practise this type of therapy in the modern world, there was a time when this approach was revolutionary. And it all came from Carl Rogers, a psychologist whose contributions to the knowledge extend across various aspects of humanistic psychology.

Given that personal growth is one of the therapy outcomes, recently, a model of a personal growth process was introduced, which stems from the organismic valuing process developed by Rogers. Led by Mia Maurer from Lund University in Sweden, the team developed an alternative to the PGI. This model explores personal growth as a sociocognitive embodied process that works in ongoing cycles of change. The socio-aspect highlights the social environment's role in individuals' personal growth process. The cognitive aspect relates to the changes in thinking, and the embodied aspect brings in psychological changes and their embodiment. The process is not linear in that it is chaotic and iterative. It is gradual in that it takes time and is holistic, as it is embedded into all systems surrounding the individual, including social and cultural dimensions.

When undergoing the process, individuals progress from a place of psychological safety towards wellbeing. Wellbeing is defined as authenticity, harmony, and life satisfaction. Authenticity is a coherence between the person we are inside (e.g. emotions, thoughts, beliefs, values) and our public persona. Harmony refers to being able to balance and be flexible when integrating various facets of our lives. Life satisfaction is being satisfied with the course of our lives and how it turned out to be.

The authors identified a range of shifts that occur throughout the process that lead to wellbeing. These are developing self-awareness and being open to experiencing change without putting up defences. Without that openness, the change cannot happen. Another shift relates to having existential courage to face adversities in life with all its ups and downs. The next shift is the sense of autonomy or having an internal locus of control, whereby an individual is no longer externally directed but realises that they take a driver's seat on their life journey. The following shift relates to taking responsibility for the self and others, whereby an individual becomes aware of their thoughts and values or their behaviour's impact on others. Finally, the next shift is the experience of self-compassion and compassion towards others, whereby an individual can be their best friend and be given unconditional positive regard towards others.

The foundation of the personal growth process lies in practice. It was developed with practice in mind; therefore, it can easily be adapted to other practical domains. This could be the apparent approaches of therapy and coaching, as well as less obvious approaches in the workplace when leaders could start with psychological safety and then slowly help their team move through the process of change that would lead to the personal growth of the team members. I have seen this enacted in one organisation. I delivered a range of workshops for them, and a few people in different groups talked about how other team members transformed into colleagues and employees. They attended six workshops delivered once a month and returned as different, more compassionate people. I asked the Learning and Development manager what exactly they did during the six workshops that made such a difference, and she told me that they followed a process similar to the one described by Maurer and saw their lives transforming. Through self-awareness, openness, existential courage, and compassion, the journey to wellbeing transformed individuals and had a ripple effect on their teams, facilitating personal growth in their personal lives and work.

References

Maurer, M. M., Maurer, J., Hoff, E., & Daukantaitė, D. (2023). What is the process of personal growth? Introducing the personal growth process model. *New Ideas in Psychology*, *70*, 101024. https://doi.org/10.1016/j.newideapsych.2023.101024

Resilience

Systemic resilience

I have a problem with the traditional view of resilience, which is the ability to protect ourselves from the negative impact of stress or bounce back from adversity. This perspective implies that until you've recovered, you are incomplete. For example, in *Journeys from Childhood to Midlife*, Emmy Werner and Ruth Smith describe resilience as a protective factor that buffers our reaction to stressful events. Similarly, in *The Emotional Life of Your Brain*, Richard J. Davidson and Sharon Begley argue that the speed of communication between the pre-frontal cortex and amygdule indicates resilience. So, the faster we engage in resilient behaviour, the more resilient we are. In both cases, resilience is centred around our reaction to stressful events. The onus is on us to "fix" ourselves and return to the status quo.

Yet, when I look at my friends and my family, I see resilience more as a process during which even the more resilient people have days when they struggle, followed by days when they feel better again, only to relapse. After all, life is beautifully messy, and we are impacted by the entire web of systems that influence our decisions and outcomes. This is why I really like this systemic theory of resilience. It acknowledges the process, not only the outcome of resilience.

Michael Ungar sees resilience not as a character trait (you are or you are not resilient) but as a dynamic process of interaction between an individual and a system. Resilience means that an individual is able to access and negotiate the resources from their environment, such as social support and social services.

For example, taking a child from the Hawaii study I mentioned earlier (book by Werner and Smith), the type of protective factor they mention is the child's personality that makes them connect with people, engage in education, or have one good adult. But what if a child's personality is not that agreeable? What if they struggle to connect with others? This may prevent them from having that one good adult in their corner or result in being kicked out of school. Ungar's model, however, firmly shifts the responsibility of a resilient child onto the system within which a child exists. He asks a question about what the system can do and how the system can be adapted to help a child engage in resilient behaviour. Here, we explore the accessibility of the system resources and the quality of those that would help a child stay on course.

Taking this perspective on resilience allows for a multisystemic process of resilience that involves a range of factors; a person is only one of them. The positive outcomes come from the interaction between the system and the individual. Therefore, to improve individual resilience, we need to strengthen the system, not put all the onus on an individual to toughen up in the face of a broken system.

A child's resilience can be, therefore, seen as a bridge. It is expected to hold steady regardless of the weather. Traditional approaches focus on providing the child with the skills to weather the storm. At the same time, Ungar's approach shifts focus to the engineers who built the bridge. Have they done their work right? He encourages us to explore the materials used for building this bridge, the support structures underneath this bridge, and the process of regular maintenance. The bridge can sustain its survival and strength only when all these support systems are in place. Resilience means reinforcing the supports, not blaming the bridge if it collapses.

References

Ungar, M. (2018). Systemic resilience. *Ecology and Society*, *23*(4).

Master resilience training

One of the first programmes that emerged in the wake of the positive psychology movement was the Penn Resiliency Programme, which aimed to increase young people's resilience capacity. I remember at the time learning that it significantly reduced depression and suicidal ideations among adolescents, which was a huge accomplishment. Also, through a series of cognitive-behavioural techniques, it build on young people's resilience to an extent where their resilience kept improving year on year over three years. Subsequently, the programme was validated in various countries worldwide. I remember that the one country where it showed a negative impact was the Netherlands in Europe. Other than this, even though the programme's effectiveness may have been lower outside the US, it generally led to positive results.

Then, a meta-analysis of the programme was conducted, which is crucial for understanding any programme impact. Led by Stephen Brunwasser et al. (2009) from the University of Michigan, it showed that there is no evidence to suggest that the Penn Resiliency Programme was superior to other psychological approaches that aim to reduce depression. Also, they reported that the programme's effects may not be as significant as previously thought. Overall, the results were good, and the programme offered a great alternative to the other approaches.

By then, the US Army has signed an agreement to roll out this approach to the soldiers and their families. A series of articles about the programme's rollout to improve resiliency were published. The article, led by Karen Reivich et al. (2011) from the University of Pennsylvania, USA, explores the background of this ten-day programme and its content. The modules are based on CBT approaches, such as coping with catastrophic thinking and changing our deeply held beliefs that are no longer useful to us. However, it is also supplemented with positive psychology research-based practice. For example, interventions such as cultivating gratitude or recognising character strengths are introduced. Strategies for managing relationships, such as capitalising on the good news, are included. Explanatory styles are also explored as a basis for practising optimism.

Overall, the soldiers' feedback on the programme was very positive, but due to the confidentiality clauses, only limited information is published about its effectiveness. For practitioners, however, this programme is an excellent example of how positive psychology science can be smoothly integrated with traditional approaches. It also offers an opportunity to develop resiliency skills as the programme continues to be delivered worldwide, and individuals can be trained to do it.

References

Brunwasser, S. M., Gillham, J. E., & Kim, E. S. (2009). A meta-analytic review of the Penn resiliency program's effect on depressive symptoms. *Journal of Consulting and Clinical Psychology*, *77*(6), 1042–1054. https://doi.org/10.1037/a0017671

Reivich, K. J., Seligman, M. E., & McBride, S. (2011). Master resilience training in the US army. *American Psychologist*, *66*(1), 25.

Resilience programmes

Justin Laiti is a Fulbright-funded PhD scholar at our Centre for Positive Health Sciences in Ireland. He is just finishing his research, which involved adolescents co-creating a heart-rate variability wrist device to collect bio-data and alert them if their stress levels are too high. Interestingly, when co-designing the device with students, Justin reported how small things mattered to them, such as the ability to change the wristband colour to suit their mood or limiting buttons so they don't get distracted. Students also did not want social media connected to the device. They wanted the device to do one thing only: help them manage their stress. I found this fascinating. We assume that young people prefer devices with all bells and whistles, yet less is better for them when asked. This is the most outstanding value of a co-design approach. Sadly, in positive psychology, we create programmes for students based on what we believe is good for them and rarely ask their opinions. I appreciate the European UPRIGHT project, which co-designs a resilience programme with students.

UPRIGHT stands for the Universal Preventive Resilience Intervention Globally implemented in schools to improve and promote mental Health for Teenagers funded by the EU. Its reach spans across Denmark, Spain, Italy, Poland, and Iceland. Academics such as Dora Gudrun Gudmundsdottir and Hans Henrik Knopp have been involved in it. The article led by Roxanna Morote Rios from the Norwegian University of Science and Technology, University of Peru, explored the process of co-creation of this important programme. It involved a range of participatory workshops with over 200 people, and almost 800 respondents to a survey. The stakeholders taking part in the co-creation process were adolescents, parents, teachers, and other school staff. The insights gained from these workshops and the survey were instrumental in shaping the programme, providing valuable information on the needs and preferences of the target audience. Given it was a whole-school programme, it was important to gain insights from everyone.

The UPRIGHT programme is a dynamic initiative that is still ongoing. Researchers and educators plan to engage with approximately 6,000 adolescents aged 12–14 and their families to help them develop resiliency skills. The thorough process of co-designing this programme is a testament to the commitment of professionals to develop a solution that truly suits the school community's needs. Simple questions, such as "Can you imagine a situation in which this skill could be useful to you?", have generated responses that are not only insightful but also invaluable for the programme's development. Despite the challenges posed by the diversity of educational policies and resources across the EU, the UPRIGHT programme is set out to become a model that can be adapted and implemented in various other countries.

As I read this paper, I couldn't help but be inspired by the potential for a resilience programme co-designed with stakeholders from a variety of cultures worldwide. Not a programme designed in one region and evaluated in others to see if it fits, but a programme truly co-designed with young people from all cultures. The potential for learning from each other and the inclusivity that such a programme could foster in our global learning community are truly exciting.

References

Morote, R., Las Hayas, C., Izco-Basurko, I., Anyan, F., Fullaondo, A., Donisi, V., Zwiefka, A., Gudmundsdottir, D. G., Ledertoug, M. M., Olafsdottir, A. S., Gabrielli, S., Carbone, S., Mazur, I., Królicka-Deręgowska, A., Knoop, H. H., Tange, N., Kaldalóns, I. V., Jónsdóttir, B. J., González Pinto, A., & Hjemdal, O. (2020). Co-creation and regional adaptation of a resilience-based universal whole-school program in five European regions. *European Educational Research Journal*. https://doi.org/10.1177/1474904120947890

Character strengths

Truth be told . . .

Character strengths have been out there since the beginning of positive psychology. Created as an anti-DSM (Diagnostic and Statistical Manual of Mental Disorders), the taxonomy of strengths was a starting point for understanding what is good about people. However, an even more exciting aspect of my strengths was the ability to apply them. I remember the beginning of the strength application when we tried to figure out how to do it. First, we were encouraged to focus on our signature (most developed) strengths; then, a study showed that focusing on the lesser strengths gave us a wellbeing boost; hence, the type of strengths didn't seem to matter as much as the practice itself. Then, an avalanche of publications, mainly books, offered a range of potential and existing strength-based interventions to improve wellbeing, which we could all try for ourselves and our clients. This is why this paper is of such importance, as it pulls together all the studies that explored strength interventions and established the shared benefits they had.

This meta-analysis focused on the signature strengths (Schutte & Malouff, 2019). Of 2,431 academic papers, 29 studies have been selected from 14 papers. The amalgamation of the results from these studies showed that strength interventions positively impacted a range of outcomes. Firstly, they were associated with more strength use. Secondly, they improved the experience of positive emotions, life satisfaction, happiness, and general flourishing. Finally, they were associated with a reduction in depression. Many of the studies had a long-term follow-up, meaning that the impact was sustained over a more extended period. At the same time, many participants were unwilling to continue with the interventions, with as many as 70% of people in one particular study not sustaining their activity. This could be due to the cognitive effort required to complete some of these activities.

This article is essential for both researchers and practitioners. The researchers' perspective highlights the need to conduct more high-quality research. It also raised the question as to what could be done for people to sustain their practice. In Seligman and team's article in 2005, a strength-based intervention showed the most promising results. The researchers speculated that it was because it may have been an enjoyable activity for participants, which they chose to continue with it past the experiment. The question remains why, in other studies, participants did not feel the same way. Does it have anything to do with their commitment to wellbeing or knowledge of positive psychology? Or are there other reasons at play that stop them from continuing? Can anything be done when presenting these activities to clients to help them stick with them for longer?

This article is important for practitioners as it highlights the aggregated benefits of strength-based interventions, which may increase the efficacy of the activities, just like a placebo effect. Also, finding ways to make this activity part of life rather than just a one-off intervention requires a lot of thinking about integrating it smoothly. With this in mind, this article can provide some invaluable information that practitioners can use to improve their practice.

References

Schutte, N. S., & Malouff, J. M. (2019). The impact of signature character strengths interventions: A meta-analysis. *Journal of Happiness Studies: An Interdisciplinary Forum on Subjective Wellbeing*, *20*(4), 1179–1196. https://doi.org/10.1007/s10902-018-9990-2

Full range of experiences

What I have always loved about teaching positive psychology at the third level was the type of students this field has attracted. They are some of the most fascinating people I have met, with many exciting stories to tell. At some point throughout the process, we encourage students to share with others reasons why they began their studies or what studying positive psychology meant to them. Their stories are always heartwarming, exuding resilience and virtue. They often have experienced life's ups and downs and found the strength to keep going. At some point through this process, they decided to enhance their education, which is how we usually meet. They are often drawn towards positive psychology as it offers the tools needed to live a good life. One such tool is character strengths.

Ryan Niemiec, whose name has become synonymous with character strengths, is a chief science and education officer at VIA Institute on Character – a non-profit organisation dedicated to bringing the science of character strengths to the world; he collects knowledge, application, and curious facts about all 24 character strengths. In the same way, he loves collecting vintage and rare Pez dispensers. His books are a treasure trove of research-based ideas on what is good about character strengths. One such idea is an exploration and reflection on primary functions of character strengths at times of adversity and opportunity. The objective of these functions is to help individuals thrive in life. Thriving, in this case, refers to life fulfilment in relation to personal development (physical, psychological, or social) and success (good relationships, health, and achievements). The three functions of character strengths in situations of opportunity are:

1. Priming function – this function occurs before an event. Imagine you are about to enter a room full of people to share your work idea with them. You are

understandably nervous but also excited about this opportunity, as it may lead to getting your project started. Before you enter the room, reflect on your strengths and the personal qualities you could leverage when presenting your idea. This act of priming, focusing on your strengths, has been shown in several studies to be a powerful tool. Therapists who became aware of their clients' strengths were more likely to focus on them during a therapy session, leading to more significant outcomes and improved relationships. Therefore, reflecting on or verbalising your or other people's strengths before an event can boost confidence and ensure positive outcomes.

2. Mindfulness function – this function takes place during an event. It relates to training attention, such as becoming mindful of the situation. Given that we are drawn towards negativity, as negativity is stronger than positivity, our initial perspectives on a situation may be harmful. We may see the adverse outcomes of a situation. However, refocusing attention on the positive and being mindful of the strengths in a given situation is another way to amplify the impact of strength interventions on wellbeing. This mindful strength could relate to listening to someone talking mindfully using the strength of emotional intelligence, giving a presentation mindfully while practising the strength of zest, or problem-solving mindfully, using the strengths of perspective.
3. Appreciation function – this function for amplifying wellbeing relates to strength-spotting and realising why strengths matter. Therefore, it is about appreciating the strengths we have and the strengths of others. For example, it is a partner telling their spouse how much they appreciate their strength of kindness or reflecting upon the strength of leadership a person used when dealing with an emergent situation. Appreciation of strengths is an essential tool for enhancing the impact of strengths on wellbeing.

The three functions of character strengths in situations of adversity are:

1. Buffering function – character strengths, such as courage, wisdom, and perseverance, serve as a buffer against adversity. For example, when courage is used, it protects individuals against experiencing negative emotions. In addition to the general function of buffering, specific strengths like wisdom are also associated with buffering against adversity. For example, a strength of judgement is beneficial during problem-solving, protecting individuals against making unwise decisions. A strength of perspective offers individuals insight, which protects them from making rash decisions. Thus, they function as buffers against adversity before a negative situation occurs.
2. Reappraisal function – character strengths are a way to review the situation, reappraise it, and see it differently during adversity. For example, one of my close friends recently attended an arduous court hearing. He was unfairly dismissed and decided to pursue fairness through court instead of cowering. His former employer played dirty throughout. They lied under oath, showed no signs of reconciliation, and understandably, caused a lot of distress. During the process, my friend told me: *Some might say that what I do today is a sign of*

stupidity, throwing yourself in the mouth of a lion. But I choose to see it differently; I dare to pursue fairness and the judgement to analyse the details that inform my decisions. I have the leadership to ensure that situations like this do not happen to anyone else in this organisation in the future. This simple reframing, or reappraisal during the adverse situation, gave him the strength to keep going and eventually win, ensuring that he was the last person in this company to be treated unlawfully.

3. Resilience function – there are several definitions of resilience, ranging from bouncing back to posttraumatic growth (PTG) and seeing it as a range of resources we negotiate to overcome adversity. Throughout the literature, character strengths are associated with a range of these definitions, with all significant theories showing the specific strengths associated with higher levels of resilience. They include hope, zest, perseverance, and many others. Using character strengths to improve future resilience is one of their functions.

These six functions of character strengths offer a solid foundation for research and, more importantly, practice. They highlight situations in which strengths could be used and offer suggestions for their application. Ryan Niemiec highlights the need to recognise the significant function of these strengths during times of calm and storm. Character strengths are like the tools in the craftsman's toolbox, waiting to be used. It is what we do with them that matters.

References

Niemiec, R. M. (2020). Six functions of character strengths for thriving at times of adversity and opportunity: A theoretical perspective. *Applied Research in Quality of Life, 15*(2), 551–572. https://doi.org/10.1007/s11482-018-9692-2

The overuse, underuse, and optimal use of character strengths

In my thirties, I sought more challenges at work when a recruitment agent put me forward for a role in Paris, France (I live in Dublin, Ireland). While I was super excited about the job, I was hesitant about relocation, so I approached the process cautiously. To my surprise, I advanced through the first stage of the interview (and negotiated that I would be in Paris only 3 days a week) and then the second stage (and negotiated that I would learn French as part of my job). Eventually, it was just me and another candidate shortlisted. At this point, I didn't want to waste anyone's time, so I checked my commitment to it. *Did I want it, or should I withdraw from the race?* I decided to go for it with all the zest I could muster, and there was plenty of it there. Sadly, they selected the other candidate. When I asked for feedback, they responded, "You were too enthusiastic". This experience became my lesson on the impact of overused strengths.

When Christopher Peterson from the University of Michigan, USA and Martin Seligman from the University of Pennsylvania, USA set out to develop a taxonomy of character strengths, they had one question in mind: What is best in human beings? This question resulted in the creation of six virtues and 24 character strengths, and millions worldwide completed a survey. However, another big question is, what should we do with our survey results? This is the main focus of Ryan Niemiec's article, ways in which we can avoid underusing or overusing our strengths.

We have all developed some strengths; however, when we do not actively use them, they become missed opportunities for personal growth or meaningful connections with others. There are many reasons why we do not use our strengths. For some, it is simply due to their need for awareness of strengths. In such cases, completing a strength survey on www.viacharcter.org can raise awareness and spring them into action. For others, a lack of opportunity to use strengths prevents them from engaging with them. Take leadership, for example. It might not be a strength that some people practise daily. Only when an opportunity arises can they use their leadership strength to guide others. Another reason for underusing strengths could lie in individuals fearing that they would be judged for using their strengths. For example, the strength of "love and be loved" might be embarrassing for some people in specific situations, such as the workplace; it is underused regularly.

However, intentionally enhancing character strengths can lead to many benefits, such as improved wellbeing, productivity, or physical health outcomes. The underuse of character strengths is often linked to an individual's capacity to apply them, which is twofold. The mindset capacity involves awareness and a proactive approach to using strengths. The behavioural capacity involves an ability to take action and use strengths in different situations. When individuals underuse their strengths, it is helpful to spur them into action by addressing one of the two capacities.

While underusing strengths is not suitable for us, neither is overusing them. Many strengths are valuable for us, such as perseverance, kindness, and humour. However, when they are overused or used in the wrong context, they may have a negative impact on people. For example, perseverance can be associated with stubbornness; too much kindness can be disingenuous, and too much humour, especially in an inappropriate situation, can be seen as disrespectful or considered bullying.

The simple solution is in the "golden mean", in other words, moderation in using strengths. Too much and inadequate use of strengths is associated with negative impact. Practising moderation in strength use is essential to improve wellbeing and performance.

References

Niemiec, R. M. (2019). Finding the golden mean: The overuse, underuse, and optimal use of character strengths. *Counselling Psychology Quarterly*, *32*(3–4), 453–471. https://doi.org/10.1080/09515070.2019.1617674

The three-factor model of virtue

Christopher Peterson, a professor of psychology at the University of Michigan, dedicated two years of sabbatical to advancing his legacy of character strengths. His efforts led to the development of a taxonomy of character strengths and the writing of a key book about it. Despite all the significant work he put into it, Peterson always viewed strengths as "work in progress". Over the years, researchers explored the possibility of adding new character strengths, but their proposals were rejected because they did not fit the 10-point inclusion criteria.

Robert McGrath, a clinical psychologist specialising in statistical methods in psychology and psychological measurement, analysed data from over 1 million participants who completed the character strengths questionnaire. His findings suggested that instead of the six virtues initially proposed by Peterson, there are statistically only three overarching virtues across the 24 character strengths. Furthermore, some strengths did not fit neatly into these categories or showed overlap. McGrath's three-factor framework simplifies human virtues into manageable categories, which the authors likened to characters from The Wizard of Oz:

1. Scarecrow: These cognitive strengths reflect intellectual and wisdom strengths, such as judgement, creativity, or perspective.
2. Tin Woodsman: These strengths are tied to emotional connections, such as empathy, kindness, or love.
3. Cowardly lion: These strengths focus on courage and perseverance, including bravery, zest, and leadership.

From a research perspective, this article highlights the importance of replicating and further exploring the psychometric structure of the 24 character strengths. Practically speaking, using the Wizard of Oz characters makes the virtues relatable and can easily engage clients in a conversation about strengths and virtues. They make virtues more accessible to people.

References

McGrath, R. E., Greenberg, M. J., & Hall-Simmonds, A. (2018). Scarecrow, tin woodsman, and cowardly lion: The three-factor model of virtue. *The Journal of Positive Psychology*, *13*(4), 373–392. https://doi.org/10.1080/17439760.2017.1326518

Character strengths in 75 nations

I grew up fascinated by the adventures and the romance of the FBI agents Fox Mulder and Dana Scully in the *X-files*. In the 1990s, I watched every episode enthusiastically, wondering what it would be like to meet an Alien. I saw it as an entertaining fiction rather than reality. Yet in a recent documentary, a NASA scientist claimed that Aliens *certainly* exist, and she speculated as to what they would think of humanity, given how poorly we treat each other and our planet Earth. Listening to her, I couldn't help but wonder the opposite. Despite all the wars, tragedies, and selfishness, we are good people capable of incredible things. I wondered what strengths the extraterrestrial beings would admire about us. An article by Robert McGrath offers some insights into this.

Over a million people across 75 nations completed the VIA Inventory of Strengths; honesty was the most highly endorsed strength. Human beings value and practise "honesty" above all else and endorse "fairness" in second place. These traits drive us to fight for injustice and be honest with ourselves and others about our convictions. Kindness also ranks highly, which balances out humanity's honesty. It ensures that despite our need for truth-telling, we pursue it compassionately so that our words are not unnecessarily hurtful.

The other two strengths we practise regularly are "judgement" and "curiosity". Together, they are a wonderful mix that allows us to think critically about what we hear and see and stay inquisitive about the facts rather than coming to conclusions based on mere assumptions. Overall, this article portrays humanity as awe-inspiring. People who pursue fairness and stand up for others when required. People who are honest but do it with a tint of kindness so that others do not get hurt. People who can think for themselves and ask questions instead of making thoughtless judgements. This is the kind of humanity I am proud to belong to.

The less frequently endorsed character strengths are self-regulation (monitoring and controlling our urges), modesty (being humble about our abilities), prudence (moral gauge), and spirituality (believing in a greater power). It is important to note that these least endorsed strengths do not make them weaknesses about humans or diminish our value. Some of them are a product of modern times, whereby societal priorities pushed them back to the background of our consciousness. Others might be strengths we don't usually get a chance to use daily, which is why they are the least endorsed.

So, if agents Mulder or Scully get to speak with Aliens in the next series of X-files, I hope they will share some of the insights from Robert McGrath's article about what is right with humanity. It is also a fantastic resource for exploring the strengths of specific nations included in this assessment. It seems Ireland is filled with people boasting high levels of social intelligence, perseverance, and modesty, which goes perfectly with the nation's history. So maybe there is something about where we came from and who we have become. If you're curious, I encourage you to check out the top strengths of your country. It is an inspiring way of looking at nations.

References

McGrath, R. E. (2014). Character strengths in 75 nations: An update. *The Journal of Positive Psychology*, *10*(1), 41–52. https://doi.org/10.1080/17439760.2014.888580

The additional components of wellbeing

Hope

A couple of decades ago, I was going through a very difficult time – the darkest time in my life. Filled with not one but five traumatic events that all piled up over a short space of time, I found it difficult to cope. I remember at the time reflecting on how different life was before the traumatic events happened. I tried to figure out what I had back then that I lacked amid my grieving. This is when I realised that I seemed to have lost hope. It was such a profound realisation that I still remember where I was sitting and what I was doing when it popped into my head. As soon as I faced it, I began to consider how my hope was enacted pre-trauma and what changes I could make in my current life to bring hope back to me. I always felt that hope was a starting point for my recovery. It was as if I were going down one way, and suddenly, I realised that there were alternative routes I could follow, so I took them, even though I had no idea where they would take me.

There are many different types of hope theories, but one that is possibly most prevalent within positive psychology is Charles Snyder's (2002). He explores hope not as an emotion, the way Barbara Fredrickson has done in some of her studies. Instead, he considers hope as a goal-oriented pattern of thinking. According to the theory, hopeful thinking comprises pathways and agency.

Pathway, in the context of hope theories, refers to the process of identifying alternative routes to achieve our goals. It involves envisioning what we hope to achieve and then devising a plan to make it a reality. Without this plan, our goals remain mere wishes, unlikely to materialise. The agency, on the other hand, is about firmly believing that we can instigate the change required to get there. Together, they are hope.

As such, when stuck in a rut for a good while, I tried to dream of a destination, my best possible self or at least a good possible self that would be distant from where I was. Once I figured it out, vaguely, I planned a pathway. I didn't know which route to take, so I brainstormed ideas. I even got my friends involved in helping me figure out a pathway, as it was complicated to be creative at the time. I rejected some ideas if I believed I couldn't make them happen and revisited them when I felt better. I started with the small changes that I knew I could instigate, such as eating more nutritious food. I had lost weight then, so getting back on a good food plan was essential and enjoyable. I then created a social plan and committed to not saying "no, maybe another time" when friends reached out to me to spend time together. Finally, I committed to practising at least one positive psychology intervention a week that allowed me to bring back some positivity into my life. All these were pathways I established that I believed I could change. And it all started with hope.

References

Snyder, C. R. (2002). Hope theory: Rainbows in the mind. *Psychological Inquiry*, *13*(4), 249–275.

Passion for activities

I was invited as a guest speaker to an MBA programme at Trinity College Dublin. I have done it many times, so I kept changing a topic I discussed yearly to keep myself challenged and entertained. My brief was always the same: discuss a positive psychology topic that students might find useful. So, this one day, I arrived half an hour ahead of time, and the programme leader brought me into the classroom. I sat quietly at the back and began listening to the previous speaker. Her topic was about the importance of MBA students developing a passion for their work. She said there was no point in getting out of bed without having passion for what we do. As I listened to her, I cringed, as ironically, a talk I prepared for the students that day was about the dangers of passion. These dangers included burnout, neglect of other important aspects of life, and a skewed work–life balance.

For decades, psychologists have explored the concept of passion, particularly in relation to passionate love and human relationships. However, the passion we feel for our daily activities has received far less attention. This is where Robert Vallerand's research added a significant value. His Duality of Passion model highlighted how passion can influence our wellbeing in both positive and negative ways, offering valuable insights for personal growth and self-awareness.

Obsessive passion occurs when the passion for an activity controls us. Imagine sitting at a table with your family, yet being restless because you feel like you should be doing something else, something associated with your passion, such as training for a marathon, studying, or working. This type of passion is driven by extrinsic motivation, meaning that you aim to avoid shame and prove to yourself or others that you are capable of doing it. While the activities you are obsessively passionate about can lead to flow experiences, you may find it challenging to replicate flow in other spheres of your life. Flow is a state of complete absorption in an activity, where time seems to fly, and you are fully focused and enjoying the process.

Harmonious passion, on the one hand, is well integrated into our lives. We feel in control and tend to engage in the activity out of intrinsic motivation. We are capable of experiencing flow when engaging in an activity we are harmoniously passionate about. However, we also have other activities that allow us to experience flow. This type of passion allows for balance, enabling individuals to experience flow across multiple areas of life. For instance, someone passionate about their career can also find fulfilment through sports, hobbies, or social activities, preventing one pursuit from dominating their identity.

While both harmonious and obsessive passion lead to successful outcomes and high achievement, only harmonious passion positively impacts wellbeing. When individuals experience obsessive passion, it is often associated with exhaustion, feeling drained, and experiencing lots of negative emotions, such as guilt or shame, or, in some cases, leads to long-term health problems.

When I presented this theory to MBA students, it challenged their view of passion as being always beneficial. Together, we explored situations when their passion had caused them more harm than good. Once aware of it, their obsessive-passion-related stories poured out indiscriminately. Recognising the balance between harmonious and obsessive passion is crucial for improving and maintaining our wellbeing. While we are familiar with the benefits of harmonious passion, interventions to reduce obsessive passion and cultivate harmonious passion need to be developed. Hopefully, future research will help us understand the practice of harmonious passion. For the time being, we can rely mainly on our awareness.

References

Vallerand, R. J., Blanchard, C., Mageau, G. A., Koestner, R., Ratelle, C., Leonard, M., Gagne, M., & Marsolais, J. (2003). Les passions de l'ame: On obsessive and harmonious passion. *Journal of Personality and Social Psychology, 85*(4), 756–767. https://doi.org/10.1037/0022-3514.85.4.756

Authenticity

For the first decade of my career, I was a practitioner. I enjoyed what I was doing, but I always felt something was missing. One day, during my lunch break, I ventured into the Guinness Storehouse in Dublin, Ireland, for a lunchtime talk about authenticity. During the talk, I heard a story that resonated with me. It is as if the story of a man who was not true to himself was, in fact, a story about me. That talk changed my life. Within three months, I quit my job and pursued my dreams, which have led me to become the person I am today.

Being authentic requires effort. Over time, we may become disconnected from ourselves due to the responsibilities and choices we've made about our lives. More importantly, people around us might be used to the alienated selves we have become and do not want us to change. We often postpone addressing that our life is heading in a direction we don't want, even though we know it's not what we desire. But then, when we finally choose to embrace authenticity, our journey is not always smooth. It's filled with positive and negative emotions as we navigate this challenging and uncomfortable process of becoming authentic selves.

According to the tripartite model (Wood et al., 2008), authenticity is defined as consistency between our experiences, awareness, and outward behaviour and communication. The three aspects of authenticity involve the following:

1. Self-alienation – this is a state when we no longer know ourselves. We feel out of touch with the person we have become. A perfect balance between our conscious awareness and actual experience is almost impossible. However, we need to understand how we feel to be authentic. When we have to hide the way we feel inside, or we don't even know ourselves well, this is when we experience self-alienation, which can lead to psychopathology.
2. Authentic living – this state relates to doing what we strongly believe in, regardless of the consequences. It is about living according to our values, standing up for what is important to us, feeling free to express our emotions, and, in general, feeling that what we do every day is good for us.
3. Accepting external influences – this aspect of authenticity relates to the extent to which we are being influenced by others. Whether we are people-pleasers or follow the rules as a norm, we may be susceptible to external influences that

prevent us from being ourselves, regardless of how we feel about it. It is about not being swayed by what other people think or how they expect us to behave and doing it our own way.

Last month, Prof. Christian van Nieuwerburgh and I had the pleasure of sharing a meal with Prof. Stephen Joseph, one of the authors of this theory of authenticity. We spent quality time discussing our authentic longings, the people we have always hoped to be versus those we have become. We concluded that as we grow, our authentic selves keep emerging stronger and stronger, yearning to be heard. Our authenticity is like a bird in a cage that wants to be set free. Free to spread our wings, free to shed our feathers, and free to be who we were meant to be.

References

Wood, A. M., Linley, P. A., Maltby, J., Baliousis, M., & Joseph, S. (2008). The authentic personality: A theoretical and empirical conceptualization and the development of the authenticity scale. *Journal of Counseling Psychology*, *55*(3), 385–399. https://doi.org/10.1037/0022-0167.55.3.385

Religiosity and spirituality

A few years ago, I read an interesting book *Religion for Atheists*, by the philosopher Alain de Botton. He is an atheist who does not try to prove that God does not exist or ridicule the idea. Instead, he acknowledges that religion can be a beneficial source of wellbeing and should not be disregarded. By not attending to the formal religious rituals, atheists may be losing out on the psychological, emotional, and social benefits it offers. Ultimately, his suggestion is to approach atheism as a "pick and mix" by taking all that is useful from religion and providing us comfort without the need to engage in the whole belief system and, for example, having a Christmas tree for the Christmas holiday, without the beliefs associated with Christianity.

Religion is a topic that often sparks heated debate. While de Botton advocates for a "gentle atheism", there are many fervent atheists who argue that religion is harmful and unnecessary. Some have even gone as far as to petition the VIA institute on character strengths to remove "religiosity" from its taxonomy. Their argument is that one can be spiritual without adhering to religious practices. This controversy has led to the removal of "religiosity" from the VIA survey, replaced entirely by "spirituality".

When exploring religion and spirituality in positive psychology, selecting only one paper to represent it is challenging. Hundreds of articles have been published about aspects of spirituality and its beneficial impact or the linkage between positive psychology's religious and secular approaches to interventions such as forgiveness. This is why I've selected two articles that are the most cited and relevant to this topic. The first is a systematic review led by Yoichi Chida et al. (2009) from University College London, UK. It explores the impact of religiosity and spirituality across 69 studies. The findings show that individuals who are spiritual or who practise religion live longer. However, this was only true for the healthy population; there were no differences between those with spiritual or religious beliefs and those who were already unwell. Moreover, spirituality and religiousness protect a healthy population from cardiovascular disease. Therefore, the psychological and emotional processes influenced by religion and spirituality offer protection against disease.

James Day (2010) from the Catholic University of Louvain, Belgium, offers a potential explanation for these processes. He explores the psychological literature from the times of the grandfather of psychology, William James, to see the impact of spiritual practices on wellbeing. He explains how religious and spiritual beliefs are created in children and how they develop further in adults. He examines practices associated with religion and spirituality, such as prayer meditation, and their impact on engagement and psychological wellbeing. He reviews a range of positive emotions evoked by spiritual and religious practices, such as happiness, wonder, awe, and joy. This article focuses mainly on religion and its development.

Recently, a special issue of Frontiers in *Positive Psychology* focused on spirituality. They featured many interesting articles, such as a unique exploration of spirituality through engagement with nature in the Arctic wilderness by Helga Synnevåg Løvoll and Knut-Willy Sæther from Volda University College, Norway. However, one that I will delve deeper into explores the association between spirituality, character, and flourishing. A team led by Tom Ford et al. (2023) from Columbia University, USA, conducted research with 763 participants and used a PERMA profiler to assess flourishing. The results showed that spirituality was consistently associated with character strengths, and those with high levels of spirituality and character reported greater flourishing.

This finding highlights the significant role of character strengths in spirituality. It suggests that the interventions developed for character strengths could potentially serve as effective interventions for spirituality in the future. Interestingly, individuals with highly developed strengths and spirituality often engage in religious practices. This implies that while the removal of "religiosity" from the VIA character taxonomy may have appeased its critics, it does not negate the fact that religiousness continues to play a significant role in spirituality and psychological flourishing.

References

Chida, Y., Steptoe, A., & Powell, L. H. (2009). Religiosity/spirituality and mortality. A systematic quantitative review. *Psychotherapy and Psychosomatics*, *78*(2), 81–90. https://doi.org/10.1159/000190791

Day, J. (2010). Religion, spirituality, and positive psychology in adulthood: A developmental view. *Journal of Adult Development*, *17*(4), 215–229. https://doi-org.elib.tcd.ie/10.1007/s10804-009-9086-7

Ford, T., Lipson, J., & Miller, L. (2023). Spiritually grounded character: A latent profile analysis. *Frontiers in Psychology*, *13*, 1061416. https://doi.org/10.3389/fpsyg.2022.1061416

Self-compassion

A few years ago, one of my colleagues, a psychotherapist, attended a weekend workshop on self-compassion. The objective was to learn about the process and, more importantly, experience it. It was delivered by an academic specialising in self-compassion at one of the universities in Ireland. Afterwards, my colleague raved about it, although he admitted that the workshop took a lot out of him emotionally. We were supposed to meet the following Monday for lunch to discuss it, and he never turned up. I wondered what happened to him. So, I rang him to enquire if he was okay. My phone call woke him up. After the workshop, he went home, ate his dinner, and had an early night. By the time I woke him, he was asleep for 20 hours. This was the time he needed to recover after doing all the psychological and emotional work. This had never happened to him before or since. So was the impact of self-compassion on his body.

Self-compassion is a process of being touched by and embracing our suffering. Sometimes, we choose to disconnect from it, as it hurts too much. Self-compassion is associated with releasing the pain we experience through self-kindness. Instead of being self-critical and hurtful to ourselves, when practising self-compassion, we don't offer judgement but try to understand our inadequacies and failures.

Self-compassion comprises three elements. First, it is about self-kindness and extending kindness and understanding to ourselves when we suffer, make a mistake, or are in pain, rather than self-criticism. We aim to be our own best friends. Second, it is about shared humanity and recognising that our experience of suffering is similar to what everyone feels. Everybody suffers; it is human to feel such pain, and we are all in it together. As such, this perspective helps us feel connected to others rather than isolated from them. Third, mindfulness is holding painful thoughts and feelings in our minds without overidentifying them.

This process is complex, and practitioners who are not experienced in guiding clients through it should avoid it. However, it can be a transformative process given the right environment and guidance. Kristin Neff, the author of this paper, has written several books about self-compassion and its application in daily life. She also offers a range of videos and activities on her website. Since this paper was published, the concept of self-compassion has grown exponentially. A lot of research was published, and several interesting systematic reviews and meta-analyses are available to read. If you are interested in this topic, you are about to embark on an exciting journey of self-discovery.

References

Neff, K. D. (2003). Self-compassion: An alternative conceptualization of a healthy attitude toward oneself. *Self and Identity*, *2*(2), 85–101. https://doi.org/10.1080/15298860309032

Coping with challenges

Stress mindset

Over a decade ago, I was invited to deliver a series of events for a state organisation in Ireland. I delivered a 3-hour training session for over 1,000 employees and talked to them about a stress mindset. During the programme, I introduced them to Cognitive Behavioural Therapy (CBT), and we discussed some beliefs that prevented them from embracing stress. The programme was so popular that the organisation asked me next year to do part 2 of this event, and I had an opportunity to hear the employees' stories of what changes they implemented after the event.

All the stories were fascinating but one in particular stuck. It was a story told by a unit manager with over 20 employees reporting to him. His job became so stressful and impacted his personal life that he left the organisation. My training course was the last course he planned to do. It could not have harmed – he thought. During the session, he realised how stressed he became, and even though he showed up home after work, his mind was always elsewhere. To protect his family, he tried desperately to push back all that happened at work, but soon, his lack of sleep and messy mind got in the way of enjoying his family life. He told us that one day, when sitting at a kitchen table, he yelled at children for nothing. That day, he knew it was either his work or his family – no other option. However, the session changed his perspective; he saw another option – changing himself. He embraced stress and began dealing with it more effectively; a year later, he was still at his job and had no intention of leaving. He loved what he did but started doing it differently, and all this was due to the stress mindset workshop.

Stress mindset research derives from a study conducted in 2012 by Keller and a team, in which the researchers found that while the amount of stress we experience matters, our approach to stress is just as significant. In this study, the researchers surveyed almost 30,000 people and asked them how stressed they were and how harmful they perceived stress. The risk of dying of those who were very stressed and saw stress as harmful increased by 43% in 8 years. Whereas for those who had a lot of stress but did not consider it harmful, their risk of dying increased by only 8%. Therefore, this study showed how we think about stress and how it impacts our choices of stress strategies.

Further studies by Alia Crum from Stanford University have shown that when we consider stress harmful, we avoid experiencing it and tend to get even more stressed about it. Subsequently, we are less likely to use effective coping strategies. Instead, we bury our heads in the sand, hoping it will disappear. We are also more likely to reach out for a glass of alcohol or focus our attention not on the source of stress that needs to be eliminated but on our symptoms of stress. Thus, we get stuck in a vicious cycle. On the other hand, when we are not afraid of stress and see it as helpful, our coping strategies are more active as we explore the source of stress and search for resources to help us and people to assist us.

These studies are of utmost importance for practitioners as they highlight the need to discuss stress not only in the context of its prevalence, but also to explore its positive and negative aspects. This comprehensive understanding of stress can significantly improve our stress mindset. Merely realising the impact of our stress mindset and consciously choosing to embrace it can make a substantial difference to our health and wellbeing. After all, what we fear is often what we create. By shedding light on the dual nature of stress, we can enlighten and inform ourselves, leading to a more balanced and effective approach to stress management.

References

Crum, A. J., Salovey, P., & Achor, S. (2013). Rethinking stress: The role of mindsets in determining the stress response. *Journal of Personality and Social Psychology*, *104*(4), 716–733. https://doi.org/10.1037/a0031201

Keller, A., Litzelman, K., Wisk, L. E., Maddox, T., Cheng, E. R., Creswell, P. D., & Witt, W. P. (2012). Does the perception that stress affects health matter? The association with health and mortality. *Health psychology: Official Journal of the Division of Health Psychology, American Psychological Association*, *31*(5), 677–684. https://doi.org/10.1037/a0026743

Posttraumatic growth

My grandmother, a woman of remarkable resilience, was the first positive psychologist I have ever known. She was barely 18 when the WW2 began, and instead of following her passion for singing and drawing, she got up every morning to fight for her country. The war robbed her of her youth, her family, and friends. Yet despite this, she remained compassionate and zestful for the rest of her life. I remember her always having a good word to say about everyone and spreading love everywhere she went. Even though she experienced the atrocities of the war, she grew post-trauma. When the war began, she changed priorities and created a home for her husband and six children. She followed her passions and was fully aware and proud of her character strengths. In other words, she experienced posttraumatic growth (PTG).

The concept of PTG was introduced in the 1990s by Richard Tedeschi and Lawrence Calhoun. It described the experience of positive change following a major life crisis. The authors argued that those who experience PTG report changes in one or many of the life domains:

1. **Appreciation of life** – they begin appreciating life more than they have done before. They value it and treasure it. This is what happened to my granny. She loved life and everything about it. She appreciated what she had in life and was grateful for her family, home, and peace.
2. **Relationship with others** – individuals with PTG become very close friends with some people who become their dearest confidants, true friends. At the same time, some may say they realise who their real friends are, and their relationships with others break down. For my granny, the war was the beginning of a beautiful friendship with her best friend. They saw each other regularly and supported each other until their death. Every time I walked into the room where they were talking, it was as if an invisible string between them held them tight. Their conversation, demeanour, was much different than when she conversed with others.

3. **New possibilities in life** – people with PTG are able to see opportunities in life they have not seen before. For my granny, it was an opportunity to find a beautiful home in the middle of Warsaw she defended so fervently, seeing opportunities for her husband who opened his shoe-making business and opportunities for her children whom she gave the best life she could imagine, standing back beside them when needed.
4. **Personal strength** – after a traumatic event, people with PTG realise they are stronger than they thought they were. I remember my granny reflecting on this after telling us stories about the war. She talked about acting in a way that she never thought she was capable of, yet she did it as there was no other option.
5. **Spirituality** – people experiencing PTG become aware of forces beyond themselves. They experience spiritual change. Some start going to church or change their religion. Others pray more, yet some feel that the universe protects them and that they feel a connection with a greater power. My granny was raised with religious beliefs and weekly visits to church. However, after the war, she lost her love for religion, but she sustained her faith by developing her spirituality.

These changes, part of the natural process of coping with trauma, unfold uniquely for each individual. They take their own time, and cannot be rushed. This highlights that PTG is not a one-size-fits-all solution but a personalised growth journey.

Note

1 See her eulogy in the *International Journal of Wellbeing*.

References

Tedeschi, R. G., & Calhoun, L. G. (2004). Target article: "Posttraumatic growth: Conceptual foundations and empirical evidence". *Psychological Inquiry*, *15*(1), 1–18. https://doi.org/10.1207/s15327965pli1501_01

3 The overview of positive psychology applications

What differentiates the positive psychology field is its dedication to applying the research in an accessible way. Positive psychology applications have become mainstream as we continue to explore the best ways to improve individuals' and communities' wellbeing. We will begin this chapter by exploring how circumstances, environmental factors, and other elements impact our wellbeing. This includes concepts such as personality, socio-economic background, and genetics. Regardless of what interventions we apply, many of us have an advantage or disadvantage for wellbeing. Then, we will delve into selected positive psychology interventions, such as counting your blessings, savouring, kindness, or humour. This section will provide insights into the range of interventions that are available for practice. Finally, we will explore the key studies assessing the effectiveness of these interventions in improving health and wellbeing. This will include the first assessment of a happiness programme in 1977, progressing through to today. This chapter will help readers understand the tools available in positive psychology and how to engage with the research, whether it's through non-intentional (e.g. personality) or intentional (e.g. structured interventions) means.

Wellbeing without interventions

Spread of happiness

My son loves science. He loves putting on his white coat and goggles, pulling out his gigantic test tubes and dropper pipettes, and spending hours mixing up colours and other potions. Recently, we played with a simpler activity that gave him a lot of joy. We put Skittles on a plate in a circle, gently poured hot water onto the plate, and saw a rainbow of colours appear. The colours stood like stripes on their own, and in some places, they mixed up. They reminded me of happiness and how proximity to happy people can influence our subjective wellbeing.

This is a folk tale that many of us have heard since our childhood. However, a while back, two sociology researchers provided evidence of the existence of the happiness contagion. They drew from a longitudinal study with almost 5,000 participants that spanned over 20 years from 1983 to 2003. In this study, happiness was measured using four questions: "I felt hopeful about the future", "I was happy", "I enjoyed life", and "I felt that I was just as good as other people". Participants

DOI: 10.4324/9781003530596-3

were followed up 7 times during the research, which involved networks of family, friends, work colleagues, and neighbours. The objective of the analysis was to explore the impact of changes in happiness on the network's wellbeing.

The results showed that happiness extends to three degrees of separation. In other words, our happiness will impact not only our direct friends but also their friends and our friends' friends' friends. Specifically, when our friends who live within 1 mile become happier, we are 25% likely to become happier too. The effect is even more powerful when mutual friends who live nearby become happier, as they are 63% more likely to boost our happiness. Thus, our friends' happiness can significantly predict our future happiness.

Similarly, if our friends' friends become happier, it will make us 9.8% likely to be happier. And if our friends' friends' friends, who we do not personally know, become happier, it will make us 5.6% more likely to be happier. This is a very curious finding as it demonstrates that our social environment dramatically impacts our happiness regardless of what action we take ourselves to be happier. It also allows us to explore the chain reaction of how the network we spend time with impacts us, even if we are not directly in contact with them.

It is helpful to mention that the same applies to unhappiness. When our friends are going through challenges, it is understandable that it will impact their network, too. This is why, life traumas need to be shared, so that we can support our close ones when they or their friends are going through rough times. Keeping their spirits up can help them regain their strength and keep going.

The situation is similar with family members, especially those living nearby. Siblings' happiness increases our chance of happiness by 14%, and our happier spouses increase our chances of happiness by 8%. Similarly, when our next-door neighbour's happiness has increased, we are 34% more likely to be happier. This research suggests that while a network of people we hang out with is essential for our happiness, what matters even more is the proximity of that network. People living nearby are more likely to impact us than when they live long-distance. Another critical factor is the sex. Our happiness seems to be impacted more by people of the same sex. Hence, same-sex friends are more likely to make each other happier than spouses.

The findings from this research are very hopeful for the future of happiness application. There is constant encouragement for researchers and practitioners to use positive psychology as a way to improve communities and societies. This research indicates that given the contagious nature of happiness, it may be possible to do so by helping one person at a time, who can spread happiness throughout their immediate network. This could help communities flourish by supporting each other's mental health. Happiness blooms in proximity; as one heart lifts, many more take flight.

References

Fowler, J. H., & Christakis, N. A. (2008). Dynamic spread of happiness in a large social network: Longitudinal analysis over 20 years in the Framingham heart study. *BMJ (Clinical Research Ed.)*, *337*, a2338. https://doi.org/10.1136/bmj.a2338

Positivity offset

A European friend of mine has recently spent a month in Ireland, and upon arriving back home, he sent me a text saying he was experiencing withdrawal symptoms from not being around the positive and smiley people in Dublin. To him, it seemed like everyone in Ireland was in a good mood, whereas everyone back home seemed to be in a perpetually bad mood. Interestingly, when I asked Irish people about their own wellbeing, they had a similar view about themselves thinking that they were less happy than other Europeans. Why is it that we tend to perceive ourselves as being in a worse mood than we are? Is it because we know ourselves so well and are more aware of the moments when we are not feeling our best?

An article published by Ed Diener and colleagues explored the reasons why so many studies are showing that, on average, people tend to be in a good mood. Regardless of their socio-economic status, or whether they live in abundance or struggle with difficult circumstances, they seem to be in a good mood. In general, people are in mildly positive mood when no strong emotional events are happening in their lives, such as change of job, getting married, graduating, or going on holiday. This is explained by a psychological concept of positivity offset, which means that we tend to interpret neutral situations in our lives as mildly positive. But the big question is why that happens.

According to the authors, the positivity offset is not just a psychological quirk, but a survival strategy ingrained in our evolutionary history. It's associated with adaptive behaviours, a trait that has helped our species not just survive, but thrive. The authors identified three main benefits of people being in a positive mood, shedding light on the origins of this universal human experience.

1. **Social connection:** When in a positive mood, we tend to attract people and subsequently receive higher levels of social support, a crucial resource during difficult times. But it's not just about attracting others. Even when alone, a good mood can persist for those with high levels of sociality. A positive mood is also predictive of successful long-term relationships, boosting self-confidence and likability.
2. **Work and employment:** Those who are in a good mood tend to be rated by their managers more favourably. They also receive more excellent customer reviews and tend to engage in more helpful behaviours with their colleagues. Good mood also predicts higher income and lower unemployment rate. Those who experience good moods tend to be more creative and productive and control their emotions more effectively.
3. **Health, longevity, and fertility:** Good-mood people tend to be more fertile, have a better immune system, and be healthier later in life. They have more energy in life; they can cope with stressful events more effectively and engage in healthier behaviours that sustain their wellbeing.

Therefore, it seems like a good mood is advantageous in many aspects of our lives, which may be motivating for us to maintain it for survival. It is important to note the difference between mood and emotions. The mood is more dispositional, unfocused, and objectless than emotions. In other words, mood is a general feeling that is not tied to a specific event, while emotions are specific reactions to specific events. Therefore, you might get up in a good mood and not know why you feel this way, but when you experience a burst of positive emotions, you can quickly pinpoint them to the good news you've just received.

References

Diener, E., Kanazawa, S., Suh, E. M., & Oishi, S. (2015). Why people are in a generally good mood. *Personality and Social Psychology Review: An Official Journal of the Society for Personality and Social Psychology, Inc*, *19*(3), 235–256. https://doi.org/10.1177/1088868314544467

Personality neglect

My little boy is an introvert, just like our whole family. When I was in school, I tended to be a quiet child, enjoying my own company, and for years I have had just one best friend with whom I sat in the school garden during the break and enjoyed our quiet chats and nature while the whole school was buzzing with children screaming and bouncing everywhere. My son is the same. For him, less is more. He has a best friend with whom he enjoys spending time and needs to recharge his batteries after school in complete silence. Then, he comes alive again.

Yet, because we live in an extroversion-loving society, with schools being pressured to focus on their pupils' social wellbeing and mistakenly believing that it means more friends, some teachers insist that a child should expand their social network. If a child has only one friend, teachers start viewing this in terms of deficit: what is wrong with a child? Focused on enhancing wellbeing and diagnosing what is wrong with children, we forget that they all have personalities and might not be desirable to society. Still, they are there, making them beautiful people, not children who need to be "fixed". Similarly, the article about personality neglect highlights the need to consider personality too.

In this article, Jordi Quoidbach from the University of Liege, Belgium, and Elizabeth Dunn from the University of British Columbia, Canada, demonstrated that it is not only others that forget we have personalities that drive our attitudes and behaviours, but we also tend to neglect our own personalities when predicting our future happiness. In a series of studies with students and adults, the researchers showed that people who were already quite happy and optimistic tended to underestimate their happiness after positive events. Similarly, neurotic people tended to overestimate their pleasure after positive events, hoping that these events will have significantly more positive impact on their happiness than they actually did. This error in judgement happened because none of them considered their personality when predicting how happy they would be. This lack of consideration could be due to a lack of self-awareness or simply a failure to recognise the influence of their personality in that moment of prediction. By becoming more self-aware, we can better understand how our personality affects our happiness in the future, empowering us to make more accurate and fulfilling life choices.

These findings offer some interesting practical implications. Given the error of judgement we make by not considering our personality, when we think of the future, our dreams, and ambitions, we need to keep our personality in mind. If we tend to be happy people anyway, chances are that whatever happens in the future, we will find a way to feel happy and might be ecstatic when good life events happen. Thus, regardless how much we plan that holiday, or a gig we hope to attend, it will be a happy event for us. We can save our energy and don't even need to make a huge amount of effort as the impact will be likely very positive. On the other hand, if we do not have a happy disposition, we might have to work a little harder on this. So, perhaps we should reduce our expectations as to how much happiness we can gain from a potentially good event; otherwise, we might be disappointed. Also, we might put more effort in planning the event, especially in relation to the small annoyances we can reduce, so that we can avoid some of its negative impact. By managing our expectations and understanding the role our personality plays in our happiness, we can build resilience and prepare ourselves for the ups and downs of life.

References

Quoidbach, J., & Dunn, E. W. (2010). Personality neglect: The unforeseen impact of personal dispositions on emotional life. *Psychological Science*, *21*(12), 1783–1786. https://doi-org.elib.tcd.ie/10.1177/0956797610388816

Very happy people

Imagine what it would be like to be very happy. What would your life circumstances be? What would be your social network? What would you do every day as a very happy person? What thoughts would you have? How would you speak? How would you walk? What would your posture be like? I recently came across an audio recording by Paul McKenna, a British hypnotist who guides people towards improved happiness. He believes that imagining what happiness looks like can lead towards it by enacting it. However, there is an alternative way of exploring what it is like to be happy, such as reading positive psychology articles about the happiest people.

David Myers and Ed Diener (1995) explored characteristics through longitudinal research conducted with 5,000 people, whereby their sample was the people who have maintained their high levels of happiness over a decade. The research showed that very happy people tended to have certain traits that supported their happiness, such as higher levels of self-esteem and a sense of personal control; they were more optimistic and often extraverted. Also, they had many close and supportive relationships. Broken marriages and unsupportive relationships were associated with lower levels of happiness.

The happiest people in this study were also those who had something that occupied their mind – their hobby, their work. It put them in a state of "flow", a concept introduced by psychologist Mihaly Csikszentmihalyi, where they lost themselves in those activities. Flow is a mental state in which a person is fully immersed in a feeling of energised focus, full involvement, and enjoyment in the process of the activity. As opposed to a state of mindless passivity that did not engage them and made them less happy. That engagement fuelled their meaning in life and drove their purpose. Finally, religiosity or having faith is also associated with higher levels of happiness, as this helps people belong and is associated with a range of adaptive behaviours that fuel their happiness. Thus, this was the first study that explored this exquisite group of people, and from there, more research was conducted to understand their lives, which would help researchers design interventions to support people in becoming happier.

In another article published about the happiest people (Diener & Seligman, 2002), the researchers found that very happy people tended to be highly social and have stronger social and romantic relationships. The reasons for it could have been partially because of their personality traits, which made them more extraverted, more agreeable, and less neurotic. Thus they were less likely to sweat the small stuff. Even though they did not have any more "objectively defined as positive events" in their lives, meaning events that are universally considered positive such as a promotion or a wedding, nor did they engage in more physical activity that would improve their positive emotions, they felt more positive about life without feeling too ecstatic, meaning that they could regulate their emotions well.

Subsequent research, including a replication of the original study by Diener et al. (2018), has shown that another crucial component of happiness is living in a happier society. This environmental factor, which is often outside of our individual control, plays a significant role in our overall happiness. It's a reminder that our happiness is not just a personal matter, but is also influenced by our society. After all, the country we are born in and the community we are part of can shape us into the people we are today.

References

Diener, E., & Seligman, M. E. P. (2002). Very happy people. *Psychological Science*, *13*(1), 81. https://doi-org.elib.tcd.ie/10.1111/1467-9280.00415

Diener, E., Seligman, M. E. P., Choi, H., & Oishi, S. (2018). Happiest people revisited. *Perspectives on Psychological Science: A Journal of the Association for Psychological Science*, *13*(2), 176–184. https://doi-org.elib.tcd.ie/10.1177/1745691617697077

Myers, D. G., & Diener, E. (1995). Who is happy? *Psychological Science*, *6*(1), 10–19. https://doi-org.elib.tcd.ie/10.1111/j.1467-9280.1995.tb00298.x

Why are some people happier?

I have a group of three friends I have known for the past 20 years. One of them is always happy-go-lucky. No matter what happens in her life, she embraces it wholeheartedly and smiles at the end. The second one is anxious and cautious. She is visibly pleased when something goes her way and very concerned when it doesn't. Yet the third friend is cynical no matter what happens to her. She prepares for the worst, and apart from some fleeting moments of pure joy, I have not seen her fully embracing happy. Ironically, as a person looking in, I objectively see their lives as happy. They deal with daily life challenges as most people do, but overall, they live a good life.

The previous article in this section answered what happy people do in life. This article, however, is one of the most-read articles in positive psychology and explores *why* some people are happier. In my friends' context, one seems always happy, whereas another is rarely happy, yet their lives are objectively similar. Why is their perception so different?

According to the literature review conducted by Sonja Lyubomirsky over 20 years ago, the answer to this question lies in a range of processes. Firstly, genetics play a role in how people respond to happy events. However, what also matters is the cognitive processes they engage in. For example, some have developed optimistic thinking or self-reflection that helps them embrace opportunities in life. Others who have not might be unable to interpret the events in their lives in a positive way.

Another important process that impacts happiness is their motivation. Individuals who tend to set up goals that are intrinsically motivating – such as fostering meaningful relationships, pursuing personal growth, or contributing to their community – tend to be happier. On the other hand, when someone pursues extrinsic goals, especially those relating to the pursuit of fame or wealth, they tend to be less happy.

Lyubomirsky highlighted that certain daily behaviours are also the reason why people are happier. For example, engaging in activities each day that foster wellbeing, such as exercise, meditation, or spending time with loved ones, tends to explain why some people are happy. These types of behaviours need to be self-reinforcing, meaning that they should bring about a sense of accomplishment, pleasure, or connection to create a feedback loop that enhances wellbeing.

This article was published at the early stage of the positive psychology research. It provided some really important information that we can nowadays add to. It has created a good foundation for creating interventions that enhance wellbeing and a good life. For instance, it has influenced the development of positive psychology interventions that focus on cultivating optimism, fostering meaningful relationships, and promoting self-reflection, all of which have been shown to enhance happiness and wellbeing.

References

Lyubomirsky, S. (2001). Why are some people happier than others? The role of cognitive and motivational processes in well-being. *American Psychologist*, *56*(3), 239–249. https://doi.org/10.1037/0003-066X.56.3.239

Nostalgia

For as long as I can remember, I have always wanted to be a mum. Yet, despite my desire, it wasn't meant to be by the time I reached 40 years old. I tried to reconcile my dreams of motherhood with the notion that it would never happen to me. To ease the pain, I continued to engage in daydreaming, which helped me cope with the emptiness I felt. However, sometimes, it made my heart sore even more. I couldn't understand why it had such a varied impact on me. This is when I came across a study led by Dana Kotter-Grühn from Max Planck Institute for Human Development, Germany, where Paul Baltes and his team conceptualised the notion of "life longing" or as it is referred to in German *Sehnsucht*, and I applied it to childlessness and my longing to be a mum.

Sehnsucht is a longing we experience for a utopian state, resulting in bittersweet feelings. For instance, we may experience a longing to speak to someone who has already passed away or a longing to succeed at something important to us that is either in the future or is not likely to happen. It could also be longing for a child that was never born or will never be born. That process of longing helps us cope with our challenges more effectively, but only when we control it. For example, when I know that it is just my imagination, and I can stop it at any time and return to my "real" life. When I gave myself these short moments of daydreaming, it felt so good and was worth the short-term sadness that followed.

The research on Sehnsucht slowed right after Paul Baltes's passing, but recently, a concept similar to Life Longing, that is, nostalgia, has emerged. The difference between them lies predominantly in the time orientation. While Life Longing extends across the past, present, and future, nostalgia relates to having bittersweet memories of something that happened to us in the past.

The article led by Kristin Layous from California State University, USA (2023), identified nostalgia as a possible pathway towards wellbeing. The authors draw upon cross-sectional research and some experimental studies showing that reflecting upon the past can improve wellbeing in the here and now. That feeling of joy mixed with sadness improves connections between people, enhances the experiences of positive emotions and boosts our positive thoughts. However, it's important to remember that, similar to Sehnsucht, nostalgia needs to be somewhat controlled so that it does not lead to negative consequences. This control empowers us to use nostalgia as a tool for our emotional wellbeing.

So, if I were to bring back my longing for a child and frame it as a nostalgic memory, I could recall a time when I got unexpectedly pregnant at the age of 43 and gave birth to my son. I recall the joyful moments of getting to know him and figuring out how to best look after him. I feel joy knowing he is now in my life but also a tint of sadness that those early days of nappies, breastfeeding, and holding him close to me all the time are now behind me. I remember his baby smell, how small and wriggly his body was, and my daily tears of joy and gratitude about having him. These memories bring me immense joy, uplifting my spirit. They also bring a tinge of sadness because I will never hold my newborn again. But for now, I choose to close my eyes for five minutes and replay in my mind's eye the joyful moments shortly after he was born.

References

Kotter-Grühn, D., Scheibe, S., Blanchard-Fields, F., & Baltes, P. B. (2009). Developmental emergence and functionality of Sehnsucht (life longings): The sample case of involuntary

childlessness in middle-aged women. *Psychology and Aging*, *24*(3), 634–644. https://doi.org/10.1037/a0016359
Layous, K., & Kurtz, J. L. (2023). Nostalgia: A potential pathway to greater well-being. *Current Opinion in Psychology*, *49*. https://doi-org.elib.tcd.ie/10.1016/j.copsyc.2022.101548

Money and happiness

My mum and dad have always had opposing views about the money. My dad claimed that having money made him happier as it allowed him to do things he wouldn't be able to do otherwise. My mum, however, said money had nothing to do with happiness. Instead, she kept talking about love and education being the most important values and how nothing else matters as long as we have people we love and can continuously develop ourselves. Regardless of my parents' views, this topic has been of interest to many researchers, which is why Ed Diener from the University of Illinois and his son Robert Biswas-Diener wrote an article about it.

The authors argue that while money can enhance wellbeing to some extent, its impact is nuanced. Money plays an essential role in satisfying our basic needs. We need it to live and have safety, shelter, and food for sustenance. When we have our basic needs met, our subjective wellbeing increases. At the same time, beyond that, any additional income yields diminishing results. Our culture also impacts the influence money has on our wellbeing. The correlation between income and happiness in affluent countries is not as significant as in poorer nations. Therefore, other elements of wellbeing, such as relationships, our sense of meaning in life, or personal values, need to be considered as they have a more substantial impact on our wellbeing than money.

The authors also attempt to explain these results using theories of adaptation and social comparisons. These theories explore our tendency to adapt to our income levels over time. They also highlighted the impact of comparing our wealth to others on our wellbeing. If we believe that our income is higher than others, it boosts our happiness. If we see others as having more income and money, it tends to reduce our happiness. Understanding these behaviours can help us navigate our own pursuit of happiness more effectively. Knowing how to change our perspective to improve wellbeing is crucial.

This reminds me of a talk about money and happiness by John Halliwell, the principal investigator of the World Happiness Report at the European Conference on Positive Psychology in Amsterdam. He told us that the report found that those in the top 1% of earners were happier than others. I remember sitting in this beautiful building in Amsterdam, wondering what being in the 1% of the richest people would be like. For the context, at the time, I was a PhD student on a scholarship, earning very little. Then, Halliwell asked us to put up our hands if we earned more than 30,000 euros a year. Most people in the room put their hands up. In response he told us that *we* were the 1%. The room fell silent, and the presentation left me with goosebumps.

We need to take perspective when thinking of money and wellbeing. Some of us must rethink wealth, privilege, and happiness assumptions. Happiness isn't just about income but about so much more than this, such as gratitude, purpose, and perspective. More importantly, this article also highlights the need for a systems approach to wellbeing and the impact of our environment on happiness. Creating government policies that enforce minimum wage and social protection systems that support those in need can positively impact their wellbeing through meeting their basic needs. This straightforward solution can change the lives of millions of people worldwide – for the better.

References

Diener, E., & Biswas-Diener, R. (2002). Will money increase subjective well-being? *Social Indicators Research*, *57*(2), 119–169. https://doi.org/10.1023/A:1014411319119

Familiarity

I love going on holidays with my family. I often book our holidays way in advance. For several weeks, I explore places, accommodations, and activities. I savour every moment of this booking process. Then, I spend additional weeks anticipating the holidays and all our activities. When we get there, I try to take in every moment to make sure my reality does not fall short of my imagination. But regardless of where I go, what I do, and with whom I do it, I also savour going back home. I enjoy returning home, sleeping in my bed, making meals in my kitchen, picking up flowers from my garden, and sitting in my favourite chair while reading a book. Familiarity makes me happy, and I'm not the only one.

In a study led by Shigehiro Oishi, researchers explored the role of familiarity in our daily experiences of wellbeing. They found that retired participants experienced a boost in positive emotions when they spent time in familiar locations, such as their homes. However, this effect was not as pronounced for those in employment. Interestingly, younger people were also found to be more inclined towards seeking novelty to enjoy life, while older individuals tended to find comfort in familiarity. This balance of novelty and familiarity in different stages of life is an interesting aspect of our wellbeing.

One thing that both young and older participants unanimously agreed on is the impact of the familiarity with people on their wellbeing. The comfort of being around people we know well is a universal source of happiness. When we spend time with our partners, we tend to experience higher levels of wellbeing than when we are with others. This finding reassures us that the people we are close to play a crucial role in our happiness, regardless of our age.

So, my excitement about going on holiday and the joy of returning home could be equivalent to having a cake and eating it. Perhaps, given that I'm middle-aged, it is lovely to have both novelty and familiarity experienced at the same time.

References

Oishi, S., Kurtz, J. L., Miao, F. F., Park, J., & Whitchurch, E. (2011). The role of familiarity in daily well-being: Developmental and cultural variation. *Developmental Psychology*, *47*(6), 1750–1756. https://doi.org/10.1037/a0025305

Positive psychology interventions

Counting blessings

Whenever I ask new students at our university to give me an example of a positive psychology intervention, 99% of the time, they mention gratitude. This is one of the most common activities that springs to mind. In its original article, Robert Emmons and Michael McCullough conducted a series of studies comparing counting blessings to counting burdens and neutral events in life. The counting blessings group reported the highest levels of wellbeing compared to the other groups. This article was the beginning of an avalanche of research on this topic.

The original instructions for this activity asked participants to think back over the past week and write down up to five things they are grateful for. Following this study, researchers have experimented with this activity in many different ways. Some have specified a smaller or larger number of blessings. Others have asked participants to explain why they felt grateful for them. Then, it was expanded further by asking participants to write a letter of gratitude and, in some cases, deliver it to others. As such, this activity has become standard for anyone wishing to improve their wellbeing.

References

Emmons, R. A., & McCullough, M. E. (2003). Counting blessings versus burdens: An experimental investigation of gratitude and subjective well-being in daily life. *Journal of Personality and Social Psychology*, *84*(2), 377–389.

The best possible self

What differentiates humans from animals is our ability to project ourselves into the future. All we need to do is close our eyes, and we are right there, living the life we want, doing the things we long to do and having people respond to us the way we'd like to see. Then, we can do what we want with this image on cue. We can bring it into our mind any time we want to improve our mood, or we can create many pathways that would allow us to get there. Imagination is a beautiful thing.

Laura King, a social psychologist at the University of Missouri, conducted a study where she asked people to project themselves into the future and write about their best possible selves. This was compared to writing about their most traumatic event and about non-emotional topics, which were neutral and not emotionally charged. The results showed that writing about future goals was significantly less upsetting and significantly increased subjective wellbeing. Five months after the experiment, writing about the best possible self or trauma was associated with decreased illness compared with the non-emotional control group.

This experiment has been replicated many times with different groups of participants, consistently showing a range of wellbeing improvements. One of the most inspiring twists on this activity is writing about the best possible health, originally introduced to patients with type 2 diabetes (Gibson et al., 2021). This activity focuses on health and encourages people to project themselves into a future where they are healthier than today. It's a powerful tool showing that change and growth are always possible.

When I introduced this activity to a group alongside other positive psychology interventions, it quickly became the group's favourite. They were encouraged by its simplicity and accessibility, and at the debriefing, they expressed how hopeful and in control it made them feel. Even if not practised regularly, this activity can be a powerful tool when feeling stuck in a rut, providing a sense of direction and control over one's life.

References

Gibson, B., Umeh, K., Davies, I., & Newson, L. (2021). The best possible self-intervention as a viable public health tool for the prevention of type 2 diabetes: A reflexive thematic analysis of public experience and engagement. *Health Expectations: An International Journal of Public Participation in Health Care and Health Policy*, *24*(5), 1713–1724. https://doi.org/10.1111/hex.13311

King, L. A. (2001). The health benefits of writing about life goals. *Personality and Social Psychology Bulletin*, *27*(7), 798–807. https://doi-org.elib.tcd.ie/10.1177/0146167201277003

Savouring

I love reading literature for its wise advice. Some of it is explicit when a sentence amid another sentence suddenly leaves me stunned. Other is hidden between the lines, and it may occur to me after I put the book down where the wisdom lies in the sentences. Some books show wisdom in abundance, just like Winnie the Pooh. "We didn't realise we were making memories", Winnie told Piglet. "We just knew we were having fun". This simple sentence is a depiction of the savouring intervention in positive psychology.

Savouring is a process of attending to a moment, whether in the past, the present, or the future. The difference between being mindful and savouring is that mindfulness is only about attending to the moment regardless of whether our thoughts and feelings are positive or negative. In contrast, savouring implies we are experiencing an abundance of positive emotions. Savouring is also associated with slowing down and involving all possible senses. So, it is attending to the moment and engaging all our senses in this experience. Finally, savouring requires reflection on that moment. Hence, it is about thinking about what it means to us.

Fred Bryant from Loyola University Chicago and Joseph Veroff (2007) have identified ten strategies for experiencing savouring. These include the following:

1. **Sharing positive experiences with others** – for example, telling your family about your positive experiences during the day. Do it with all the detail it deserves to help you re-experience all the emotions.

2. **Memory building** – taking a "mental photograph" while you are having fun with someone. For example, imagine you have friends over for dinner. While everyone at the table chats and food is shared abundantly, you stop and take a mental photograph of that moment, taking in all there is to take about this picture of happiness.
3. **Comparing** – compared with other people or situations you've experienced, what makes this moment so unique and memorable? Reflecting on it will help you savour it more effectively.
4. **Sensory perceptual sharpening** – have you ever experienced a situation when suddenly one of your senses is at high alert? It could be because you focus on it while ignoring all other stimuli. This is how the sensory-perceptual sharpening happens. It is as if we put a spotlight on one sense or one object.
5. **Self-congratulation** – another pathway for experiencing savouring is congratulating yourself for something you are proud of.
6. **Absorption** relates to losing oneself in an activity, which could become a pathway for savouring.
7. **Behavioural expression** is about dancing, singing, laughing, and performing other activities that can lead to savouring.
8. **Temporal awareness** is being aware of how quickly time passes. For instance, one might reflect on how quickly children grow up or how fast time goes when one is enjoying oneself.
9. **Counting blessings** is yet another pathway to savouring. It is about reflecting on how fortunate we are to have something or someone in our lives.
10. **Kiljoy's thinking** is the reverse of a savouring pathway and relates to ruminating over the temporal nature of joy. For example, some people, when they are in the middle of a joyous moment, think that it will not last forever and start worrying about what happens when the joy goes.

These are just some of the strategies that researchers have created to help experience savouring. You could use those or come up with other ones that work for you. At the same time, as with all things in life, moderation is required when searching for positive experiences we can savour. Experiencing too many positive events may reduce savouring (Quoidbach et al., 2015). This is why, when arranging your next holiday, feel free to reduce the number of places you visit but focus on how you could savour those places before you get there, while you are there and after you leave them. Less is more.

References

Bryant, F. B., & Veroff, J. (2007). *Savoring: A new model of positive experience*. Taylor Francis Group.

Quoidbach, J., Dunn, E. W., Hansenne, M., & Bustin, G. (2015). The price of abundance: How a wealth of experiences impoverishes savoring. *Personality & Social Psychology Bulletin*, *41*(3), 393–404. https://doi.org/10.1177/0146167214566189

Kindness

By now you already know my granny and understand how much she has influenced my life. During WW2, she served in the Polish underground army and took an active role in the Warsaw Uprising, reaching a Lieutenant rank. What I found fascinating about her is that despite losing most of her family and friends to war, she never talked about hatred, loss, or death. Instead, all the stories she told me and her seven other grandchildren were tales of love, forgiveness, kindness, compassion, and patriotism. Kindness is what always stuck with me. She spent the entire war helping people and then helping her children to become good people, and finally until her final days, she continued to help more people through the charity she was involved in. She used to say that the war stripped people to the core of their existence, and kindness was at her core.

Kindness refers to any actions we take that benefit others. The article led by Oliver Curry (2018) from the University of Oxford, UK, is a systematic review demonstrating the impact of kindness interventions on wellbeing. However, it also offers a range of interventions that could be practised. In positive psychology, the most popular intervention is the Random Acts of Kindness, whereby we search for opportunities in the day to do something valuable for other people, such as holding a door open for someone, complimenting someone, or helping a colleague at work, even though it is not part of your responsibility. Random acts of kindness are about having a mindset prepared to offer your support and searching for opportunities.

In addition to this intervention, we could always practise not-so random acts of kindness, whereby we plan for them. For example, we may plan to do little acts of kindness throughout the day, such as making someone lunch or a cuppa, or fewer but bigger acts of kindness, such as spending a few hours helping your friend's son who struggles with maths, or doing a local community clean-up. Other examples of not-so random acts of kindness could include volunteering at a local charity, helping an elderly neighbour with their groceries, or mentoring a younger colleague at work.

Apart from performing acts of kindness, other interventions expanded towards the whole-range of kindness-related activities. These include keeping track of kindness you perform, or recalling acts of kindness you've performed, or observing acts of kindness in other people. Keeping track of kindness involves maintaining a journal or a digital record of the kind acts you perform or witness. This practice can help you reflect on your actions, appreciate the impact of kindness, and inspire you to continue spreading kindness.

These "kindness" interventions are not exhaustive. Whichever ones you choose, what matters is putting your effort into them and doing it mindfully. Beware, however, which acts you select, as they might not have the same effect. Consider, for instance, buying someone a present versus offering them a gift of time. A present might be easier, but will it have the same impact on both the recipient and you?

Finally, one of my friends set out to pay forward, be kind to a stranger, and buy coffee for the next person who entered the coffee shop. She thought it would be a pleasant surprise if the barista told them they were getting a free coffee, as an act of kindness. But her act of kindness backfired as the barista couldn't understand why she was doing it, and by the time the next customer walked in, it was no longer an anonymous act of kindness she was after. So, the timing and circumstances matter when selecting your acts.

References

Curry, O. S., Rowland, L. A., Van Lissa, C. J., Zlotowitz, S., McAlaney, J., & Whitehouse, H. (2018). Happy to help? A systematic review and meta-analysis of the effects of performing acts of kindness on the well-being of the actor. *Journal of Experimental Social Psychology*, *76*, 320–329.

Benefit finding

When we were in our twenties and thirties, my friends and I enjoyed dating and having fun. Some of us fell in love quickly and fell out of love just as easily. However, one of my friends, in particular, was always very cautious about giving her heart away to anyone. One day, she met a guy, and after a long time of dating, she finally realised she was in love with him, and then things moved swiftly. They moved in together and started planning for the future; three months later, what seemed like out of nowhere, he broke up with her. Given her cautious nature, we thought she would find it particularly hard to cope with it, but we were all surprised with how well she coped. Soon after the breakup, she kept talking about the benefits of splitting up, and the list became longer and longer as time passed.

Benefit-finding is a natural process of recovery from traumatic or upsetting situations. By attempting to see the benefits of the dire situation, we make it meaningful and valuable for our development or life. Many studies have explored benefit-finding, but one particular research that is often discussed in this context was conducted by Laura King and Kathi Miner (2000). They asked participants to write about either their traumatic events, given that expressive writing is a well-established intervention, or the benefits of their traumatic events. Their research showed that both approaches showed health benefits compared to a control group that did nothing. Specifically, their visits to a doctor decreased over five months following the intervention.

Interestingly, when in another group participants wrote about both positive and negative aspects of their trauma, the impact was not lasting and soon dissipated. It was significantly lower than writing about traumatic events when participants allowed themselves to express all of their negative emotions and significantly lower than writing about the benefits of trauma, which was filled with many more positive emotional expressions. Thus, in this study, mixing good and bad had only a small benefit to people.

This activity has been further developed, with parts added and reframing. For example, it was used as a "One door closes, another door opens" activity (Gander et al., 2013), whereby participants are asked to reflect upon the opportunities that present themselves after life disappointments. Another twist on this activity is exploring what might have happened and searching for ways it could have been worse (Kennedy et al., 2021). It is also important to note that the benefit-finding activity can be done not only for one-off traumatic or disappointing events but life circumstances, such as dealing with chronic illness. In this case, we could do a "benefit reminding" activity (Tennen & Affleck, 2005), whereby reflecting on the ongoing pain of our circumstance, we might remind ourselves about the benefits of our illness.

For my friend, whose relationship dissolved so suddenly, exploring the benefits of the breakup was a coping strategy she used. Interestingly, two decades later, she continues to see it in this way. It is a testament to the long-term advantages of benefit-finding, helping her see her relationship as a stepping stone on her life journey.

References

Gander, F., Proyer, R., Ruch, W., & Wyss, T. (2013). Strength-based positive interventions: Further evidence for their potential in enhancing well-being and alleviating depression. *Journal of Happiness Studies*, *14*(4), 1241–1259.

Kennedy, C., Deane, F. P., & Chan, A. Y. C. (2021). "What might have been . . .": Counterfactual thinking, psychological symptoms and posttraumatic growth when a loved one is missing. *Cognitive Therapy & Research*, *45*(2), 322–332. https://doi-org.elib.tcd.ie/10.1007/s10608-020-10156-7

King, L. A., & Miner, K. N. (2000). Writing about the perceived benefits of traumatic events: Implications for physical health. *Personality and Social Psychology Bulletin*, *26*(2), 220–230. https://doi.org/10.1177/0146167200264008

Tennen, H., & Affleck, G. (2005). Benefit-finding and benefit reminding. In C. R. Snyder & S. J. Lopez (Eds.), *Handbook of positive psychology* (pp. 584–597). Oxford University Press.

Character strengths

I have to admit – it took me quite some time to truly embrace the idea of character strengths. I found the research on character strengths intriguing, but initially, I had many reservations about it. During my early days of learning about positive psychology, three college friends and I met weekly to discuss our insights about the applications of positive psychology. Every week, my friends spoke enthusiastically about the glorious effect of using their character strengths on their wellbeing. I listened to them with curiosity but remained unconvinced. To me, it felt like a redundant exercise. After all, I was already using my strengths daily, so what was the point in overusing them? That perspective stayed with me until I began to approach my strengths in a slightly different way.

One of the first activities advocating strength use was for individuals to complete a strengths questionnaire and use their signature (top) strengths differently. This activity consistently shows improvements in wellbeing and is considered as one of the core positive psychology interventions.

However, Rene Proyer and the team from the Department of Psychology at the University of Zurich, Switzerland, who have contributed with abundant research on strengths, designed an experiment that allowed us to see strengths differently.

They asked participants to use either their signature (top) strengths or their lesser strengths. Interestingly, both approaches positively impacted participants' wellbeing for up to 3 months after the experiment and reduced depression in the short term. The findings also revealed that those with already well-developed strengths benefitted more from challenging themselves to work on their lesser strengths. Those with underdeveloped strengths gained more from using their signature strengths. This insight may explain why I was initially so reluctant to practise my signature strengths. I love a challenge, and the activity was just not challenging enough for me.

Furthermore, research consistently demonstrates that practising character strengths impacts wellbeing. Recently, Fabian Gander and colleagues (2024) published research showing that such practice not only improves wellbeing but also develops our character strengths. In essence, using strengths has an overall positive impact on many aspects of our lives.

Over the years, I have begun to embrace the use of strengths, especially when I am in a tricky situation or when I procrastinate; I find a creative way to use my strengths to get the job done. While I don't necessarily practise them as interventions, I make sure that I do what makes me happy each day. For example, I try to spread love (the strength of Love and Be Loved), put myself in situations that allow me to practise my Zest, regularly spend time in nature (Love of Beauty and Excellence), and enjoy spotting strengths in people around me. So, for me, strengths are not as much of an intervention but a way of looking at the world differently.

References

Gander, F., Wagner, L., & Niemiec, R. M. (2024). Do character strengths-based interventions change character strengths? Two randomized controlled intervention studies. *Collabra: Psychology*, *10*(1). https://doi.org/10.1525/collabra.108604

Proyer, R. T., Gander, F., Wellenzohn, S., & Ruch, W. (2015). Strengths-based positive psychology interventions: A randomized placebo-controlled online trial on long-term effects for a signature strengths-vs a lesser strengths-intervention. *Frontiers in Psychology*, *6*. https://doi.org.elib.tcd.ie/10.3389/fpsyg.2015.00456

Humour

My husband is, without a doubt, the funniest man I know. He sees the world very differently from most of us, and suddenly, out of nowhere, he reframes what he sees and makes everyone laugh. My husband has ADHD, so his mind travels a million miles an hour. He considers it his superpower and why he perceives a situation's funny side before everyone else catches up to him. He is known for his humour at work, where he sees it as part of his job to release the tension during tough meetings. At home, his humour is cheeky as he plays pranks on all of us, including the dog, and the children love the distraction very much. Even though sometimes I give out to him about it and plead for him to be more serious, I do love it, too.

Humour, a powerful tool in positive psychology, offers a range of interventions that can significantly impact our wellbeing. In this article, the authors (Wellenzohn et al., 2016) explored several humour-based interventions, each designed to be easily incorporated into our daily lives. These interventions include:

1. Identify three funny things each evening that you experienced during the day
2. Recall one hilarious thing and write about it in detail
3. Count the funny things that happen to you during the day and then record the number of funny things you've experienced each evening
4. During the day, notice funny things and add other humorous things, like reading jokes, watching funny clips on social media, or reading comic books
5. Think of a stressful event during the day and try to reframe it humorously

These five examples demonstrate how humour can release tension and improve wellbeing throughout the day and evening. The study asked participants to practise one of these interventions daily for a week. The results showed that all interventions led to immediate improvements in happiness. Importantly, three of these interventions continued to show benefits 6 months later. These were listing three funny things, noticing funny things, then adding new humorous activities, and counting the funny things that happened during the day. This suggests that with consistent practice, humour can have a lasting positive impact on our wellbeing.

For some, humour comes naturally, much like my husband. For others, it may require more effort. It's important to note that not all humour is beneficial. Research suggests that self-deprecating humour can backfire in certain situations, and sarcasm or aggressive humour is generally not associated with wellbeing. Instead, practising affiliative humour that makes other people laugh without hurting them is essential. Make wise choices about using humour that would serve you and others well.

References

Wellenzohn, S., Proyer, R. T., & Ruch, W. (2016). Humor-based online positive psychology interventions: A randomized placebo-controlled long-term trial. *The Journal of Positive Psychology*, *11*(6), 584–594. https://doi.org/10.1080/17439760.2015.1137624

Optimism

In his book *Learned Optimism* Martin Seligman demonstrated the ABCD technique from the CBT, which ultimately aimed to enhance optimism. The technique is focused on changing people's beliefs about their life events into more optimistic by considering the consequences of those beliefs, then disputing them and exploring alternative, more optimistic beliefs.

While CBT is best known for improving optimism, a systematic review of interventions identified many activities that result in increased optimism (Malouff & Schutte, 2017). These include Best Possible Self, meaning-making programmes, or a psychodrama stress management programme. However, one that we will explore today is an article by Hadassah Littman-Ovadia and Dina Nir (2014) about "Looking forward to tomorrow".

In this activity, you are asked to think of three good things, these could be items, events, or people that you will be experiencing tomorrow. Write them all down and then select one activity you would like to practise. Now, try to imagine this one activity in as much detail as you can muster. Draw upon the heart-felt feelings you experience when thinking of it. This simple activity can help you feel happier but also boost your optimism.

References

Littman-Ovadia, H., & Nir, D. (2014). Looking forward to tomorrow: The buffering effect of a daily optimism intervention. *The Journal of Positive Psychology*, *9*(2), 122–136. https://doi-org.elib.tcd.ie/10.1080/17439760.2013.853202

Malouff, J. M., & Schutte, N. S. (2017). Can psychological interventions increase optimism? A meta-analysis. *The Journal of Positive Psychology*, *12*(6), 594–604. https://doi-org.elib.tcd.ie/10.1080/17439760.2016.1221122

Forgiveness

My client has been married to his partner for over a decade. They have been through thick and thin. Being gay in Ireland before it was legalised and embraced by society was not easy. Then, out of nowhere, he found out that his partner cheated on him with someone else. I asked him how he felt about it. He said he forgave him but did not forget it. I asked him what it felt like to forgive. He said that he told him that because they had been together for so long and had gone through so much, he would let it go, but the next time it happened, it would be a different story. Did my client forgive?

We teach children forgiveness by pleading that when someone does something terrible to them and apologises, they should say, "Thank you, I forgive you", and the matter is closed. However, this type of forgiveness is decisional and does not seep into the emotional state. True forgiveness exists emotionally when thinking about the transgression no longer makes us angry, sad, frustrated, or experiencing other negative emotions. Instead, we are at peace with it and experience neutral or sometimes even positive emotions. For instance, when a friend betrays our trust, and we can genuinely forgive them, we no longer feel the same hurt or anger towards them.

Forgiveness is often misunderstood as condoning the offense, as if we're letting the wrongdoer off the hook. But in reality, forgiveness is a deeply personal act. It's about taking control of our own emotions and thoughts, and not letting the actions of others continue to hurt us. It's about releasing the negative impact of the offense and moving forward, stronger and more resilient. It's a transformative process that can give hope and optimism to those who are struggling with forgiveness.

Over the years, I have heard of many interventions that may facilitate forgiveness. One that I really liked was a school intervention. Teachers created a forgiveness garden on school premises. Children could go to this garden any time they wish and leave a stone of forgiveness behind that was weighing on their shoulders. Within a month, the garden was filled with stones.

Everett Worthington's REACH forgiveness programme is one of the most famous programmes developed to facilitate forgiveness. It takes 6 hours to complete and can be done in a group, with a therapist, or as a do-it-yourself activity. One well-known activity from this programme is writing a letter of forgiveness to someone who has wronged you.

The programme comprises five steps:

1. **Recall the hurt** – during this stage, individuals close their eyes and try to remember the transgression in detail without allowing self-pity.
2. **Empathise** – the second stage encourages extending empathy to the person who did you wrong. It is about putting yourself in the transgressor's shoes.
3. **Altruistic gift** – in this stage, you recall a time when you did something wrong to someone and were forgiven by them.
4. **Commit to forgiveness** – express your willingness to forgive someone, perhaps by writing a letter of forgiveness.
5. **Hold on to forgiveness** – think of ways to maintain it and remind yourself to do so.

Many years ago, when studying for a master's in positive psychology, I wanted to practise all the interventions our module leader suggested. One of them was writing a letter of forgiveness. Of all the interventions, this was the one that I kept procrastinating until one day when I sat on a train from Dublin to Cork (Ireland) and decided to write a letter of forgiveness to someone who had hurt my feelings. I can still remember the impact the letter had on me. I felt lighter and was filled with compassion. By the time I arrived at my destination, I picked up my phone and spoke with the person I forgave. She didn't know what I was going through. It didn't really matter. That letter of forgiveness was not for her but for me. Until then, many unsaid things were festering inside me, creating resentment that impacted my relationship with her. I was apparently very quiet. But as soon as the letter was finished, all the negativity inside me was gone. It was one of the most powerful interventions I have ever done.

One thing to note is that not everyone experiences the same sense of relief after completing this activity. Over the years, when I encouraged students to do it, some reported they felt guilty writing a letter of forgiveness as it assumed they had not contributed to some of the wrongdoing. They felt that by forgiving, they failed to take responsibility for their own actions. This is obviously not the case in all situations, but it's a reminder that forgiveness is a deeply personal process. Beware that some situations could make the process of forgiveness more challenging. Especially, when we find it hard to forgive ourselves.

References

Worthington, E. L., Jr., Witvliet, C. V. O., Pietrini, P., & Miller, A. J. (2007). Forgiveness, health, and well-being: A review of evidence for emotional versus decisional forgiveness, dispositional forgivingness, and reduced unforgiveness. *Journal of Behavioral Medicine*, *30*(4), 291–302. https://doi-org.elib.tcd.ie/10.1007/s10865-007-9105-8

Meaning and purpose

In Ireland, we do not pay any bills associated with water consumption. In some countries, water charges were introduced decades ago, and they've become part of life. However, when the Irish government attempted to charge the citizens for water a few years ago, the usually quiet nation rebelled against it. We use water every day. We cannot live without it. Yet, when was the last time you talked to someone about water? We do not usually talk about the value of water at all. It is always there in the background, sustaining our existence. However, when the Irish nation disagreed with the government on the water charges, everybody on TV, radio, bus stop, workplaces, playgrounds, and all other places talked about water. Life's meaning is similar to water. It is not something we talk about every day, yet it drives our activities daily. It is always in the background, and sometimes, bringing it up to our consciousness helps us experience more life meaning.

One unique activity that has managed to do this is one led by Michael Steger who created a "Through the windows of the soul" intervention. Participants in this intervention were asked to take 9–12 photographs of things that made their lives meaningful over a week. Then, a week later, they were asked to review their pictures and explain the significance of each one.

Despite its simplicity, this activity has led to improvements in wellbeing. Participants reported increased positive emotions, life satisfaction, and a greater sense of meaning in life. Moreover, they experienced a decrease in negative emotions. All these positive changes were a result of reflecting on what made their lives meaningful and explaining the significance of their photographs.

While this activity is a promising example of a simple intervention that can enhance wellbeing, it's important to note that the sample size in this study was relatively small. Therefore, more replications of the study are needed to confirm these results. In the meantime, based on the preliminary findings, this activity in all its forms could be a valuable tool to integrate in daily life by exploring situations and opportunities to identify what matters to us and then reflecting on their significance.

References

Steger, M. F., Shim, Y., Barenz, J., & Shin, J. Y. (2014). Through the windows of the soul: A pilot study using photography to enhance meaning in life. *Journal of Contextual Behavioral Science*, *3*(1), 27–30. https://doi-org.elib.tcd.ie/10.1016/j.jcbs.2013.11.002

Nine beautiful things

One of my son's character strengths is his love of beauty. I first noticed it when he was four years old, standing at the window, his eyes filled with awe as he watched the sunset – "mammy" he said, "look how beautiful it is". His joy and wonder were infectious. Over the years, he often stopped and admired the tree canopies, noticed the birds singing, the intoxicating smell of the forest, or ran around the Glendalough (Ireland) hiking tracks, stopping every now and then to admire the beauty of nature. His interest in beauty also extends to art, as he loved being in the Louvre when we holidayed in Paris (France). Given that this is also one of my top strengths, we are often in this awesome experience together. For us, seeing that beauty of nature, or art, comes naturally. For others, it does not. Yet, even if it is natural to us, sometimes when we feel off and reflect on the reasons for it, we may realise that we have missed practising our strength of beauty. So, doing interventions that may bring us back to our passions, or help us develop "the love of beauty and excellence" strength, can be useful. This is exactly what this article is about.

The researchers asked participants to reflect each evening for a week about nine beautiful things they experienced, three things for each of the following categories:

1. Beautiful things in human behaviour – these things involve morally valued behaviours or any of the good deeds they have done
2. Beautiful things they found in nature or their environment
3. Beautiful things in general

Following this intervention, participants experienced higher levels of happiness for up to 1 month and a decline in depression symptoms for up to 1 week.

When I think of a beauty intervention, two things strike me. Firstly, it is essential to replicate this study with a larger sample of participants, given that it was relatively small and the effect sizes of the findings were also small. This means that the actual extent of the difference between those who did these interventions, and the control group was small. Secondly, I love this Greek proverb that links this study with our character: "What is beautiful is good, and what is good will soon be beautiful". Searching for beauty around us can not only improve wellbeing in the short term but also help us become better people.

References

Proyer, R. T., Gander, F., Wellenzohn, S., & Ruch, W. (2016). Nine beautiful things: A self-administered online positive psychology intervention on the beauty in nature, arts, and behaviors increases happiness and ameliorates depressive symptoms. *Personality & Individual Differences*, *94*, 189–193. https://doi-org.elib.tcd.ie/10.1016/j.paid.2016.01.028

Awe walk

Vast forest, crowds at an anti-Brexit rally, and the starry sky – what do they have in common? All of them can evoke an incredible feeling of awe. We overuse the word "awesome" in our lives to the extent that it has lost meaning. However, research on the concept of awe is thriving. Dacher Keltner and Jonathan Haidt (2003), who first conceptualised awe, defined it as a complex emotion that emerges when we are exposed to something vast that makes us feel humble and insignificant. Natural wonders like Niagara Falls, the Atlantic Ocean, or the local forest trigger awe. Also, art may evoke awe, such as Leonardo Da Vinci's *Mona Lisa*, Banksy's *There is Always Hope*, or Adele's "Someone Like You". In addition, any moral or spiritual event could result in awe. Just consider the 14th Dalai Lama Nobel Peace Prize acceptance speech as an example.

Many interventions have been developed to experience awe. However, one that has recently received a lot of attention is a simple and accessible intervention, the 15-minute "Awe walk" (Sturm et al., 2022). This intervention doesn't require any special skills or equipment. Participants were asked to go for a walk once a week for 8 weeks. They took the walks alone and were asked not to use their smartphones unless they wanted to take a photograph. They were also encouraged to search for places that offered vastness and novelty in them, to help participants experience awe.

Compared to a control group that was asked to go for a walk, the group engaged in the "Awe walk" experienced more awe during their walk and reported feeling more joy and pro-social emotions, which resulted in pro-social behaviours such as helping others, sharing, or comforting others. This positive impact on their wellbeing continued even after the walk, with the pro-social emotions persisting and a decrease in distress in their lives. Thus, the addition of a search for awe during a walk can lead to significant improvements in wellbeing, offering hope for those seeking to enhance their mental health.

At the same time, participants in the control group who didn't need to put much effort into searching for and experiencing awe, tended to go for more walks during the same time. This raises an interesting question – could the effort put into the "awe walks" deter people from frequent engagement in physical activity? More research needs to be done to confirm this, sparking curiosity and further exploration in the field of psychology and wellbeing.

References

Keltner, D., & Haidt, J. (2003). Approaching awe, a moral, spiritual, and aesthetic emotion. *Cognition & Emotion*, *17*(2), 297–314. https://doi.org/10.1080/02699930302297

Sturm, V. E., Datta, S., Roy, A. R. K., Sible, I. J., Kosik, E. L., Veziris, C. R., Chow, T. E., Morris, N. A., Neuhaus, J., Kramer, J. H., Miller, B. L., Holley, S. R., & Keltner, D. (2022). Big smile, small self: Awe walks promote prosocial positive emotions in older adults. *Emotion*, *22*(5), 1044–1058. https://doi.org/10.1037/emo0000876

Courage

My cousin is one of the most courageous people I know when it comes to physical courage. Since childhood, she has always pushed the boundaries of comfort and surprised everyone with her courage. This led her to dive deeply into a 5-hour narrow cave climb that only she and her friend dared to enter; while other experienced climbers did not dare. She pushed her fear aside when paragliding in the Grand Canyon. She also challenged herself when climbing Kilimanjaro in Tasmania. While her courage is for audacious activities, many of us need the courage to attend to less extreme everyday life-related matters. This is where the intervention, designed to help individuals build courage in their daily lives, comes in.

Through the work of Amanda Kramer and Richard Zinbarg from Northwestern University, USA, we've discovered a powerful tool for personal growth. By recalling a time when we faced our fears with courage, we can actually increase our likelihood of making more courageous decisions in the future. This intervention also holds the promise of a more courageous tomorrow.

I'm happy to test this intervention in any prosaic-type of situations, such as asking someone a difficult question, learning a new and challenging skill, or standing up for someone in a tricky situation. I think I will leave the big courageous acts to my cousin.

References

Kramer, A., & Zinbarg, R. (2019). Recalling courage: An initial test of a brief writing intervention to activate a 'courageous mindset' and courageous behavior. *The Journal of Positive Psychology*, *14*(4), 528–537. https://doi-org.elib.tcd.ie/10.1080/17439760.2018.1484943

Reframing the ordinary

My beloved dad passed away suddenly when he was in his early sixties. One of the last pieces of wisdom he shared with me was a reminder that our lives shrink with age, making each day more valuable than the day before. He encouraged me to live my life to the fullest and squeeze all the juice out of it. His advice resonated deeply with me and was revived when I recently saw a "life calendar". It showed an estimated number of days we have left before we die versus how many days are already behind us. Given that I am in my fifties now, the picture did not look too good for me, so my dad's advice popped into my mind. The activities that reframe the ordinary follow the same sentiment.

The less time we have, the more valuable it becomes. This is why, in the first experiment, Jamie Kurtz (2008) from James Madison University (USA), asked college students to take 10 minutes to write about one of the four topics: the friends they have in college, the campus, the college activities in which they participate, or their overall college experience. However, she has also asked students to consider that they have very little time left to graduate, only about 1,200 hours. The researcher found that priming participants by reminding them of time scarcity resulted in higher subjective wellbeing levels over 2 weeks and more engagement in college activities.

A more recent study about scarcity (Layous et al., 2017) requested that participants reflect on the area where they live and think of people, restaurants, and other places they love. Then, they were asked to imagine that in 30 days, they would be moving out of there. During the month, they were encouraged to do all the things they would miss once they move away. This simple reframing activity resulted in improvements in life satisfaction and positive emotions.

It may seem counterintuitive, but the act of imagining a loss, even if it is only a fictional activity, can be a powerful motivator to live our lives to the full. It can inspire us to make the most of the time we have left, fostering happiness. This may be one reason why, according to some reports, our happiness tends to increase as we age.

References

Kurtz J. L. (2008). Looking to the future to appreciate the present: The benefits of perceived temporal scarcity. *Psychological Science*, *19*(12), 1238–1241. https://doi.org/10.1111/j.1467-9280.2008.02231.x

Layous, K., Kurtz, J., Chancellor, J., & Lyubomirsky, S. (2017). Reframing the ordinary: Imagining time as scarce increases well-being. *The Journal of Positive Psychology*, *13*(3), 301–308. https://doi.org/10.1080/17439760.2017.1279210

Personality

Amy Cuddy's TEDx talk has made headlines. At 19, she survived a serious car accident that left her with a head injury affecting her IQ. Despite this, she persevered, earning a PhD and a position at Harvard University. In her talk, she shares her experience with imposter syndrome and the value of "faking it until you make it", a testament to her incredible resilience.

Intelligence is often seen as a fixed trait. Similarly, personality is perceived as unchangeable. We tend to describe individuals as more conscientious or introverted than others and assume that these traits will remain stable over time. However, research indicates that our personality evolves, particularly in response to some traumatic events we experience. Additionally, growing research explores how individuals can adopt new thoughts and behaviours to benefit from characteristics that do not come naturally to them.

Let us take extraversion as an example. Extraversion is a propensity to seek stimulation from our social environment, whereas introversion is associated with needing and seeking less social stimulation. Introverts tend to recharge their energy levels in quiet and prefer one-to-one relationships with a smaller group of people. Conversely, extroverts tend to become more energised when surrounded by others and prefer more frequent social contact that boasts large groups of people. This distinction between introversion and extraversion is a concept in understanding the potential benefits of personality-based interventions, given that social connection is one of the pathways for improved wellbeing.

While research continues to explore personality-based interventions, one study by Seth Margolis and Sonja Lyubomirsky from the University of California, USA, is a key one. Participants were asked to behave as if they were introverted or extroverted for 1 week. Their wellbeing was assessed on days 1 and 8 and a 1-week follow-up. The findings showed that adopting introversion led to a decline in wellbeing, whereas acting extraverted enhanced it. Specifically, changes were found in the participants' experience of positive emotions, connectedness, and flow, which is a state of being engrossed in an activity to an extent when we lose the sense of who we are, where we are, and who we are with. Curiously, the personality measures also showed differences before and after the interventions, meaning that small behavioural changes can influence not only our wellbeing but also our self-perceived traits.

As an introvert, I find these findings fascinating. Over the years, I have naturally engaged in extraverted behaviour not as a wellbeing intervention but as a way to navigate situations where being extraverted was more beneficial to me, such as teaching or attending networking events. While these moments often put me in a good mood and may have improved my wellbeing, I could never escape my true nature. My greatest joy always came from going home and recharging my batteries. So, while it is the route to wellbeing is intriguing, my authentic self rebels against it a little.

References

Margolis, S., & Lyubomirsky, S. (2020). Experimental manipulation of extraverted and introverted behavior and its effects on well-being. *Journal of Experimental Psychology. General, 149*(4), 719–731. https://doi.org/10.1037/xge0000668

The effectiveness of positive psychology interventions

This is how it all began

The first ever happiness programme was created in the 1970s by Michael Fordyce, an eccentric professor of psychology who everyone loved. He completed his PhD in the topic of happiness in 1972 and then went on to study it for decades. His true passion, however, was teaching and making his students happy. A true hedonist, after he retired, he spent years travelling around Europe and enjoying *la dolce vita*. When I was a student of positive psychology, we had reports of him living in Spain. One of my fellow students decided to contact him and he kindly agreed to meet her to share some of his life's insights. This experience was one of the highlights of her life.

Until the Fordyce programme was first published, many researchers doubted whether happiness could be changed at all. Even Freud has famously said that the best we can hope for is to turn misery into common unhappiness. Until 1977, nobody had done it as part of research. Roll on 50 years, and according to *The Lancet*, we have never spent as much money on wellbeing as we do now, and the costs of mental health are estimated to rise further to $6 trillion by 2030. This cost is greater than the cost of cancer, diabetes, and respiratory disease combined. And it all started with the Fordyce programme, which made people believe that changes in wellbeing were possible.

The programme comprised nine fundamentals (1977), further expanded to 14 when assessed for its long-term impact (over 28 months) (Fordyce, 1977). The fundamentals included such components as:

- Spending more time socialising
- Developing an outgoing, social personality
- Becoming more active
- Lowering expectations and aspirations
- Developing positive, optimistic thinking
- Getting better organised and planning things out

- Eliminating adverse problems (especially stop worrying)
- Becoming more present-oriented
- Valuing happiness
- Developing positive thinking
- Keeping busy

Today, many of the topics discussed in the programme we take for granted, some of the topics we continue to promote for happiness, yet some of them we have evidence that may impact people negatively. Nonetheless, at the time, the programme was revolutionary.

A few years later, the programme was expanded and assessed long term, over 9 and then again 28 months, and it showed that participants continued to report higher levels of wellbeing (Fordyce, 1983). This was the beginning of the wellbeing programme design. While it stagnated for over a decade, the field of positive psychology has revitalised it, leading to an enormous impact. We now have many programmes developed, although not all are as effective. We could learn from some of the simplicity of this programme when introducing positive psychology interventions.

References

Fordyce, M. W. (1977). Development of a program to increase personal happiness. *Journal of Counseling Psychology*, *24*(6), 511–521. https://doi-org.elib.tcd.ie/10.1037/0022-0167.24.6.511

Fordyce, M. W. (1983). A program to increase happiness: Further studies. *Journal of Counseling Psychology*, *30*(4), 483–498. https://doi.org/10.1037/0022-0167.30.4.483

Psychological interventions to increase happiness

The first time positive psychology interventions were tested as part of positive psychology was in an article written by Martin Seligman and a team. They have reported on the progress in positive psychology and one topic they covered were interventions. At the time, they did not even call them "positive psychology interventions", just "psychological intervention to increase happiness". They said that from over 100 interventions promoted by the self-improvement industry, they distilled around 40 of them that are good enough for using in research. From them, they have further selected five, and reported on the results. The assessments used were a depression scale and the Steen Happiness Index, which to that date was unknown and did not have any information published about its validity.

Five 1-week interventions were selected and compared against a placebo group that were asked to write about their early memories every night for a week. The first intervention was a gratitude visit, whereby participants were asked to write and deliver a letter of gratitude to someone who was kind to them but they had never got an opportunity to thank them for it. The second intervention was writing down every day three good things that went well that day. The third one was writing about a time when the participants were at their best and what strengths they engaged in during this time. The fourth intervention related to using signature strengths in a new way, after completing, what we know now as VIAcharacter.org assessment. Finally, the fifth intervention was to complete a survey, identify their strengths, and try to use it more frequently during the next week.

All these interventions are well known nowadays, and we have been researched for decades. However, back then, they were very new and exciting, as we began learning about ways to improve wellbeing by engaging in those interventions. What was particularly encouraging was that two of the activities increased happiness and decreased symptoms of depression for not only a week, but 6 months. They were using signature strengths in a new way and three good things. What made these two activities so impactful over a longer period of time was the frequency with which participants continued to use them after the experiment ended. Thus, these new activities were a foundation of a speciality within positive psychology that explored positive psychology interventions and their mechanisms.

References

Seligman, M. E. P., Steen, T. A., Park, N., & Peterson, C. (2005). Positive psychology progress: Empirical validation of interventions. *American Psychologist*, *60*(5), 410–421.

Replication

I found this article fascinating when it was first published because it hinted at something important about the relationship between positive psychology and wellbeing. Our interest in positive psychology could, in itself, amplify our wellbeing. This is almost like a placebo effect. Simply believing in the effectiveness of positive psychology interventions can make them more effective. This was great news for me and anyone involved in positive psychology research. But it made me wonder about everyone else. Should we provide evidence of the benefits to wellbeing before people practise interventions? Shall we work on their motivation to do it instead of implementing it cold face?

Myriam Mongrain, a professor at a Canadian university specialising in clinical psychology, and Tracy Anselmo-Matthews, a clinical and rehabilitation psychologist, decided to replicate the famous experiment Seligman and colleagues (2005) conducted about the impact of positive psychology interventions. Given that Seligman et al. have reported long-term positive impact of positive psychology interventions on participants with depression and Mongrain and Anselmo-Matthews were interested in the impact of these interventions on the clinical population, they designed a study that followed similar guidance to the original research but improved the scientific rigour of Seligman and team's research.

The researchers included two positive psychology interventions from the previous study that showed the highest impact, that is, "Three good things" and "Using signature strengths in a new way". They have also changed the control group and added another control group to test the effectiveness of activities. In the original paper, the control group was asked to recall memories; however, in the replication article, the authors point out that recollection can increase understanding, self-acceptance, and happiness, so they added positive memories to the instructions. Thus, the objective of tweaking the original control group was to examine where there was anything special about the two positive psychology interventions apart from improving participants' positive self-representations. They also created another control group that reflected on their early memories without much emphasis on the positive or negative.

Here are their details of conditions:

Three Good Things (Seligman et al., 2005):

We often dwell too much on what is wrong than right in our lives. While reflecting on the negative events can help us learn and grow, excessive focus on them can lead to anxiety and depression. This is why, it's important to develop a habit of thinking about the good in our lives. Every day over the next week, list three things that went well for you and try to explain why they happened.

Using signature strengths in a new way (Seligman et al., 2005):

Honesty, loyalty, perseverance, creativity, kindness, wisdom, courage, and fairness are just some of the character strengths valued across cultures. Identifying and using your character strengths can enhance life satisfaction in work, love, and play. This exercise has two parts. First, complete a 45-minute questionnaire to identify your strengths. Then, for one week, apply your character strengths in new ways and report your experiences.

Positive Placebo Control Group (Mongrain & Anselmo-Matthews, 2012):

Reflecting on our past can improve our self-acceptance and wellbeing, especially when we recollect positive experiences. For the next week, take 10 minutes each night and write about your early positive memories.

Early Memories Control Group (Mongrain & Anselmo-Matthews, 2012):

"The unexamined life is not worth living (Socrates)". Reflecting on our past can improve our self-acceptance and wellbeing. For the next week, take 10 minutes each night and write about your early memories.

Similar to the original study, the results showed wellbeing improvements in the gratitude and strength activities that extended up to 6 months post-intervention. However, improvements were also found in the Positive Placebo control group, making it a new PPI. The positive memories have improved how individuals have viewed themselves, thus leading to positive outcomes.

Another interesting finding from this study was that the decrease in depressive symptoms was not as significant in the experimental groups compared to the control group. Also, the improvement in happiness was not as significant as in the original study. The researchers explained these differences by pointing out their changes to the control group. Also, in the original study, participants had higher motivation to engage in activities and showed significant interest in positive psychology. They were recruited from the "Authentic Happiness" website which at the time was a hub of positive psychology research. They were also likely to read Martin Seligman's book *Authentic Happiness* before completing these exercises, as the link to the website was promoted via the book. In contrast to the replication study, where participants were randomly selected; thus, their motivation to do it was different.

I found this study fascinating, as it highlights the significant role our beliefs play in enhancing the effectiveness of interventions. It's intriguing to see how much our mindset and expectations can shape outcomes, particularly in the context of wellbeing. The placebo effect is a powerful force that influences us daily, often without our conscious awareness. It has been extensively studied in the medical field in drug trials. However, positive psychology interventions are just as sensitive to it as other forms of placebo.

References

Mongrain, M., & Anselmo-Matthews, T. (2012). Do positive psychology exercises work? A replication of Seligman et al. (2005). *Journal of Clinical Psychology*, *68*(4), 382–389. https://doi-org.elib.tcd.ie/10.1002/jclp.21839

Seligman, M. E. P., Steen, T. A., Park, N., & Peterson, C. (2005). Positive psychology progress: Empirical validation of interventions. *American Psychologist*, *60*(5), 410–421. https://doi.org/10.1037/0003-066X.60.5.410

Practice-friendly meta-analysis

There was a time in my life when I knew this paper inside and out, having read it more times than my favourite book. It was the first and most important paper for both researchers and practitioners, a groundbreaking exploration of the first decade of research on positive psychology interventions. This paper guided us in ways in which positive activities could help alleviate depressive symptoms – a convincing argument for any sceptics who found positive psychology too positive. The article was particularly useful for clinical psychologists and psychotherapists, as it offered them key insights that could enhance their therapeutic practices.

The review included 51 interventions. At the time, it provided an essential resource for anyone studying positive psychology. It offered a comprehensive perspective on the types of positive psychology interventions that can improve wellbeing. It was the first of many systematic reviews that followed and set the stage for future research in the field. While more data is available, this review continues to serve as a reminder of how it all began and the ongoing relevance of our work.

One of the important findings from this paper was that therapists' use of positive psychology interventions with their clients resulted in the highest improvements in wellbeing compared to group therapy or self-administered interventions. Also, the authors found that longer interventions yielded better results, prompting researchers to recommend that interventions should best be designed as long-term solutions.

The results of this study also highlighted that positive psychology interventions were effective for individuals with depression. The findings suggested that those who were depressed benefited more from them than non-depressed individuals. Interestingly, they appeared to be more effective than traditional therapeutic approaches, which was good news to anyone wishing to use them as part of the therapy.

At the time of publication, this article caused a stir. It was widely welcomed, especially for those who were invested in positive psychology and found it to validate their work. However, subsequent research showed that perhaps some results of this study may have been overly optimistic. To explore these developments further, let's take a look at a systematic review on the same topic led by Linda Bolier.

References

Sin, N. L., & Lyubomirsky, S. (2009). Enhancing well-being and alleviating depressive symptoms with positive psychology interventions: A practice-friendly meta-analysis. *Journal of Clinical Psychology*, *65*(5), 467–487. https://doi.org/10.1002/jclp.20593

Meta-analysis of randomised controlled trials

For many years, I have been a part of the "Friends of Positive Psychology" email exchange. It was created by the University of Pennsylvania and allowed Martin Seligman to share news with all interested in positive psychology. The email exchanges are less active now, but at one point in time, it was a very useful source for sharing some of the main developments within positive psychology. We often read about new and exciting papers published by colleagues worldwide via this group. One such paper shared by someone was the second systematic review exploring the impact of positive psychology interventions on wellbeing and illbeing. When it came out and was announced via the Friends of Positive Psychology email, it created a lively discussion with one person critiquing it fervently. Let's discuss the reason for this critique and the findings from this review.

The paper follows a review of 51 academic articles conducted by Sin and Lyubomirsky just a few years earlier. Linda Bolier et al. (2013), a researcher at the Trimbos Institute in the Netherlands and a specialist in mental health research, led a meta-analysis that included just over 30 articles, significantly fewer than Sin and Lyubomirsky. This sparked criticism, with some accusing her of carelessly excluding studies. However, this criticism was unwarranted. The articles were carefully selected, and Bolier and colleagues conducted a thorough quality assessment, resulting in more stringent papers' inclusion and exclusion and fewer papers.

This study confirmed that, indeed, positive psychology interventions that were available to date were effective in improving subjective wellbeing, psychological wellbeing, and improving symptoms of depression. However, it also noted that the effective sizes, so the actual impact of the change, were smaller than reported by the previous review, as lower-quality studies tended to have high effect sizes. The significant contribution of this review was the confirmation that positive psychology interventions are effective, even if only the most rigorous research was included. Given that they are low-cost interventions, this news was excellent for the clinical and non-clinical populations.

Following the study, researchers led by Eugenia Gorlin et al. (2018) from Boston University conducted an additional analysis of the interventions explored by Bolier and colleagues. This analysis was a topographical map approach to treatment efficacy. The researchers planted a range of interventions onto a map and explored the number of studies and their effect sizes. They found that interventions focused on the future, such as goal-pursuit or learning optimism, reported a much higher positive impact than interventions focused on the past or present.

From the practice perspective, it is essential to select interventions that best suit individuals and their needs. This individualised approach respects each client's unique circumstances and values mental health professionals' expertise. However, given the positive impact of future-oriented interventions, there is an opportunity to further explore and enhance this approach. For a practitioner, all these studies offer a bag of tools they can dip into to improve their own or their clients' wellbeing.

References

Bolier, L., Haverman, M., Westerhof, G. J., Riper, H., Smit, F., & Bohlmeijer, E. (2013). Positive psychology interventions: A meta-analysis of randomized controlled studies. *BMC Public Health*, *13*, 119. https://doi.org/10.1186/1471-2458-13-119

Gorlin, E. I., Lee, J., & Otto, M. W. (2018). A topographical map approach to representing treatment efficacy: A focus on positive psychology interventions. *Cognitive Behaviour Therapy*, *47*(1), 34–42. https://doi.org/10.1080/16506073.2017.1342173

A mega analysis of wellbeing programmes

I love whodunit stories, but not the gruesome type. I have devoured Agatha Christie's and MC Beaton's books – they relax me. What I like about them is the clues that authors leave behind for us to deduce who committed a crime. They are like pieces of puzzle. They may mean one thing on their own, but when mixed with others, their meaning changes. As we collect them on our way to the last chapter, it becomes clearer who the villain is. What is great about those books is not the end but the process of discovering clues. The same applies to meta-analyses. Their clues are the academic papers published on the topics they discuss.

Recently, there has been an influx of comprehensive systematic reviews and meta-analyses about the effectiveness of positive psychology interventions. Alan Carr from University College Dublin, Ireland, has spearheaded two of the most extensive reviews. The first review (2021) delves into the impact of positive psychology interventions on individual wellbeing. A staggering 347 studies were selected, encompassing over 72,000 participants. What's noteworthy is that over 70% of the studies included in this research focused on non-clinical populations, but the team also saw fit to include individuals with a range of other conditions, from mood disorders to chronic pain and beyond.

A broad list of interventions was included in this review, such as practising gratitude, practising forgiveness, doing exercises that create an optimistic outlook (e.g. best possible self), savouring, life review, recalling recent events or appreciating the present moment, identifying and using signature strengths, being kind to others, writing about positive, meaningful, or successful experiences, practising meaning-making, humour (e.g. recalling three funny things), setting highly valued goals (e.g. writing an obituary, eulogy, or legacy letter), solution-focused coaching, relationship strengthening, appreciating, beauty/nature, active constructive responding, rehearsing positive statements, volunteering, practising humility, and finding flow. In addition, programmes based on positive psychology were included, such as wellbeing therapy and positive psychotherapy.

The results of this review showed that positive psychology interventions were effective in improving wellbeing, quality of life, stress, as well as reducing the symptoms of anxiety, depression, and stress. The differences before and after the intervention ranged from minor to moderate. However, the good news is that when the wellbeing was re-assessed at follow-up, participants maintained higher levels of wellbeing on average 3 months after the intervention. This lasting effect is very encouraging.

The second "review of reviews" included 198 systematic reviews and meta-analyses about the effectiveness of positive psychology interventions. However, its inclusion criteria went beyond the usual interventions, including mindfulness, mind-body, and exercise-based programmes. They involved 4,065 studies with 501,335 participants – it is a mega review, as the title suggests. This review showed that positive psychology interventions had a small to moderate impact on wellbeing, quality of life, strengths, depression, anxiety, and stress. That impact continued up to an average of 7.5 months. The most effective interventions were those that mixed body and mind approaches, such as yoga. Also, the longer the participants were involved in the interventions, the more effective they were, primarily when delivered face-to-face instead of online.

Given the criticisms that positive psychology has a "floating head" approach to wellbeing, whereby we are only concerned with changes to the mind, extending interventions towards the body-related interventions that keep the entire body, not only the head, engaged is understandable. The "floating head" approach refers to a criticism that positive psychology focuses solely on mental changes, neglecting the potential benefits of engaging the entire body in interventions. Perhaps positive psychology should explore more the impact of combining some of the body-related interventions for improved wellbeing and health results.

References

Carr, A., Cullen, K., Keeney, C., Canning, C., Mooney, O., Chinseallaigh, E., & O'Dowd, A. (2021). Effectiveness of positive psychology interventions: A systematic review and meta-analysis. *The Journal of Positive Psychology*, *16*(6), 749–769. https://doi.org/10.1080/17439760.2020.1818807

Carr, A., Finneran, L., Boyd, C., Shirey, C., Canning, C., Stafford, O., Lyons, J., Cullen, K., Prendergast, C., Corbett, C., Drumm, C., & Burke, T. (2024). The evidence-base for positive psychology interventions: A mega-analysis of meta-analyses. *The Journal of Positive Psychology*, *19*(2), 191–205. https://doi.org/10.1080/17439760.2023.2168564

4 The approaches to maximising the impact of positive psychology application

The intentional activities that improve wellbeing come with additional conditions. Their effectiveness is governed by a range of factors such as how the interventions are presented, designed, or performed. In this chapter, we will begin by exploring the most common approach to practising wellbeing interventions, which is online. We will identify what is the optimal number of interventions that should be practised, and other nuances associated with improving online engagement. Next, we will delve into the world of mechanisms that influence the effectiveness of interventions. These mechanisms are like a gauge that can either minimise or maximise their performance. We will dig deeper into the main frameworks that guide the positive psychology intervention application, explore the impact of context, and theories that amplify the impact of interventions on wellbeing. Finally, we will stress the exploration of the process of change that occurs when applying positive psychology. We will explore models that explain the readiness for change, motivation, and self-control. This chapter will deepen readers' knowledge and create a foundation for developing skills to maximise the impact of any application in positive psychology.

Wellbeing online

Online positive psychology interventions

My university colleagues in the positive psychology field have once designed a comprehensive wellbeing programme. It contained the best interventions in positive psychology, starting with knowledge-enhancement, developing skills, and practising interventions. Their content was awe-inspiring. Even though I love this area of research very much, I don't think I could develop a more comprehensive programme than this. Yet, despite their best efforts, the programme failed at the efficacy testing stage because the way it was designed and delivered to participants did not work. Real life, combined with an online intervention, needed additional considerations, such as cyberpsychology research-base. Yet cyber psychologists were not involved in its design.

Fortunately, Acacia Parks has explored this topic in more detail and provided some reflection on the design of interventions online. In this paper, she identified three specific factors that could impact the efficacy of an intervention.

DOI: 10.4324/9781003530596-4

1. **User engagement** – attrition is a vital issue in online design. When individuals do not engage in an intervention, no positive change is reported, so it is important to keep them engaged. According to the author, when interventions are part of research, the attrition is lower than in real-life design. So, it is particularly important to consider in real life.

Three factors impact user engagement. Firstly, relative advantage relates to something that the website offers that other websites do not have. For some, it could be social networking, and for others, it could be word of mouth. Something special and unique about the site is essential to keep people engaged.

Secondly, it is compatibility between the user and their goals and preferences. This is why tailoring interventions to the users' needs is paramount. If someone likes exploring the past, perhaps the best possible self-activity could be conducted by reflecting on the best possible self in the past. If someone likes going outside, perhaps activities can be explored that involve connecting with nature.

Thirdly, it is observability, which refers to the user's ability to assess their progress. When they can see clear progress on their journey, they are more motivated to be engaged and keep going, which will, in turn, positively impact their results. Thus, user engagement is an important concept to consider in online courses.

2. **Dosage** is yet another factor that impacts the effectiveness of interventions. Many of the interventions offer one activity to practice, for example, gratitude. However, research indicates that those searching for happiness apps prefer to practise several interventions simultaneously. In fact, those who practise four activities tend to report the best results. Also, to encourage people to stay on the site for as long as possible, we need to create opportunities for them to interact with online content. The balance of the interaction that suits the person and their time on it matters here. The preference for both the number of activities and time spent can vary among individuals.

3. Finally, **user choice** is the third factor that matters when designing online interventions. The author suggests that it is essential that activities are designed for users' preferences, but users also like having access to additional activities if they wish to draw on them. They might not choose well, but they still like the choice. For example, popular activities, such as goal setting tend to be less effective, yet users gravitate towards them. Therefore, it is crucial to offer these preferred activities while also guiding users towards interventions that have a greater positive impact.

These guidelines are critical for designing any online intervention associated with wellbeing. They show the need to do it wisely to keep participants interested, keep them returning to the site, and give them choices, regardless of how effective it is for them.

References

Parks, A. C. (2014). A case for the advancement of the design and study of online positive psychological interventions. *The Journal of Positive Psychology*, *9*(6), 502–508. https://doi-org.elib.tcd.ie/10.1080/17439760.2014.936969

Everyday treatment in natural setting

We have recently conducted research with alumni of positive psychology and asked them if they used online applications for wellbeing. The vast majority did not. At the same time, when I once asked a room full of laypeople about their use of wellbeing apps, it created a buzz in a group with many people sharing their favourite wellbeing apps. Thus, the interest in learning about wellbeing or even improving wellbeing via smartphones is thriving. This is why positive psychologists and app designers are eager to collaborate. However, introducing positive psychology interventions online is challenging in helping users improve their wellbeing and stay engaged. This is what this article is about.

Mobile-enabled interventions, positive activities delivered via smartphone devices, hold immense potential. Ecological momentary interventions, treatments people complete during their daily lives, can be a game-changer. Imagine the impact of activities people can complete using their mobile phones in their daily lives and natural, real-life settings. While they are potentially significant media for engaging with positive psychology interventions, Yerin Shim from Chungnam National University in South Korea and colleagues (2022) explore the literature relating to their use to maximise their impact on wellbeing. Specifically, they view smartphone use by examining three characteristics and challenges.

1. **Mobile:** They encourage exploring mobile technology hardware with all the components tested to meet participant needs. This consideration also includes software designed to enhance users' experience. It may include shortening the interventions to ensure more engagement.
2. **Ecological:** The design must be relevant to the participant and the context within which they practise interventions. As such, it should be validated with users to ensure that it does what it should, that is, improve their wellbeing, consider their environment, and determine how often they engage with their smartphone. This validation process, which relies heavily on user feedback, is crucial in the co-designing process of effective mobile interventions.
3. **Momentary:** The designers must explore such intricacies as the frequency of notifications to help them engage with the positive psychology interventions to an optimal level. Alternatively, it explores when those notifications should be sent for maximum impact.

These three considerations are crucial for developing a successful mobile phone app to improve participants' wellbeing. Over the last two decades, designers frequently contacted me, asking me what interventions they should list on their apps, presenting the interventions they already included, and asking me to give them an endorsement. However, I have always declined these requests because they were asking the wrong questions. Rather than focusing solely on *what* interventions to include, the emphasis should be on *how* these interventions should be designed and adapted for digital platforms. Face-to-face and mobile interventions are not comparable, so more consideration should always be given to the "how" rather than the "what" content of the smartphone apps. Shifting the focus can lead to more effective and transformative app design process.

References

Shim, Y., Scotney, V. S., & Tay, L. (2022). Conducting mobile-enabled ecological momentary intervention research in positive psychology: Key considerations and recommended practices. *Journal of Positive Psychology*, *17*(5), 708–717. https://doi-org.elib.tcd.ie/10.1080/17439760.2021.1913642

The mechanisms of positive psychology interventions

Person-Activity Fit model

The first and currently the most prevalent model for practising positive psychology interventions is the Person-Activity Fit model (Lyubomirsky & Layous, 2013). It aims to explain why performing positive activities makes people happier. It posits that there are activity features and person features that influence its effectiveness. The activity features encompass all activities related to the dosage of activities performed daily or a few times a week. Importantly, there is a wide variety of activities that are being practised, offering individuals the freedom and flexibility to choose activities that suit them best. Another aspect of the features across activities relates to the trigger that makes a difference when it comes to the activities, in that some may trigger positive emotions, whereas others may not. Also, social support is of great value as some activities may draw upon social support while others might not.

In addition to the activity features between the activities, activities offer various perspectives, for example, past, future, or present. Some may be other-oriented, whereas some could be self-oriented. Some activities are social, whereas others are reflective. All these choices make a difference.

Several key aspects influence interventions' effectiveness within a person's features. One such factor is motivation, which is the drive and the effort individuals choose to exert when practising them. Personal desires and goals often shape motivation, and they play a significant role in the effectiveness of the interventions, creating a sense of agency. The more motivated an individual is to complete an activity, the more effective the intervention.

Another important factor is efficacy belief – whether individuals believe the activity will increase their happiness and whether they can practise selected interventions. Additionally, the baseline of their affective state matters. Some individuals naturally experience many positive emotions, whereas others do not. Those who tend to experience fewer positive emotions are likely to gain more from these activities.

Personality is yet another person's feature that makes a difference. Some personalities are more likely to induce improvements in wellbeing. For example, extraversion is associated with higher levels of wellbeing and may impact the practice of positive activities. Similarly, social support matters. The more supported by their family and friends when practising interventions, the more likely individuals are to sustain their practice and improve their wellbeing. Finally, demographic factors impact the effectiveness of interventions, such as gender, country of origin, and similar. These are just some factors associated with the person's characteristics impacting intervention outcomes.

The Person-Activity Fit model offers a comprehensive and flexible framework for applying positive psychology interventions. Its effectiveness has been validated in a few studies, and its versatility and adaptability explain why it is widespread across positive psychology. However, recently, research began to emerge that challenges some of the initial presuppositions of the model and offers refinements and additional insights that have not been explored in the model. Also, my colleague and I (Burke & Giraldez-Hayes, forthcoming) have conducted a systematic review of mechanisms of practising positive psychology interventions and were surprised with inconsistent results and scarcity of replication of studies upon which this and similar theories were based. We certainly need more research in this area to understand how we can practise positive interventions more effectively.

References

Burke, J., & Giraldez-Hayes, A. (forthcoming). Factors impacting positive psychology interventions: A systematic review of the literature.

Lyubomirsky, S., & Layous, K. (2013). How do simple positive activities increase well-being? *Current Directions in Psychological Science*, *22*(1), 57–62. https://doi.org/10.1177/0963721412469809

Context matters

My son loves nature. We often picnic at the botanic gardens and watch the seasons change. Given his interest, I signed him up to a forest school. After a few classes, the teacher told me he didn't engage with a group. When we got home, I asked him what had happened. He told me that other boys were teasing him, so he chose not to play with them. Then, the teacher, seeing him play on his own, insisted he rejoin them. He refused to do it, and she got cross. I moved him to another forest school. After three classes, I asked the teacher how he got on. "Wonderfully", she said. "He is funny, and loves playing rough and tumble with other boys. We are having a great time together". The same child, the same activity, a different context, and the outcome was so different. We often underestimate the context's impact on our thoughts, emotions, behaviours and tend to attribute too much to the individual's stable characteristics, which may lead us to thinking that something is "wrong" with people, but context does matter – a lot.

Context is the basis of the article written by Ciarrochi and colleagues (2016). They believe that the lack of contextualised interventions in positive psychology is the source of criticism of the field. As such, they argue that the majority of positive psychology interventions are focused on content; that is, we encourage people to change how they think, by introducing content such as gratitude thinking, or optimistic reframing. This approach may seem overly forceful to some of them, coercing them into doing what is not natural for them. The authors warn against it, especially in the school context, where adults have significantly more power over children. This is why, they introduce the concept of "context-focused positive psychology interventions", which are interventions that take into account the individual's environment and personal values, allowing for a more authentic and flexible approach to positive psychology.

These interventions treat the causes of behaviour stemming from the environment, not individuals. The positive psychology approach to thinking optimistically, being grateful, or experiencing higher positive emotions is seen as a historical context drawn from individuals' genetic predispositions. As such, the goal of creating context-focused positive psychology interventions is to create an environment that allows individuals to practise autonomy and choose what is meaningful for them and help individuals learn skills that allow them to adapt flexibly to the environment, which will, in turn, help them to reach their potential.

This new approach to creating interventions and practising them taps into the process of change that ultimately helps improve wellbeing. It is a necessary departure from the de-contextualisation of the majority of positive psychology intervention approaches, where we force people to think in a certain way to improve wellbeing. It is a critical step towards dealing more adequately with negative emotions and experiences. For example, when people go through challenges, instead of trying to refocus them to look at the positive side of the situation, we could acknowledge their negative emotions and help them navigate through them. This approach values not just positive states, but also the flexible behaviours authentic to the self, while seeing positive states as outcomes of such behaviours.

In one sentence, most content-focused positive psychology interventions focus on pursuing positive states, such as positive emotions. In contrast, context-focused positive psychology interventions focus on engaging in personally valued activities even if they do not always produce positive emotions or other outcomes. It is a way of balancing the positive outcomes with the individual's needs and values.

This approach has significant implications for practitioners. It's not just about considering context when suggesting interventions but also about reflecting on the interaction between the context and the individual with whom we work. This personalised approach is the key to designing more effective positive psychology interventions, one activity at a time.

References

Ciarrochi, J., Atkins, P. W. B., Hayes, L. L., Sahdra, B. K., & Parker, P. (2016). Contextual positive psychology: Policy recommendations for implementing positive psychology into schools. *Frontiers in Psychology*, *7*.

Five domains

My distant cousin is a magician. He has a YouTube channel that attracts hundreds of thousands of followers. Magic has been his passion ever since he was a child. I love some of his tricks because I often do not understand how they work. I have seen many magic shows by some famous magicians, such as Dynamo, David

Blane, or Darren Brown, and they usually leave me happy and satisfied but baffled. In fact, I enjoy not knowing how they did it, as it would take the magic of their shows away. While it is helpful in magic not to know why action creates a reaction, in positive psychology, we need to explore the mediating factors to help us understand why interventions work and design the most impactful wellbeing activities for people.

This five-domain model derives from the existing research in positive psychology. Reuben Rusk and Lea Waters explored over 18,000 articles in the field of positive psychology and, from them, identified five distinct themes: (1) Attention and awareness, (2) Comprehension and coping, (3) Emotions, (4) Goals and habits, (5) Virtues and relationships. These themes relate to psychological and social functioning (psycho-social) which refers to processes, state, and events that mediate wellbeing. Mediating factors are those that explain how two variables are related, for example, how doing a positive psychology intervention is related to the wellbeing improvement. Let us now go into the five domains identified in this article.

Attention and awareness refer to the regulation of attention, be it controlled or automatic, to focus on something. This includes topics such as mindfulness, rumination, and imagery.

Comprehension and coping are the processes of identifying links between the past, present, and future and making sense of them. They also involve applying these processes to aid our coping capabilities in the face of adversity. Topics relating to this domain include attribution, growth, resilience, and adversity reappraisal.

Emotions are the present-moment experiences of emotion, an ability to identify and associate them with present and past situations. These topics include mood, reactivity, and facial expressions.

Goals and habits relate to persisting in exploring values that guide our behaviours and habits and exploring the skills associated with setting goals and maintaining habits. Topics within this domain include efficacy, decision-making, grip, lifestyle changes, and behavioural change.

Virtues and relationships are about long-term social relationships as well as brief connections. They include relationships between individuals and community organisations, as well as the virtues and behaviours that impact the quality of relationships.

The wellbeing interventions in positive psychology impact each one of these five dimensions. For example, you may perform acts of kindness, as a positive activity, impacting your relationship with someone you were kind to (Virtues and relationship dimension). However, they are also heavily dependent on the environmental and biological factors. To what extent they are effective depends, for instance, on where they are practised, such as the workplace, or the types of people you are practising them with and the extent to which both parties are open to engaging in this intervention. Thus, the positive outcomes of any positive psychology interventions occur by impacting one of the four domains, which are subject to environmental and biological factors.

This model is an excellent platform for exploring how interventions impact people. We may know that an intervention resulted in enhanced wellbeing, but exploring the five domains will pinpoint which psycho-social functioning was triggered that resulted in the change. Two interventions may create an improvement in wellbeing. However, one may show more extensive improvement than another. This could be because of the five psycho-social functioning domains; one triggered only one dimension, whereas the other triggered several dimensions simultaneously. Thus, this model could explain why one intervention is more effective. The findings from the model will also help us design the most impactful intervention that will tap into several psycho-social functions.

References

Rusk, R. D., & Waters, L. (2015). A psycho-social system approach to well-being: Empirically deriving the five domains of positive functioning. *The Journal of Positive Psychology*, *10*(2), 141–152. https://doi.org/10.1080/17439760.2014.920409

Sustained positive emotions

Think back to some of the reasons why you continue to engage in your daily habits. What do you get out of it? For example, one of my friends loves doing a gratitude activity. She is in her fifties now and has done it since she was a teenager, almost every day. Another friend of mine loves running. Every day, she goes for a run and takes her favourite route. For me, it's my morning cup of coffee. I usually wake up at around 5 am when our home is completely quiet. I make myself a hot cuppa, curl up on a sofa with a dog at my feet and a cat on my lap, and savour it for 10–15 minutes. When I miss my morning ritual for any reason, my day feels incomplete. It's a small but meaningful practice that sets the tone for everything that follows as it gives me a boost of positive emotions.

The role of positive emotions has been explored in several studies. However, given that this article came up as one of the top positive psychology papers, I decided to include it in this volume. It was published by Barbara Fredrickson et al. (2008) who led a study that showed not only the sustainability of positive emotions following a meditation practice, but also their sustainability over time.

In this experiment, participants were divided into two groups: one that practised Loving Kindness meditation and another that did not. They measured their experiences of positive emotions every day for a week and then a week later, when they were asked to complete a battery of psychological tests to assess various aspects of wellbeing. The results showed that participants reported an increase in experiencing positive emotions each day. That experience resulted in a range of additional resources, a spill-over effect a week later, such as increased mindfulness, life purpose, and social support, and a decrease in typical symptoms of illness such as headaches, chest pain, or congestion.

I enjoyed reading this study as it explained *why* we enjoy and continue engaging in some activities. According to the researchers, experiencing a burst of positive emotions while engaging in an activity we enjoy makes it more likely for us to continue. This continuous engagement could lead to further positive emotions and other positive psychological changes, creating a loop of positivity sustained over time. Therefore, they act as fuel and a mechanism for making positive changes.

References

Fredrickson, B. L., Cohn, M. A., Coffey, K. A., Pek, J., & Finkel, S. M. (2008). Open hearts build lives: Positive emotions, induced through loving-kindness meditation, build consequential personal resources. *Journal of Personality and Social Psychology*, *95*(5), 1045–1062. https://doi.org/10.1037/a0013262

The will and the way

I have a strong interest in positive psychology interventions. When I come across a new activity, I always try it out, and afterwards, I reflect on how it influenced my thoughts and feelings and whether it had any obvious impact on aspects of my wellbeing. I also consider who might benefit from an intervention and explore its alternative applications. Sometimes, I play around with an activity by tweaking it slightly. This practice and personal reflection process, driven by my passion for positive psychology and wellbeing, keeps me fully engaged and motivated. My practice is very different from that of someone new to positive psychology.

This is why one of the main criticisms of the first article on positive psychology interventions (Seligman et al., 2005) was the sample used in the study. Participants were recruited from a website dedicated to wellbeing, meaning they were already highly interested and motivated to practice these interventions, just like myself. While our specific motivations may have differed, we all shared a strong commitment to engaging in positive psychology practices and improving our wellbeing, which is why our outcomes may have been amplified. The participants in this study did not accurately represent the general public, particularly those who might encounter these interventions randomly without prior interest or motivation.

Lyubomirsky and colleagues (2011) designed a study to address this criticism and examine the impact of self-selection of positive psychology interventions among the general public. The study focused on two interventions: a gratitude activity and writing about the best possible self. Their findings showed that participants who had self-selected activities, compared to those who had not self-selected, reported higher levels of wellbeing after the intervention. However, the effect did not last until a 6-month follow-up.

Another interesting finding was that being motivated to become happier was an essential ingredient for improving wellbeing, and it mattered at the 6-month follow-up. On the other hand, assigning a positive activity to participants who did not have intrinsic motivation to do it did not sustain their practice or positive outcomes. This research highlighted the importance of self-selection and motivation when practising positive psychology interventions.

This paper provided essential insights for positive psychology practitioners supporting the Person-Activity Fit model developed by Lyubomirsky and Layous (2013). It also offered some valuable insights to researchers exploring the optimal applications of positive psychology interventions. However, the study had limitations. Firstly, the sample of participants included in this study was a large group of US undergraduate students, meaning that the group was not representative of the population. Also, the effect sizes of these findings were small. Even though the study gave us some great insights into practising positive psychology interventions, the findings must be replicated to confirm their validity.

References

Lyubomirsky, S., Dickerhoof, R., Boehm, J. K., & Sheldon, K. M. (2011). Becoming happier takes both a will and a proper way: An experimental longitudinal intervention to boost well-being. *Emotion*, *11*(2), 391–402. https://doi.org.elib.tcd.ie/10.1037/a0022575

Lyubomirsky, S., & Layous, K. (2013). How do simple positive activities increase well-being? *Current Directions in Psychological Science*, *22*(1), 57–62. https://doi.org/10.1177/0963721412469809

Seligman, M. E. P., Steen, T. A., Park, N., & Peterson, C. (2005). Positive Psychology Progress: Empirical Validation of Interventions. *American Psychologist*, *60*(5), 410–421. https://doi.org/10.1037/0003-066X.60.5.410

Adaptive mental mechanisms

I have a friend who is one of the most resilient people I have ever known. We've been friends for almost 30 years, so I have seen her in many life's ups and downs, and her mental strategies work perfectly to help her cope with adversity as it happens. As a medical doctor, she frequently faces emotionally challenging situations – delivering difficult diagnoses, caring for terminally ill patients, and dealing with loss. On top of that, her personal life hasn't exactly been a bed of roses. Yet she meets each challenge with dignity and humour, managing to keep her emotions in check. When the time is right, she allows her to process her experiences deeply, reflecting on the meaning of suffering in the broader context of her life. This is what the article by George Vaillant is all about.

We usually rely on three universal types of coping strategies during challenging times. First, we seek help from others by drawing on our social network. Second, we engage in conscious cognitive strategies to navigate challenging situations. For some, it may involve reframing the situation in a more positive way or getting to the root of the problem and then tackling it. However, there is also a third approach to coping with adversity, and it relates to adaptive mental mechanisms, which aim to reduce our distress when a challenging event happens. They do it by distorting our perception of what is happening inside ourselves and outside. In other words, it is a form of healthy denial that helps us understand the situation and engage in conscious strategies for coping with adversity.

These strategies, called defences, serve as a highly adaptive mental mechanism. They are fully independent of our upbringing and what social or demographic status we hold. When we find ourselves in a helpless situation, they help us regulate the perceptions associated with the situation. Most importantly, they serve as powerful transformative agents in real-world situations, offering hope and inspiration. Let us explore them in turn.

Anticipation is a powerful coping strategy that relates to both thinking and feeling about the future. It prepares us to deal with life's consequences, making us feel proactive and in control. It is about worrying in advance and trying to figure out what could go wrong so that we can prepare for it. Anticipation before challenging situations is a healthy adaptive mechanism that helps us cope more positively when bad things happen in our lives.

Altruism is about providing support to others and showing kindness. It is a strategy that sees dealing with tough situations as a way to give back to those in need. For example, a man who experienced abuse from his partner could start volunteering in homeless shelters as an automatic adaptive coping strategy.

Humour is yet another way of automatically dealing with a challenging situation. This is my favourite coping strategy, and it happens so automatically that I sometimes find it hard to catch it. I remember once I was a passenger in a car that was crushed on the side of the road. We ended up in a ditch with a car on its side. After checking that we were all okay, my automatic reaction was to laugh and crack a joke, to which the driver reacted severely. I apologised, as my intention was not to ridicule anyone or any situation, but it was my way of releasing the tension and fear I experienced during a crash.

Sublimation is the ability to redirect attention from an unacceptable impulse, such as shouting, aggressive behaviour, or verbally abusing someone during an argument, to a more socially acceptable reaction. For example, when angry, you may choose to go for a run rather than have an unnecessary argument with your spouse. This is how you can direct your attention towards a more useful action.

Suppression is a form of stoicism. It is associated with postponing paying attention to a challenge, especially from an emotional perspective. For example, when being let unfairly go from a job, a person might be filled with an avalanche of emotion. Still, they would suppress it and take the news with dignity, asking questions and then back at home, allowing for the emotions to surface. If they had not suppressed them, the situation may have ended up being particularly challenging, filled with aggression, arguments, and actions that they might regret in the future. Thus, unlike pure unhealthy denial, it is a process of suspending attention to the challenge or its consequences, only to deal with it afterwards.

Vaillant (2000), who wrote this paper, argues that these mechanisms can be considered part of positive psychology as they promote positive outcomes, such as increased love and the ability to play or work effectively. At the same time, they serve well as ways to reduce conflict during a challenging situation, thus allowing us to grow and minimise negative impact simultaneously. It is like navigating a storm with a sturdy ship. Our chances of getting through it and growing through the experience are much higher when we use these coping strategies.

References

Vaillant, G. E. (2000). Adaptive mental mechanisms: Their role in a positive psychology. *American Psychologist*, *55*(1), 89–98. https://doi.org/10.1037/0003-066X.55.1.89

What determines happiness?

I remember the day I was in the Dublin city centre, Eason's bookshop. It was 2010 and a new yellow covered book was prominently displayed on the table with all the latest publications. I picked it up and did not believe my luck. It was the latest book by Professor Sonja Lyubomirsky about the "how" of happiness. I bought it and read it with delight. One thing that I found striking about it was its pragmatism and simplicity. The graph she presented, which explored what determined happiness, was a revelation. She claimed 50% of our happiness was determined by genetic factors, 10% by the circumstances, and 40% by intentional activity, which is why she argued positive psychology interventions work. This practical model made me feel empowered, although in the back of my mind I wondered where individual differences fitted in all this.

A year later, Sonja published a paper explaining the model in more detail (Lyubomirsky et al., 2005). She drew on years of research in behavioural genetics, according to which happiness is "determined" by individuals' set point. This means that some of us who are of less happy kind have this set point set at a lower level, whereas those with higher happiness levels have this set point set up at a higher level. The good news was that despite the circumstances, we could all increase our happiness levels if we engaged in activities that allowed us to do it. This model, when published, went viral. It became popular with trainers, psychologists, and really anyone who wanted to understand how positive psychology interventions work. It created hope that we can increase happiness, inspiring many, but infamous among anyone working in epigenetics.

Epigenetics is a field of genetics that explores not only the impact of genes on individuals' attitudes, beliefs, affect, and behaviour and the bi-directional effect of genes. As such, when we interact with an environment, our genes are either activated or not. The issue that some in the field had with Sonja's work was the concept of genetic determinism. This is the belief that our genes determine our behaviour and traits and that we have little control over them. However, our genetics is a predisposition, which can be activated or deactivated depending on our environment. For example, some people may have a genetic predisposition against lung cancer, but their gene is not activated because they do not smoke and tend to spend much time breathing in clear air. Other people who do smoke and have a predisposition to develop cancer, yet some without a predisposition smoke a pack of cigarettes a day and do not develop any lung cancer. Therefore, given the idea of genetic determinism she promoted, Sonja received considerable criticism, forcing her to write an updated version of this article.

Over a decade later, she published her updated thinking about the sustainable happiness model and pie chart (Sheldon & Lyubomirsky, 2021). The authors admitted that empirical studies showed that they have overestimated the impact of positive psychology interventions (intentional activities), especially in long-term wellbeing. They also admitted agreeing with the extensive criticism and deemed the model redundant. However, they refocused readers' attention back to the original objective of that pie, which was to illustrate that people can engage in intentional activities that would influence their happiness. They have also drawn readers' attention to the new models developed, which provided a more nuanced perspective on this issue, for example, the Hedonic Adaptation Prevention model (Sheldon & Lyubomirsky, 2012) and Lyubomirsky's Positive Activity Model (Lyubomirsky & Layous, 2013).

You may wonder why I included this model, given that it has reached its shelf life. The reason is that it is still out there in publications and presentations of non-academics who have heard of it, find it useful, and continue to perpetuate its ideas. As a practitioner, it might sometimes be difficult to keep up with all the research to truly engage in research-based practice. However, it's our responsibility as professionals to not only understand what models are useful but also recognise and address those that have become redundant.

References

Lyubomirsky, S., & Layous, K. (2013). How do simple positive activities increase well-being? *Current Directions in Psychological Science*, *22*(1), 57–62. https://doi.org/10.1177/0963721412469809

Lyubomirsky, S., Sheldon, K. M., & Schkade, D. (2005). Pursuing happiness: The architecture of sustainable change. *Review of General Psychology*, *9*(2), 111–131.

Sheldon, K. M., & Lyubomirsky, S. (2012). The challenge of staying happier: Testing the hedonic adaptation prevention model. *Personality and Social Psychology Bulletin, 38*(5), 670–680. https://doi.org/10.1177/0146167212436400

Sheldon, K. M., & Lyubomirsky, S. (2021). Revisiting the sustainable happiness model and pie chart: Can happiness be successfully pursued? *The Journal of Positive Psychology, 16*(2), 145–154. https://doi.org/10.1080/17439760.2019.1689421

The Elements Model

It has been two decades since I enrolled in a Masters in Applied Positive Psychology. I was in one of the first cohorts, and I loved every minute of it. In my second module, we were asked to practise positive psychology interventions. And when I explore the interventions that existed back then and compare them to the interventions today, the difference is not too significant. We currently have more evidence for their effectiveness and many tweaks have been made to them. Still, we continue to rely heavily on the first generation of interventions that included such activities as gratitude, acts of kindness, or using strengths differently. This is also what James Pawelski, the leader of the Masters in Applied Positive Psychology programme at the University of Pennsylvania, noticed.

Teaching about the interventions for so many years, he noted how we tend to have a very narrow focus when designing positive psychology interventions. We focus, say, on enhancing one component of wellbeing, such as life satisfaction, rather than considering a broader spectrum, more comprehensive impact that incorporates a number of components. We also tend not to integrate interventions with each other. For example, we have separate gratitude and separate strength interventions. What about combining them to explore their effectiveness. More importantly, James Pawelski points out the crucial role of cultural differences when designing interventions. He emphasises that a one-size-fits-all approach is not effective and that we need to consider cultural nuances to ensure the interventions are truly impactful. In summary, he highlights the need to rethink how interventions are designed and encourages researchers and practitioners to create more interventions. To do so, he created the Elements Model that aims to aid our intervention design.

The Elements Model encourages a more holistic approach to designing interventions. It suggests that merging interventions and targeting more than one aspect of wellbeing could increase their efficacy and result in higher wellbeing impact. However, the Elements Model is still at an early stage of development and needs more empirical testing. The urgency and significance of this empirical testing cannot be overstated. Researchers' potential contributions to this testing are crucial to ensure the model's viability. Practitioners could also use this model to play around with the positive psychology interventions they already know and create one that suits them or their clients best. Let us now explore how it is recommended to work.

The author has broken down the intervention design into elements to build it into a cohesive intervention. The elements of positive psychology interventions are:

Desired Outcome: The intended effect of the change within the target system, for example, increased happiness, enhanced life meaning, improved relationships, and more engagement in life. In other words, they are the components of wellbeing and other positive outcomes we wish to influence through an intervention.

Target System: The area where the change takes place. This may relate to psychological systems such as attention, motivation, thinking, and affect, physiological systems such as heart rate and respiration, or physical systems such as posture. Knowing what systems an intervention impacts can help us understand its impact.

Target Change: The specific change sought within a particular wellbeing domain, for example, higher self-efficacy, increased self-determination, a more optimistic outlook, greater sensitivity to a partner, and improved teamwork. This is the change that we want to see in individuals.

Active Ingredient: The factor that drives change in the target system, for example, shifting an individual's attention towards the positive or becoming more mindful about state, goal setting, or challenging beliefs. The active ingredient is what makes the change happen.

Activity: The specific intentional actions upon which the positive psychology intervention is based, for example, writing, speaking, thinking, playing a game.

Here is an example of how a well-known activity, such as writing about "the best possible self", can be broken into elements:

Desired outcome: Increased hopefulness
Target system: Thinking and affect
Target change: Higher levels of hope
Active ingredient: Shifting attention towards positive
Activity: Writing down

James Pawelski encourages researchers and practitioners to think of interventions in this way so that we can mix and match the various elements, which would create more effective interventions and expand on them. Why not spend a day playing around with them? This could result in improvements that go beyond the expected positive outcomes.

References

Pawelski, J. O. (2020). The elements model: Toward a new generation of positive psychology interventions. *The Journal of Positive Psychology*, *15*(5), 675–679. https://doi.org/10.1080/17439760.2020.1789710

Emotion regulation

Many years ago, some of my friends wanted to go to a Forbidden Fruit festival in Dublin, Ireland, which is famously the first summer festival of the season. I wasn't in a mood for it, but they twisted my arm, so I reluctantly agreed to join them. The company was great, the music was good, and the presence of my friends made the first hour of the festival bearable despite my initial feelings of being out of sorts. Being surrounded by friends and listening to music usually makes me happier, but that day it is not enough. This is when I remembered the research led by Jordi Quoidbach et al. (2015) about emotion regulation during positive events, and my attitude changed.

We all have positive experiences that, upon reflection, leave us wondering why we didn't enjoy them more than we should have. Some of us intentionally engage in positive psychology interventions, but they might not impact us as positively as they impact others. One explanation for this is individual differences, our environment, or our motivation for engaging with them in the first place. However, another possible explanation lies in how we use emotion regulation strategies to enhance our experiences. By consciously managing our emotions, we can amplify the positive impact of these moments and increase our overall sense of wellbeing.

This paper proposes five strategies to do it: (1) situation selection, (2) situation modification, (3) attentional deployment, (4) cognitive change, and (5) response modulation. Let's explore them one by one.

Situation selection – to maximise the impact of an intervention or an event, we need to carefully select a situation that is bound to make us happier. For example, to connect with your partner, you may choose to go out for dinner at a cosy restaurant, or to find work–life balance, you may decide to go hiking in a serene location, or to improve your wellbeing, you may choose to use one of the positive psychology interventions "Best Possible Self", which involves writing about you in the future when you become the best possible self and speculating how you got there.

Situation modification – to further maximise the impact of an intervention, we need to modify it to our own needs, values, and preferences. For example, when we go out for dinner with our partner, we may select our favourite restaurant or sit at a table near the window. When hiking, we might select a high-quality natural space with beautiful views. When engaging in the "Best Possible Self" activity, we may choose to write about our dreams, which we don't usually dare to mention.

Attentional deployment – this strategy relates to paying attention to what we do at this moment in time. When the mind wonders, bringing it back to the moment. For example, when sitting in a restaurant with our partner, taking in their face, the details of where we are eating, and noticing what is so good about this moment. When hiking, we become aware of our body moving, the air going in and out of our lungs as we breathe, and the wind caressing our faces. Engaging in the "Best Possible Self" activity is about becoming aware of the physiological sensations associated with our writing, perhaps our heart rate speeding up, or the feeling of warmth. It is about realising our changing emotions as we write different parts of our best possible self-journey.

Cognitive change – once we notice what is happening to us, how we think about it can impact our emotions. This strategy is about reframing positive feelings to amplify our emotional experiences. For example, when enjoying seeing our partners across the table, it is about thinking how grateful we are to have them in our lives. Hiking is about realising that what we feel when looking at nature's beauty is a pure sense of awe. Writing about our best possible self is about how much hope we have for the future.

Response modulation – the final stage of this strategic emotion regulation is modulating our response. As a result of engaging in the process, we may experience a Duchenne smile, have more sparkle in our eyes, or behave in an inviting or warm way. This state of emotional self-regulation involves the physiological impact of the process or our behavioural response. For example, when sitting at a restaurant with your partner, you may share your enjoyment of the night with them, resulting in a kiss or an offer to stay out for a drink. When hiking, you may realise how relaxed you have become and how much you've contributed to your work–life balance on that day of rummaging through the mountains. Or, when writing the "Best Possible Self" activity, you might take action on the first step towards becoming the best possible self. All these activities will create a positive loop of increased positive emotions.

Applying these five strategies will increase your positive emotions both short term and long term. They can be used at different time perspectives – for example, when anticipating some positive events, such as your holidays, or when experiencing an event as described earlier. They could also be used when reminiscing about a positive event as they would amplify the positive emotions in the present moment. For me at the Forbidden Fruit festival, this method was a fire starter for realising how lucky I was to be there with my friends and have so much fun. Almost a decade later, I still remember the burst of positive emotions I experienced that day. And the effect continues to impact me to this day. I encourage you to try these strategies in your own life and see their positive impact on your emotional wellbeing.

References

Quoidbach, J., Mikolajczak, M., & Gross, J. J. (2015). Positive interventions: An emotion regulation perspective. *Psychological Bulletin, 141*(3), 655–693. https://doi.org/10.1037/a0038648

Wellbeing literacy

Last year, I was involved in two qualitative studies in which we interviewed participants to identify the impact of their experiences on their wellbeing. One group of participants responded to a question about impact by saying, "It was grand" ("grand" is an Irish slang, meaning okay). They found it difficult to articulate their emotions, thoughts, or actions associated with wellbeing. Analysing their responses was challenging for my research team because of the lack of detail in their reflections. In contrast, the second group of participants responded to the same question with such nuances that their monologues lasted a few minutes. They were highly attuned to their feelings and thoughts. Some were even capable of describing their process of thinking in real-time, for example, "first I experienced sadness, then a thought occurred which flooded me with joy, so I experienced both sadness and joy all at the same time". Analysing their data was equally challenging, but for a different reason. While the first group had low levels of wellbeing literacy, the wellbeing literacy of the second group was very high.

Wellbeing literacy is a concept developed by a team led by Lindsay Oades from the University of Melbourne. It is defined as "a capability to comprehend and compose wellbeing language, across contexts, to use such language to maintain or improve the wellbeing of oneself, others or the world" (Oades et al., 2021, p. 1). In other words, wellbeing literacy describes how people process and communicate information about wellbeing. They believed it was a missing link rarely discussed in wellbeing practice. Yet they see it as an active ingredient influencing the outcomes of positive psychology interventions and programmes.

Their model of wellbeing literacy comprises five elements.

1. Individuals' knowledge of the content of wellbeing, what makes people happy, or what individuals need to do to improve their wellbeing. Knowledge also refers to the vocabulary they use to describe wellbeing.
2. Individuals' understanding of the multimodal texts about wellbeing. Individuals read and listen about wellbeing, watch programmes and videos relating to wellbeing, and engage in various forms of bibliotherapy, whereby they read for improved wellbeing. These texts can include books, articles, podcasts, and videos discussing various wellbeing aspects.
3. Individuals can compose multimodal text about wellbeing. For example, they can write about it or speak eloquently about it. They can create content relating to wellbeing.
4. Individuals' awareness of the impact of context on wellbeing. They can recognise the environmental influences on wellbeing and take steps to adapt to them. This includes adapting their vocabulary to the relevant content.
5. Individuals develop a habit of intentionally using the language to maintain or improve their own wellbeing and the wellbeing of others. This includes ethical considerations, such as respecting the privacy and autonomy of others when discussing their wellbeing and ensuring that the language used is inclusive and respectful.

This five-element model has been recently developed into a scale, allowing the researchers to conduct more research to expand this concept. More importantly, the focus has shifted towards applying the model in various contexts. For example, leaders in the workplace with high wellbeing literacy may incorporate wellbeing discussions into their meetings to help employees embrace good mental health. Similarly, within families, loved ones can share their personal experiences outside the home, reflect on their impact, and explore strategies for maintaining wellbeing in the face of adversity. That shared language will expand young people's awareness of wellbeing and improve their wellbeing literacy.

References

Oades, L. G., Jarden, A., Hou, H., Ozturk, C., Williams, P., Slemp, G. R., & Huang, L. (2021). Wellbeing literacy: A capability model for wellbeing science and practice. *International Journal of Environmental Research and Public Health*, *18*(2), 719. https://doi.org/10.3390/ijerph18020719

Vantage theory

Imagine you and your best friend decide to sign up to a wellbeing programme, both eager to enhance your wellbeing and support each other. You follow the programme diligently and you notice improvement in your wellbeing over time. In contrast, your friend sees only a temporary boost before her wellbeing declines. She ends up feeling like a hamster on a wheel, constantly cycling through different wellbeing courses and activities without lasting improvement in wellbeing, whereas, for you, this one course seemed to have been enough to make a positive difference in your life. In these situations, it is easy to fall into the trap of blaming people for not putting in enough effort. This is, after all, what society tends to do. We shift so much responsibility onto an individual, praise them when they do something well, and blame them when they don't. But we forget the powerful impact our genetics and the environment have on us. We may also explore the environment and whether something significantly negatively impacted their lives. However, researchers Michael Pluess and Jay Belsky approached this issue differently. Instead of focusing solely on the individual's behaviour or environment, they delved into their molecular architecture to establish whether genetic factors could explain why some people flourish after completing wellbeing interventions while others struggle.

The whole exploration began with a Differential Susceptibility theory, according to which some individuals demonstrate more genetic plasticity for experiencing positive and negative events (Belsky, 2013). It is as if we are all on a continuum between negative and positive impact of life experiences. For some people, the scale goes from 3 to 7, meaning that they stay in their moderate wellbeing, but the extreme states are not accessible to them. So, they do not get too upset about events that upset others, or they do not experience excessive happiness. For others, however, the scale goes from 1 to 10, meaning they have a greater capacity for experiencing very high or very low levels of positive and negative wellbeing. These people are often called Highly Sensitive People, and approximately a third of our population belongs to this category. They are people whose emotional range is more significant than an average person's, and further research has shown that they also have a more significant ability to change.

Following on from this theory, another theory was established. This one related to positive events only, as among those with more remarkable genetic plasticity, some people in particular reported "vantage sensitivity" (Pluess & Belsky, 2013). This means that they were able to benefit disproportionately from supportive conditions due to their genetic makeup. For example, research with children experiencing anxiety showed that those with higher sensitivity benefited from CBT significantly more compared to those without (Eley et al., 2012). Similarly, a series of positive psychology interventions introduced with female adolescents showed that those with higher vantage sensitivity benefited from the intervention even 6 months later. In contrast, less sensitive people returned to baseline within 3 months (Pluess & Boniwell, 2015).

This significant research demonstrates our genetics' impact on the effectiveness of wellbeing programmes and single interventions. Our genetic makeup does not change, but how our genes are expressed alters due to environmental influences. As such, people predisposed to positive change will be more responsive to positive environments and benefit more from wellbeing interventions. This is why, on average, an intervention may show a less significant impact when people with higher and lower sensitivity are mixed; however, if we were to isolate those with higher vantage sensitivity, the interventions could have a longer-lasting impact on wellbeing. This needs to be considered when designing any wellbeing initiatives.

References

Belsky, J. (2013). Differential susceptibility to environmental influences. *International Journal of Child Care and Education Policy*, *7*(2), 15–31. https://doi.org/10.1007/2288-6729-7-2-15

Eley, T. C., Hudson, J. L., Creswell, C., Tropeano, M., Lester, K. J., Cooper, P., Farmer, A., Lewis, C. M., Lyneham, H. J., Rapee, R. M., Uher, R., Zavos, H. M., & Collier, D. A. (2012). Therapygenetics: The 5HTTLPR and response to psychological therapy. *Molecular Psychiatry*, *17*(3), 236–237. https://doi.org/10.1038/mp.2011.132

Pluess, M., & Belsky, J. (2013). Vantage sensitivity: Individual differences in response to positive experiences. *Psychological Bulletin*, *139*(4), 901–916. https://doi.org/10.1037/a0030196

Pluess, M., & Boniwell, I. (2015). Sensory-processing sensitivity predicts treatment response to a school-based depression prevention program: Evidence of vantage sensitivity. *Personality and Individual Differences*, *82*, 40–45. https://doi.org/10.1016/j.paid.2015.03.011

The dark side of happiness

If you ask any parent what they want for their children, most will want them to be happy. The pursuit of happiness, as opposed to the pursuit of money, fame, or success, is considered in folk psychology to be an honourable goal. And let's be honest with ourselves: Who does not want to be happy? However, despite happiness being so well embedded in Western culture, there is a dark side to it that needs to be addressed, and this is what Iris Mauss from the University of Denver set out to explore.

In an article by Gruber and colleagues (2011), the researchers explored the literature on the dark side of happiness and asked themselves four questions. Let's explore them in more detail. The first question is related to the degree of optimal levels of happiness. At the same time, many of the wellbeing models are based on an assumption that the higher the happiness or wellbeing, the better; existing literature leans towards the Aristotelian notion of moderation. As such, perhaps moderation should be our aim, given that too much of a good thing could lead to adverse outcomes. For example, extreme intensity of positive emotions is associated with risk-taking, higher mortality rates, or neglecting dangers. Thus, too much happiness could be potentially detrimental to us.

The second question is related to the timing. Happiness may not always be effective in all circumstances. For example, I once was asked by a weight-loss organisation whether positive emotions were good for people who tried to lose weight. The question arose from examples of people who were happy with their weight loss, celebrated their success by treating themselves to a cake, and blamed their outcomes on emotions. In some situations, experiencing negativity can motivate or support us in tackling a difficult situation. For example, experiencing positivity or happiness would not be adaptive when in danger. Instead, fear may be a more helpful emotion. Thus, situational happiness is essential to consider.

The third question the authors asked themselves was whether there is a right or wrong way to pursue happiness. Original research led by Iris Mauss et al. (2011, 2012) showed that individuals who value happiness a lot tend to be more lonely and realise they are less happy than they thought. This makes sense to me. I remember years ago when I decided to try a range of wellbeing interventions, mainly focused on pursuing happiness. I realised I had become a recluse, so focused on making myself happy that I forgot to do my usual activities with friends. Or Schooler and colleagues (2023) found that telling people to try to make themselves happy as they listened to music made them less happy than simply listening to music, so how we pursue happiness matters.

Finally, the authors asked themselves whether there were wrong types of happiness. Happiness comprises higher levels of positive emotions and lower levels of negative emotions. However, those emotions can impact our happiness, too. For example, feeling pride that is not associated with any specific success can lead to lower levels of happiness. Similarly, not experiencing emotions such as embarrassment is usually considered harmful and leads to unhappiness. Therefore, it is important to embrace all types of wellbeing – the key is the balance between them.

These questions are fundamental for practitioners. They help them stop and think more critically about the positive psychology interventions and advice they use or recommend to their clients. Focusing on all the positive outcomes of research without considering its darker side might not be helpful and needs to be reframed.

Blockbuster movies, such as *The Pursuit of Happyness*, have perpetuated the notion of happiness as being something that can change and depend on our choices. Therefore, if we choose to be happy, we must take action and make changes, and the positive outcomes will follow. As motivating as it might be, the belief that happiness depends on an individual can also backfire. What if a person is not happy? Is it their fault they have not pursued it hard enough or not put enough effort into their wellbeing? This line of thinking can be dangerous and may lead to adverse outcomes. We need to keep this in mind as we search for happiness.

References

Gruber, J., Mauss, I. B., & Tamir, M. (2011). A dark side of happiness? How, when, and why happiness is not always good. *Perspectives on Psychological Science: A Journal of the Association for Psychological Science*, *6*(3), 222–233. https://doi.org.elib.tcd.ie/10.1177/1745691611406927

Mauss, I. B., Savino, N. S., Anderson, C. L., Weisbuch, M., Tamir, M., & Laudenslager, M. L. (2012). The pursuit of happiness can be lonely. *Emotion, 12*(5), 908–912. https://doi.org/10.1037/a0025299

Mauss, I. B., Tamir, M., Anderson, C. L., & Savino, N. S. (2011). Can seeking happiness make people unhappy? Paradoxical effects of valuing happiness. *Emotion, 11*(4), 807–815. https://doi.org/10.1037/a0022010

Schooler, J. W. Y., Ariel, D., & Loewenstein, L. (2023). The pursuit and assessment of happiness can be self-defeating. In I. Brocas & J. Carrillo (Eds.), *The psychology of economic decisions: Rationality and well-being*. Oxford Academic. https://doi.org/10.1093/oso/9780199251063.003.0003

Process of change

Synergistic Change Model

I watched an absorbing, albeit slightly bizarre, film a few years ago. It was Hitoshi Matsumoto's *Shinboru*, translated as "Symbol". A man wakes up in captivity in a white room with no windows or doors, only white walls, floor, and ceiling. Suddenly, he sees something sticking on a wall, and as soon as he presses it, random objects fall out of the walls, such as a stool, cart, or sushi. Suddenly, he is surrounded by them and on a rollercoaster of emotions driven by his determination to escape this trap. But each action he takes causes an unpredictable reaction. This part of the film reminds me of an article by Reuben Rusk and colleagues about the Synergistic Change Model, which emphasises the chain reaction of changes we make in life; sometimes, the outcomes are easy to see. Otherwise, they seem unexpected. These changes are like pushing one button, only to realise several other buttons have come out.

The Synergistic Change Model is an extension of the domains of the positive functioning framework created from a comprehensive review of the positive psychology literature (Rusk & Waters, 2015). The five domains that were identified in this framework were (1) Attention and Awareness, (2) Comprehension and Coping,

(3) Emotions, (4) Goals and Habits, and (5) Relationships and Virtues. The objective of the Synergistic Change Model is to create lasting changes in each of the five dimensions.

The core principle of the Synergistic Change Model is the dynamic nature of the interactions between domains. For instance, an increase in our awareness of how our words or actions affect others can change the quality of our relationships. Similarly, adopting new coping strategies can alter our emotional life. Thus, a change in one domain can trigger a cascade of effects in other domains, making the model a complex and comprehensive tool for personal development.

1. **Relapse** – given that a change in one domain causes a knock-on interaction between other domains, the changes these interactions cause may be negative for the domain in question. For example, I may set up a goal for myself. Through this process, I will become aware of the incongruence of my actions and values, increasing my experience of negative emotions. As a result, I might have difficulty meeting my initial goal. Thus, the interaction between the varied domains could cause a relapse in one domain.
2. **Spill-over** – these interactions between domains could also work to our advantage. For example, say that I set up a goal for myself related to relationships. Through improved relationships with people close to me, I may become more aware of my connection with them; it may encourage me to use more coping strategies associated with seeking help from others. Thus, one domain will positively impact a range of other domains.
3. **Synergy** – one challenge related to the interventions used is that they often do not last. For example, we may use an intervention that helps us experience more positive emotions; however, after a while, we may relapse, and the impact of the intervention will ultimately cease. Alternatively, we may experience a spill-over effect that will positively impact other domains. So, the intervention may cause what authors called "the tray to tip" effect, which means that non-linear change will occur, causing a more permanent change by stabilising the other domains at a higher level. This "tipping the system" concept occurs when the new behaviour or attitude becomes so well embedded in our psyche that it becomes a more permanent part of our lives.

Following this explanation, the authors of this paper explore three strategies that can support us in tipping the system:

1. Targeting pivotal elements – these domains have a particularly potent impact on other domains. They suggest that positive emotions could have that effect. However, given how different we all are, perhaps the pivotal elements are based on individuals' values, not only objective, research-based essential elements.
2. Leveraging existing strengths and values – in the spirit of positive psychology, using our strengths and all that is important to guide our engagement in interventions could be another strategy for tipping the system. For example, if what is essential to use is success, setting up goals to allow us to do it could be that

pathway. Or if we are particularly good at emotional intelligence, interventions relating to emotions may cause a positive chain reaction.

3. Targeting mutually reinforcing elements – this strategy relates to bringing together two domains that could easily support a spill-over effect. They provide an example of increasing attention to positive outcomes, which may support more optimistic thinking that can further support individuals' coping.

This complex model emphasises the importance of examining people's lives rather than just one aspect. Every action we take influences other areas of our lives, so it's crucial to consider these connections when implementing interventions designed to foster lasting wellbeing. We are part of an interconnected network, not isolated compartments. In this way, even a small action can create ripples that spread throughout the system.

References

Rusk, R. D., Vella-Brodrick, D. A., & Waters, L. (2018). A complex dynamic systems approach to lasting positive change: The synergistic change model. *The Journal of Positive Psychology*, *13*(4), 406–418. https://doi.org/10.1080/17439760.2017.1291853

Rusk, R. D., & Waters, L. (2015). A psycho-social system approach to well-being: Empirically deriving the five domains of positive functioning. *The Journal of Positive Psychology*, *10*(2), 141–152. https://doi.org/10.1080/17439760.2014.920409

Transtheoretical model of change

Are you happy? If you're not as happy as you'd like to be, would you like to make changes in your life? According to the Transtheoretical model of change (Prochaska & DiClemente, 1983), your answer to this question will indicate your readiness for change. This model, originally introduced in health psychology to explain addiction, has been applied to various habits, including those related to personal happiness. It presents six stages of change, offering a roadmap for personal transformation and growth.

1. **Pre-contemplation** is when individuals are not aware of the need to change. They live their lives oblivious to the impact of their behaviour. In the case of happiness, it may be a stage before they completed a survey assessing their wellbeing or before anyone talked to them about positive psychology and how it can help them live a good life.
2. **Contemplation** is when they have gained awareness of a problem and reflect on whether they should make any change in their lives or not. When contemplating happiness, it is the moment of realisation that perhaps their wellbeing is not satisfactory and they would like to live a different kind of life. At this stage, they are contemplating the costs and benefits of making such a change.
3. **Preparation** is a stage when they begin to reevaluate their lives and consider their environment's impact on their wellbeing or the social network and how it

influences their wellbeing. In relation to the pursuit of happiness, they are now weighing options and coming up with ideas as to what they can do to instigate changes, how they can improve their wellbeing.

4. **Action** is when they decide to do something about it. At this stage, they finally take action to make a change. In relation to happiness, it could be the time when they sign up to attend a wellbeing programme, try positive psychology interventions, or begin to work with a life coach.
5. **Maintenance** relates to the process of maintaining behaviours so that the individuals continue to engage in desirable behaviour. It involves reinforcing the behaviour that work well, self-evaluating to see the positive outcomes achieved to date, or using other techniques that help individuals persist through challenges to improve their wellbeing.
6. The sixth stage is related to a **relapse** whereby, despite attempting to lose weight, they plateau or start putting on weight, or despite trying to quit smoking, they go back on cigarettes. In the happiness pursuit, relapse is about not engaging in wellbeing activities, or self-care practices. Thus, individuals need to refocus their attention on the wellbeing journey after they have lost interest or momentum in it.

The Transtheoretical Model is commonly used to assess an individual's readiness for coaching, often introduced to positive psychology students to reflect on their preparedness for wellbeing change. However, it's important to note that the model's primary focus is on altering unwanted behaviours, like insufficient physical activity or being overweight. The model's relapse aspect is based on explicit feedback showing that the unwanted behaviour persists, and so do the health consequences of it. The examples I've provided above relate to happiness change based on actions people take to engage in self-care attempts. Just because they ceased to take action, it does not mean that their wellbeing has declined, which is what makes this model so tricky to use in positive psychology.

Real life presents a far more complex issue of wellbeing improvement than this model can fully address. Wellbeing is not as straightforward as quitting smoking, and the successes in wellbeing improvement are not easily measurable. Life is messy, and unless our goal is solely to reduce symptoms of depression, this model might not be the most effective route to pursue happiness.

Take, for example, someone who is going through a difficult time. They are stuck in a toxic relationship, work in a dead-end job, and feel generally very unhappy. They may be ready to make changes to improve their life. But who is to say that introducing a series of wellbeing activities will improve their wellbeing over time? If life circumstances keep knocking them down, no matter how many positive psychology interventions they practise, their wellbeing might not budge. Their life may temporarily feel like they are rolling an immense boulder up a hill, only for it to roll down again. Their lack of positive outcomes might be demotivating for them and have little to do with their effort and maybe little to do with having control over their life circumstances.

In contrast, when they try to lose weight, their action-feedback look is far more straightforward, so the process of change, while still challenging, is less convoluted because they can see the outcomes of their effort more immediately. This is why I believe that this model, while applicable to health interventions, might not work so well with positive psychology changes. Wellbeing isn't always driven by behaviour change and is impacted by a range of other factors that the model does not account for.

References

Prochaska, J. O., & DiClemente, C. C. (1983). Stages and processes of self-change of smoking: Toward an integrative model of change. *Journal of Consulting and Clinical Psychology*, *51*(3), 390–395. https://doi.org/10.1037/0022-006X.51.3.390

Ego depletion

Imagine you get up in the morning; it is nice and quiet before your children wake up. You take a warm shower and sit down for 10 minutes to read a book. Before you notice, the house is buzzing again; everyone is up and ready to face the day. They lean over each other, reaching out for a milk bottle; they spill the cereal and call out to you, complaining about each other. You ask them to keep it down while preparing their lunchboxes. Then, you rush them to get ready as you're running late for work, they give out to you, and you feel like telling them off, but you keep your cool. Finally, they are ready to go out; you walk them to school as they bicker along the way. You do not react. Just keep counting to ten, fifty, and a hundred. Finally, you're ready to catch a bus to work and see it coming, but the driver never sees you and drives off. It's only mid-morning, but you're already exhausted from the constant hustle. You swear out loud and don't care that people at the bus stop see you lose it like this. You've just experienced ego depletion.

The theory of ego depletion is a concept that resonates with many. It suggests that our self-control functions like a muscle (Baumeister et al., 2024). Each time we try to manage our anger, our thoughts, our emotions, a bit of our self-control is drained. And when we use this control too often in a short space of time, we reach a point where we can no longer keep it in check and we lose control. This loss of control might lead us to binge-eat when we're on a diet, or indulge in spree shopping after a rough day, regardless of our financial wellbeing. However, similar to building muscles with regular exercise, with practice, we can build our resilience to these urges and enhance our self-control making it easier to cope with daily hassles.

A meta-analysis suggests that the effect of self-depletion may have been exaggerated (Carter et al., 2015). However, in response, Baumeister and colleagues (2024) pointed out that hundreds of replications have demonstrated the ego depletion effect, and the studies that failed to show it were poorly designed. Therefore, the theory stands and its application is vast. For example, when working with clients, I found that helping them use the techniques developed by the researchers work. Practising these small acts of control can help us develop the self-control muscle, thus allowing us to achieve larger goals. These include making a list of what we spend our money on during the day and minding one's posture. A simple solution and so effective.

References

Baumeister, R. F., André, N., Southwick, D. A., & Tice, D. M. (2024). Self-control and limited willpower: Current status of ego depletion theory and research. *Current Opinion in Psychology*, *60*, 101882.

Carter, E. C., Kofler, L. M., Forster, D. E., & McCullough, M. E. (2015). A series of meta-analytic tests of the depletion effect: Self-control does not seem to rely on a limited resource. *Journal of Experimental Psychology: General*, *144*(4), 796–815. https://doi.org/10.1037/xge0000083

Self-determination theory

I was once invited to consult with an organisation to help them explain why their sales A-team, especially created for cold calling clients, were not successful, even though they all had had outstanding track record when working in other sales departments. The leadership team wondered if it was the market, their leadership, or the people they chose that did not quite fit. They asked for tips on how to help their team excel. I began interviewing their staff and their leader, observing how they work, and afterwards, I concluded that it all boiled down to the self-determination theory. The team leader of this A-team kept pushing the team into the extrinsic motivation to such an extent that they lost the enjoyment of their work, which led to lack of intrinsic motivation. Small tweaks on how the team was led and managed resulted in significant improvements.

Self-determination theory is a powerful theory of motivation that explains our varying energy levels and persistence in pursuing different tasks. When our motivation is purely intrinsic, we experience a sense of empowerment, deriving enjoyment, interest, and inherent satisfaction from our actions because we choose to do them for their own sake. We become the masters of our behaviour, regulating ourselves and driving our actions. In contrast, any form of extrinsic regulation presents a challenge, as it requires us to regulate ourselves to a certain extent.

When we are forced into a specific behaviour due to compliance, we often feel a loss of control over our situation. We become heavily reliant on external rewards to keep us going, but we also fear external punishments as a consequence of not meeting expectations. Our motivation becomes driven by others' desires and the way they reward or punish us, rather than our own interests and values. This extreme form of external regulation can lead to a sense of disempowerment and disconnection from our true desires.

An introjected regulation, which is external, is when we do what we need to do not because we are genuinely interested but because our ego is threatened. Whether we fail or succeed, we are driven by how others view us. Organisations that keep using this type of motivation on their employees demotivate some rather than lighting fire in their bellies. People in this category know they "should" be doing something, even though they might not want to do it deep in their hearts. Again, they do it to avoid punishment or perhaps to get an external award, which is also in the form of praise, showing the boss that a person can do it. As such, the behaviour might not be sustainable.

Identified regulation is an extrinsic regulation heading towards intrinsic but not quite there yet. This is when the person realises the importance of a cause; they may value it and would like to do it, but emotionally, they are not there and are not getting the intrinsic reward, the personal satisfaction or enjoyment, to keep them going. The regulation closest to intrinsic motivation, but a little step behind, is integrated regulation, when there is a congruence between the behaviour and the self; as such, we do what we want. There is also awareness about where we are and where we want to be. But what is lacking is that emotional engagement, an enjoyment we get from doing it. Once the enjoyment and satisfaction come in, we are tipping into the intrinsic motivation space, the ultimate place to be.

In a book chapter by Sheldon and Ryan, the authors argue that combining self-determination theory with positive psychology interventions is a marriage made in heaven. The self-determination theory can explain why interventions were successful, and consequently, the design of interventions can be informed by the theory. For example, to help individuals regulate themselves by using positive psychology interventions, the three important components of the self-determination theory could be considered: autonomy, competence, and relatedness.

Autonomy is the sense that we have a choice to choose the best course of action for ourselves. Autonomy in selecting positive psychology interventions, like mindfulness meditation or gratitude journaling, can significantly boost intrinsic motivation. When individuals feel they have the freedom to choose the practices that resonate with them, they are more likely to engage with it and sustain these new behaviours over time.

Competence is the awareness that we are improving our skills and knowledge and can achieve more. It is the growing sense that we know how to improve our wellbeing, develop our skills, and grow personally and professionally. It allows us to understand the benefits of our intervention practice better.

Relatedness is a component of the theory associated with social connection. It is about feeling connected or experiencing a sense of belonging. For example, when engaging in positive psychology interventions, an individual may feel a sense of community when practising wellbeing with a group of like-minded people.

The theory of self-determination is one of the key theories in psychology that can be tapped into when we do not feel motivated to do something. It helps us consider why we feel the way we feel and what changes we can make to ignite a fire in our bellies. It is a valuable theory to consider when exploring the most effective change process.

References

Ryan, R. M., & Deci, E. L. (2000). Self-determination theory and the facilitation of intrinsic motivation, social development, and well-being. *American Psychologist*, *55*(1), 68–78. https://doi.org/10.1037/0003-066X.55.1.68

Sheldon, K. M., & Ryan, R. M. (2011). Positive psychology and self-determination theory: A natural interface. In V. I. Chirkov, R. M. Ryan, & K. M. Sheldon (Eds.), *Human autonomy in cross-cultural context: Perspectives on the psychology of agency, freedom, and well-being* (pp. 33–44). Springer Science + Business Media. https://doi.org/10.1007/978-90-481-9667-8_2

Meta theory for positive psychology interventions

Positive psychology is a young field of research, so drawing on what's been there before is essential. Clinical psychologists have been developing an approach to helping clients engage in effective change processes for over a century. Therefore, it is no surprise that some of the processes of change or other types of learning should be drawn from their more advanced fields.

One approach that positive psychologists use predominantly in testing interventions is creating new interventions and testing them against the established interventions to see which is more effective. However, according to Ciarrochi and colleagues (2022), this approach has not been very practical in clinical psychology, and as such, they suggest an alternative approach. They argue that, similar to clinical psychology and psychotherapy, the field of positive psychology should shift towards evaluating specific interventions that target the process of change. Alternatively, it should tailor interventions for specific people in a specific context. This is a departure from the intervention testing, especially that of multicomponent interventions.

Targeting change process – this shift relates to a process based on explicit scientific theories. It is dynamic and often bidirectional and non-linear, meaning that change is a messy process peppered with setbacks. Individuals may experience change gradually. Sometimes the change is fast, other times, they experience periods of relapse. It is also progressive, meaning that in spite of challenges, individuals head in the right direction. It is contextually bound, meaning that what happens in one's environment influences progress. This is why regular context reappraisal is crucial for successful implementation. Finally, it is multilevel, which targets individuals at different levels, such as biological, psychological, or social functioning.

Personalised interventions – this shift relates to modifying interventions to meet participants' needs. Assumptions are made that all interventions are effective with all participants. However in reality, the process of change differs for each individual. One person has the motivation to make changes but is disorganised, and cannot focus on the end goal; the other person is organised but lacks motivation and start questioning the reason why they began the process in the first place. The interventions used for each person must be different as they address a different change process.

The authors introduce the Extended Evolutionary Meta-Model (EEMM). They argue that all models and frameworks in psychology have some evolutionary basis. The driving force behind the EEMM is variation (interventions to increase, e.g. positive emotions or optimism or improve awareness), selection (client's goal), and retention (maintaining adaptive behaviour). These forces are also set within a context, be it a workplace, school, or home. The EEMM model, therefore, acts as a meta-model within positive psychology, providing practitioners with practical steps to apply when working with clients.

The variation, selection, and retention process is applied at multiple dimensions and levels within the EEMM model. The authors suggest extending the model by six specific dimensions, including affect, cognition, attention, self, motivation, or overt behaviour. The process of change aims to undermine negative processes (e.g. reducing the experience of negative emotions) and promote positive ones (e.g. increasing positive experiences of emotions). For example, the dimension of affect (experiences of emotions) is about reducing the experience of negative emotions by exercising non-reactivity to them during a mindfulness session (undermining negative processes) and increasing positive experiences of emotions through gratitude (promoting positive processes). Thus, the authors explore each dimension in the context of these two processes. They also argue that while the negative and positive processes are distinct, they interact and impact each other.

The EEMM model, serving as a meta-model within positive psychology, is a comprehensive concept. It provides practitioners with a wealth of knowledge and practical steps to apply when working with clients. For example, if a client presents with sleeping disturbances, instead of a narrow approach like teaching them about sleep hygiene, we could explore their emotional experiences during restful and disturbed sleep. This discussion might reveal activities that support positive emotional experiences, such as socialising (at the sociocultural level) or exercising (at the physiological level). Thus, this model can guide coaches, leaders, teachers, and other professionals in helping their clients identify the domain they could work on, across the variation, selection, retention, and context, to effect lasting change in their lives.

References

Ciarrochi, J., Hayes, S. C., Oades, L. G., & Hofmann, S. G. (2022). Toward a unified framework for positive psychology interventions: Evidence-based processes of change in coaching, prevention, and training. *Frontiers in Psychology*, *12*, 809362. https://doi.org/10.3389/fpsyg.2021.809362

5 The introduction to multidisciplinary positive psychology

One of the greatest accomplishments of the field of positive psychology is its transformative spread across a range of diverse fields. In this chapter, we will explore how it has been combined with other scientific fields and how it impacted them. We will begin by exploring the fast-emerging field of Positive Health, which is the application of positive psychology within the healthcare field. It also includes examining how positive psychology concepts can support those who experience physical and mental health issues. Then, we will examine another fast-growing field of positive coaching, which brings together positive psychology science with the psychology of coaching. It has a two-directional objective for positive psychology to support coaching psychology with evidence-based tools to improve clients' wellbeing, but also coaching psychology supporting positive psychology to improve the application of the research in framework-based conversations. Next, we will delve into the new field of positive technology and explore how it can be beneficial in creating technology that serves us all well, by enhancing our wellbeing rather than impacting negatively on our health and wellbeing. Afterwards, we will delve deeper into the new science of positive education that explores how positive psychology research can be applied and embedded in educational systems. Next, we will tap into the workplace wellbeing and the field that is gaining traction in the past decade. We will explore the research behind it and ways in which it can be further developed. Following this, we will explore a new field of Wellbeing arts, which is slowly becoming a helpful exploration of how arts and humanities can be used to support wellbeing. Finally, we will describe a range of other disciplines that are developing rapidly while embracing the research of positive psychology. A sociologist once said that when you put disciplines together, they are not just a mix of both, but they start creating a diverse identity that becomes something new. This chapter is a foundation for presenting the key studies that contribute to this transformation.

Positive health

Positive health: A systematic review

A few months ago, I met with a colleague whose research and practice delved into positive health. Initially, we were both excited about our mutual interests,

DOI: 10.4324/9781003530596-5

but after 15 minutes of discussion, we began to see the differences in how we conceptualised the merging of health and wellbeing. I was focused on bringing together the fields of positive psychology and lifestyle medicine; she was focused on bringing together psycho-social models that supported health. Two years earlier, I recall a similar conversation with a group of colleagues with whom I spent hours discussing the scope of positive health. This is not unusual in academia, as we all come from different perspectives and bring different experiences and expertise. It is also beautiful to work in multidisciplinary teams where your views are considered and respected regardless of your stance. This allows you to contribute to the final concepts in some ways. This foundation makes this article exciting, as it summarises various views on positive health.

The authors (Bodryzlova & Moullec, 2023) have explored the literature for any conceptualisations of positive health. From 41 publications, they found four different approaches that fell into one- or two-dimensional conceptualisations.

One-dimensional conceptualisation of positive health

1. Positive health as wellbeing – this approach to health comes from two distinct schools of thought, one introduced by Martin Seligman and the other by Carol Ryff. For Seligman, it is a concept that emphasises health as going beyond the absence of disease, which is the foundation of the positive psychology field. He sees it as a combination of wellbeing (e.g. physical, absence of disease symptoms); biological factors, (such as Heart Rate Variability); or functional factors (such as having efficient person-environment relationships).

   For Ryff and colleagues (2004), who created the concept of Psychological Wellbeing based on eudaemonic philosophical foundations, positive health goes beyond the simple experiences of positive or negative emotions. It encompasses the person's whole life, including meaning in life, environmental mastery, or vocational wellbeing. Carol Ryff leads one of the most influential longitudinal studies in the US, which began as an examination of midlife and has now followed participants into their old age. The study measures positive health through medical, psychological, social, and other assessments, providing rich data on what it is like to experience positive health over time. The MIDUS study is an excellent example of Ryff's conceptualisation of this field.

Two-dimensional conceptualisations of positive health

2. Positive health as resilience – this approach to discussing health relates to how resilient individuals are despite their health. It draws upon the salutogenesis model of health as it's based on the thinking that individuals can resist adversities or experience wellbeing even if their health is failing, such as when diagnosed with cancer. An example of such an approach is the Health Asset Model (Morgan & Ziglio, 2007), which integrates several concepts from positive psychology and defines a health asset as a set of factors or resources that amplify individuals, communities, and populations to attain and maintain good health and wellbeing. In this case, resilience is seen as an outcome of these resources.

3. Positive health as capacities/resources – this approach is informed by Machteld Huber and colleagues (2011), who challenged the definition of health presented by WHO and saw it as managing oneself in the context of social, physical, and emotional challenges. As such, at a practical level, when a patient comes in with ailments, a positive health approach considers not only their physical condition but also their social context, for example, support and how they cope emotionally.
4. Other definitions – in addition to these three main approaches, other approaches have emerged that combine various aspects of health and positive psychology.

At the RCSI University of Medicine and Health Sciences, where I work, we would possibly fall into that "other" category. However, when this systematic review was being conducted, we were still in the early stages of conceptualising this field, hence our contributions were not included. We have been inspired by the rapid growth of a medical speciality "Lifestyle Medicine", which aims to help people change their lifestyle to improve their health. Our mission is to combine the field of positive psychology and lifestyle medicine to create a powerful tool for improving health and wellbeing. More about it later.

References

Bodryzlova, Y., & Moullec, G. (2023). Definitions of positive health: A systematic scoping review. *Global Health Promotion*. https://doi.org/10.1177/17579759221139802

Huber, M., Knottnerus, J. A., Green, L., van der Horst, H., Jadad, A. R., Kromhout, D., Leonard, B., Lorig, K., Loureiro, M. I., van der Meer, J. W., Schnabel, P., Smith, R., van Weel, C., & Smid, H. (2011). How should we define health?. *BMJ (Clinical Research Ed.)*, *343*, d4163. https://doi.org/10.1136/bmj.d4163

Morgan, A., & Ziglio, E. (2007). Revitalising the evidence base for public health: An assets model. *Promotion & Education*, (Suppl 2), 17–22. https://doi.org/10.1177/10253823070140020701x

Ryff, C. D., Singer, B. H., & Dienberg Love, G. (2004). Positive health: Connecting well-being with biology. *Philosophical transactions of the Royal Society of London. Series B, Biological Sciences*, *359*(1449), 1383–1394. https://doi.org/10.1098/rstb.2004.1521

Seligman, M. E. P. (2008). Positive health. *Applied Psychology: An International Review*, *57*(Suppl 1), 3–18. https://doi.org/10.1111/j.1464-0597.2008.00351.x

The marriage of positive psychology and lifestyle medicine

Liana Lianov is a medical doctor whose passion for lifestyle medicine grew exponentially, leading her to become the American College of Lifestyle Medicine president. She was inspired by the potential of lifestyle medicine, but it wasn't until she attended a positive psychology conference that she realised the two fields could complement each other. Just because someone follows healthy lifestyle guidelines (e.g. eats well, moves, sleeps well) does not mean they thrive in life. Similarly, just because someone thrives psychologically does not necessarily mean they are healthy. Therefore, bringing both fields made sense to her. This is when she made it her mission to instigate change.

One of the first articles she published about it was with Barbara Fredrickson and colleagues (2019). They explored ways in which positive psychology can be used in lifestyle medicine and, generally, in healthcare. Lifestyle medicine is a medical speciality that focuses on reducing the prevalence of non-communicable diseases by encouraging people to adopt healthier lifestyles. Non-communicable diseases account for 74% of global deaths each year and include such diseases as cardiovascular disease, stroke, cancer, and diabetes. Lifestyle medicine developed six pillars to slow down and reverse this trend, providing clear guidance for change. They are eating well, by significantly reducing meat consumption and adopting a plant-based diet, sleeping well by ensuring adequate quantity and quality of sleep, moving for at least 120 minutes a week, reducing or eliminating the use of substances, such as alcohol or tobacco, stress management, and fostering relationships.

In their article, the authors argued that both fields work towards the same goal of living a good life. While lifestyle medicine has behavioural approaches to improve physiological and physical health, evidence from positive psychology research points to similar improvements using positive psychology interventions. For example, gratitude and mindfulness practices reduce strokes, heart attacks, and body mass index (BMI) and exercising improves positive affect. Both fields fight the same battle; therefore, combining their resources could lead to an even more significant improvement in managing the health and wellbeing of populations.

Their voice was not the only one calling for inclusion. Other researchers also advocated for combining the fields to improve the mental health of populations (e.g. Morton, 2018). They explored the impact of positive psychology on behavioural choices, going beyond the obvious benefits of improving health and wellbeing outcomes and towards the psychological mechanisms for behavioural changes. They also discussed ways to include positive psychology in direct patient care to elicit change and give patients agency. This collaborative approach is a testament to the inclusive and community-driven nature of this field, which is rapidly gaining interest of practitioners and researchers.

Over the last few years, the RCSI University of Medicine and Health sciences has led several projects that explore this exciting connection. One of them was a book *Positive Health: The Basics* (Burke et al., 2025) that introduced the field of positive health from the perspective of combining lifestyle medicine and positive psychology. Another book was *International Routledge Handbook of Positive Health* (Burke et al., 2024), a comprehensive volume exploring this topic with top researchers in positive psychology and lifestyle medicine fields. Finally, a collaboration between Liana Lianov and myself (2024) brought together a book for physicians filled with numerous practical ideas on how they can apply positive psychology in their daily interactions with patients. These books serve as a practical guide for this rapidly growing field, empowering healthcare professionals to apply positive psychology to improve not only mental health but also the physical and physiological health of populations.

References

Burke, J., Boniwell, I., Frates, B., Lianov, L., & O'Boyle, C. A. (2024). *The Routledge international handbook of positive health*. Routledge.

Burke, J., Dunne, P. J., Byrne, E., & O'Boyle, C. (2025). *Positive health: The basics*. Routledge.

Lianov, L., & Burke, J. (2024). *Lifestyle medicine inside and out: A guide on how to apply positive psychology in person-centred medicine*. Routledge.

Lianov, L. S., Fredrickson, B. L., Barron, C., Krishnaswami, J., & Wallace, A. (2019). Positive psychology in lifestyle medicine and health care: Strategies for implementation. *American Journal of Lifestyle Medicine, 13*(5), 480–486. https://doi.org/10.1177/1559827619838992

Morton, D. P. (2018). Combining lifestyle medicine and positive psychology to improve mental health and emotional well-being. *American Journal of Lifestyle Medicine, 12*(5), 370. https://doi.org/10.1177/1559827618766482

The first evidence of a positive health approach

"Of course, it works", everyone would say when we first began to think about linking positive psychology with lifestyle medicine in empirical research. Common sense and research examining individual components of lifestyle medicine vis-à-vis wellbeing suggested it would be valid. But deep inside, we couldn't help but wonder if we were heading in the right direction. So, after years of writing theoretical articles linking positive psychology with lifestyle medicine, my colleague and I empirically explored the relationship between wellbeing and lifestyle pillars (Burke & Dunne, 2022).

Our research involved over 1,000 participants. We used two main positive psychology models of wellbeing, Keyes's Mental Health Continuum (2002) and Seligman's PERMA (2011). We compared them vis-à-vis participants' satisfaction with the six pillars of lifestyle medicine, that is, eating well, sleeping well, moving, reducing substances, stress management, and relationships. Our findings showed a correlation between these two concepts. Furthermore, those who flourished were three times more likely to use 3 to 6 lifestyle medicine pillars than those who were moderately well. Furthermore, those who flourished were nine times more likely to use 3 to 6 lifestyle medicine pillars than those who languished. Thus, a healthy lifestyle and wellbeing go hand in hand.

This important finding shows that looking after our bodies by engaging in healthy lifestyle choices could lead to psychological flourishing. Alternatively, having higher levels of wellbeing, referred to as flourishing, could lead to engaging in healthier lifestyle choices. We don't know the direction of this association yet, but we know that there is an association.

At the RCSI Centre for Positive Health Sciences, we are excited about the potential of this research to deepen our understanding of the connection between lifestyle medicine and positive psychology. From a practical standpoint, anyone using positive psychology interventions to improve their wellbeing can enhance their approach by incorporating healthy-lifestyle tools, of which there are many. The potential of combining these strategies for both body and mind is truly incredible.

References

Burke, J., & Dunne, P. J. (2022). Lifestyle medicine pillars as predictors of psychological flourishing. *Frontiers in Psychology, 13*, 963806. https://doi.org/10.3389/fpsyg.2022.963806

Positive health interventions

After joining the RCSI Centre for Positive Health Sciences, one of my first projects was leading the team in writing a book about Positive Health tools commissioned by Routledge. At that point, the centre had just been established, driven by a mission to enhance the health and wellbeing of populations using the science of positive psychology and lifestyle medicine. Our focus was very much on practical approaches to achieve this. We began our journey by defining what we meant by "positive health" and then delved into the literature to explore existing interventions. Our search criteria focused on the evidence of interventions improving physical and physiological health and wellbeing at the same time and expanded our perspective by examining interventions for non-clinical participants and individuals diagnosed with a disease.

When we began our search, we hoped to find at least 50 interventions that fitted our criteria. However, to our surprise, we found over 100 research-based interventions that showed evidence of improving health and wellbeing (Burke et al., 2022). In addition, we discovered more than 100 other approaches cited by researchers and practitioners that have not been fully tested yet, but recommended as tools for health and wellbeing. Over the past few decades, studies have consistently showed that positive psychology interventions can improve various aspects of health and using lifestyle medicine interventions can improve wellbeing, as it is viewed by positive psychology. However, what was missing was a well-informed integration of both approaches.

Around the same time, Geraldine Przybylko et al. (2021), from the Lifestyle Medicine and Health Research Centre at Avondale University College, Australia, created the first 10-week programme that combined lifestyle medicine and positive psychology interventions by alternating them each week. For example, participants were asked to practise gratitude for 1 week and eat better the following week. The results of this study showed that looking after their body and mind resulted in wellbeing boost. However, it would have been great to see similar improvements in health.

My colleague Padraic Dunne and I (2022) further expanded this research. We were interested in how combining the interventions by creating new, lifestyle-medicine-and-positive-psychology interventions in one improved health and wellbeing. To do this, we designed a 4-week programme for young people and gave them three interventions a week to choose from (Burke & Dunne, 2024). Each week was themed. For example, one week, they were learning about eating well, and the next week, they were introduced to the benefits and examples of physical activity. To support the themes, they practised interventions such as "Practise kindness to your gut this week by eating more prebiotics and probiotics". Our results showed more modest changes in wellbeing, but interestingly, they also indicated that participants' sleep quality was reduced compared with the control group. This study highlighted the importance of measuring both health and wellbeing at the same time, as we cannot assume that a combination of two good activities leads to positive outcomes.

The development of positive health interventions is in its infancy. At the same time, we see it as an exciting opportunity for individuals, communities, and populations to embrace it for a healthier future. Creating a range of interventions that combine well-researched positive psychology tools with health-related strategies provides a unique opportunity to address both health and wellbeing at the same time.

References

Burke, J., & Dunne, P. J. (2022). Lifestyle medicine pillars as predictors of psychological flourishing. *Frontiers in Psychology*, *13*, 963806. https://doi.org/10.3389/fpsyg.2022.963806

Burke, J., & Dunne, P. J. (2024). Mind meets body: Lifestyle medicine and positive psychology interventions for school. In G. Arslan & M. Yildirim (Eds.), *Handbook of positive school psychology interventions: Evidence-based practice for promoting youth mental health*. Springer Publishing.

Burke, J., Dunne, P. J., Meehan, T., O'Boyle, C., & van Nieuwerburgh, C. (2022). *Positive health: 100+ research-based positive psychology and lifestyle medicine tools for enhancing wellbeing*. Routledge.

Przybylko, G., Morton, D., Kent, L., Morton, J., Hinze, J., Beamish, P., & Renfrew, M. (2021). The effectiveness of an online interdisciplinary intervention for mental health promotion: A randomized controlled trial. *BMC Psychology*, *9*(1), 77. https://doi.org/10.1186/s40359-021-00577-8

Positive coaching

The same topics from four perspectives

Tim Lomas, a researcher at Harvard University, USA, is not a coach himself, but he became curious about how to conceptualise the emerging field of positive psychology coaching while working at the University of East London, where this innovative approach was introduced as part of a master's programme. He suggested a highly valuable activity, asking over 100 students from the first cohort of the programme to explore their perceptions of how the combination of coaching psychology and positive psychology should be structured. Their insights were fascinating, and we presented the findings at the International Congress for Positive Psychology in Montreal, Canada (Lomas et al., 2017). This session also set a foundation for Tim's subsequent article (Lomas, 2020), which delves into various perspectives on how positive psychology coaching could be perceived.

In this paper, he presents four options for integrating positive psychology with coaching psychology. The first option is a coterminous relationship, whereby coaching psychology is inherently positive and vice versa. The second perspective proposes that coaching psychology is a part of positive psychology, with coaching serving primarily as a method to apply positive psychology principles. The third view suggests that positive psychology is a minor component of coaching psychology, providing a range of tools that can be used within coaching, but with many other aspects of coaching remaining distinct. Finally, the fourth model describes an overlap between coaching and positive psychology, where the two fields are sometimes separate but also share common elements.

This paper is of particular interest to coaches and positive psychologists interested in coaching, as it provides a solid foundation for discussing what positive psychology coaching is and how it can be effectively applied. It is also a useful resource for reflecting on our beliefs associated with our practice and how they influence our relationship with clients. For those interested in the combination of these two fields, it offers a unique perspective on the role of positive psychology in other domains, making it an invaluable tool for further exploration and understanding.

References

Lomas, T. (2020). Positive coaching psychology: A case study in the hybridization of positive psychology. *International Journal of Wellbeing*, *10*(2), 1–16.

Lomas, T., Tunariu, A., Hart, R., Ivtzan, I., Burke, J., Stopforth, M., Kampman, H., Jacob, Y., Pennington, W., & Dell, P. (2017). Positive psychology coaching: Working towards a harmonious marriage of two fields. Paper presented at the International Positive Psychology Association Conference, Montreal, Canada.

What is positive psychology coaching?

For nearly a decade, we have been intrigued by the diverse perspectives on positive psychology coaching. Researchers and practitioners have contributed a multitude of definitions, each offering a unique angle on this dynamic field. This systematic review of definitions is a valuable tool for all of us, providing a comprehensive exploration of the various modes of positive psychology coaching (Van Zyl et al., 2020).

The most prevalent component in the definition of positive psychology coaching refers to identifying, using, and optimising strengths. Thus, positive psychology coaching refers to helping clients realise their strengths and then use them in a way that serves them best. The second most prevalent definition explores the focus on either optimal human functioning or wellbeing. As such, it aims to improve various aspects of wellbeing. The third most prevalent component of a definition focuses on helping clients improve their positive traits, states, and behaviour. As such, the definition of positive psychology coaching relates to exploring strengths and other positive traits, states, and behaviours to enhance wellbeing or achieve a state of optimal human functioning.

Regarding the models used, they focus primarily on strength profiling and providing clients feedback about their top strengths and ways to use them more effectively. It is also a model that centres around strengths and exploring goals that can be set up for use in daily life. Another framework explored as part of positive psychology coaching relates to reframing or reinforcement to empower individuals. This is associated with building resilience, building motivation, or rethinking how one perceives oneself and the effectiveness of one's mindset in relation to one's outcomes. Another frequent model component referred to exploring positive relationships with a client or a client's relationship with others.

This article is a practical resource for practitioners who want to apply positive psychology in their coaching practice. While it may not cover every aspect of the coaching practice, it provides a solid foundation and a clear outline of what to focus on to enhance your knowledge and skills in this area.

References

Van Zyl, L. E., Roll, L. C., Stander, M. W., & Richter, S. (2020). Positive psychological coaching definitions and models: A systematic literature review. *Frontiers in Psychology, 11*, 520603. https://doi.org/10.3389/fpsyg.2020.00793

Hard-core positive psychology coaching

I joined the University of East London as a faculty member just a few months after it combined two programmes: a Masters in Applied Positive Psychology and a Masters in Coaching. At the time, we knew very little about what happens when these both fields are brought together. At an intuition level, it made sense. However, at practical and methodological levels, we needed to figure out what it meant to practise positive psychology coaching. Within a year of joining the team, the faculty decided to explore the meaning of positive psychology coaching. However, each faculty member had varying experiences in coaching and how they used positive psychology in their practice. Subsequently, our conceptualisation of the field was different.

Before completing my PhD, for over 10 years, I worked as a coach, mainly within organisations and as long as I can remember, positive psychology was present in all my sessions with clients. The clients rarely aimed to improve their wellbeing directly. My work was mainly associated with leadership coaching, as I worked with new and existing leaders and helped them figure out what was important to them and how they could apply it in their work. In all my sessions, I used positive psychology at all times. My positive psychology perspective informed everything I did during the session. I regularly used assessments with clients, helping them figure out where they were at and how to move on. I used models informed by positive psychology and research to guide our conversations. Thus, my view of positive psychology coaching was that it was fully integrated into a coaching dialogue regardless of the topic of the conversation.

However, my colleagues viewed it differently. Some saw positive psychology as supporting coaching as usual practice. Others saw it as an alternative to the coaching as usual practice. Initially, we planned to publish a paper as a team, exploring its concept from various perspectives, but we ended up publishing separate papers as our perspectives differed so much. This is how I wrote a paper about the "Conceptual Framework for a Positive Psychology Coaching Practice" – the first such framework published (Burke, 2018).

According to the framework, positive coaching practice comprises six components: (1) Knowledge, (2) Strength-based models, (3) Positive diagnosis, (4) Optimal-functioning goals, (5) Positive psychology interventions, and (6) Positive measures.

Knowledge refers to having knowledge of positive psychology when coaching someone. Without such knowledge, we are oblivious to what is happening to our clients from a positive psychological point of view. Adequate knowledge of positive psychology allows coaches to become aware of positive processes, communicate them, and help clients work with them. Without such knowledge, coaches are blind to some critical concepts in positive psychology coaching.

Strength-based models refer to coaches using various models that focus on human strengths. This does not mean that we should not discuss the weaknesses or obstacles. True positive psychology coaching involves the strength-focused aspect as part of the process, not only the intention or outcomes.

Positive diagnosis refers to helping clients understand themselves through positive psychology. That diagnosis could include observing clients and giving them feedback as to their levels of optimism, hope, or post-traumatic growth. Alternatively, clients could be asked to complete a scale assessing various aspects of their character relevant to the coaching discussion.

Optimal-functioning goals are about helping clients not only avoid adverse outcomes but strive towards optimal human functioning in whatever aspect of their lives they wish to pursue. It is about being careful about what goals we set up and being audacious about personal development.

Positive psychology interventions relate to using interventions as activities for clients to complete; alternatively, our coaching conversation could be guided by an intervention. For example, we could explore the best possible health with a client by guiding them through an activity whereby individuals are asked to write down their health 5 or 10 years from now and imagine that they met all their health goals. What changes would they make, and how would they accomplish their goals? This intervention could become a line of questioning for a coach to explore their client's health goals and create a health plan.

The final component of positive psychology coaching, according to this model, is **positive measurement**, which refers to exploring measures used in positive psychology to either complete a client and discuss or explore the questions from a scale as a basis for client discussion. For example, Michael Ungar's model of resilience explores a range of behaviours associated with child resilience. A coach may work with a parent to explore ways in which a parent can enhance their child's resilience.

My good friend Christian van Nieuwerburgh refers to this model as a hard-core positive psychology coaching model. This is due to its hard stance on making positive psychology the centre of the client-coach conversation. However, it is essential to note that this model has not been designed to focus primarily on improving clients' wellbeing rather using positive psychology knowledge to maximise clients' outcomes.

References

Burke, J. (2018). Conceptual framework for a positive psychology coaching practice. *The Coaching Psychologist*, *14*(1), 16–25.

Practice of positive psychology coaching

My romance with positive psychology started through coaching. In my early twenties, I enrolled in a coaching diploma course, which lasted a year and exposed me to this new and exciting practice. I remember the man who taught me coaching. He was a fantastic psychotherapist whose skill in working with a client-centred approach was second to none. I loved the practical aspects of the course. However, I found it frustrating about science. At the time, coaching was just an emerging field of research and practice, so much of what he talked about was based on therapy. What really bothered me was when he demonstrated an intervention and, when I asked how he knew it worked, his response was always, "Because it worked with my clients".

Over the years, we become friends and spent hours discussing various aspects of coaching. He often teased me about my relentless need to find empirical evidence behind coaching approaches; I teased him for his disinterest in science. This was happening in the early 2000s, and it became increasingly clear to me that evidence-based practices were essential in coaching, just as they were in psychology and therapy.

Years later, when I began my Masters in Applied Positive Psychology at the University of East London, I was eager to apply my knowledge in a practical setting. In one of my first assignments, I created a range of interventions that could be used with my coaching clients, reflecting my hands-on approach. I was fortunate to transition into coaching immediately after completing my diploma, and for a decade, I have worked as a coach in various organisations, mainly with leaders. This is why I got to practise positive psychology coaching before it became widely recognised.

I was thrilled when the first book on positive psychology coaching, written by Robert Bisswas-Diener and his father, Ed Diener, was published. I loved Diener's next book, *Practicing Positive Psychology Coaching*, even more; it was super practical and sparked my continued interest and engagement in the field. Soon after, Biswas-Diener became a positive psychology coaching guru, synonymous with the field itself, as he shared some provoking and interesting articles and chapters on the topic. One of them is undeniably "The practice of positive psychology coaching", which explored what he believed mattered after 15 years of practising positive psychology coaching. He highlighted four considerations that amplify positive psychology interventions' success in coaching.

1. The need to avoid prescribing interventions. It is easy to do so when you know positive psychology and have experienced the benefits of interventions. But people are different. So, the author discourages prescribing interventions and instead encourages a more nuanced approach, whereby the sessions are client-centred, and the positive psychology knowledge of interventions can bolster the coaching practice rather than become a prescribed solution. This client-centred approach, I believe, is what truly respects the individuality and uniqueness of each client.
2. Meta-intervention refers to the broader approach used for applying research in practice. Coaching itself can become this meta-intervention due to coaches' ability to create a supportive environment, setting up norms that encourage such qualities as openness, confidentiality, and non-judgment. This coach's way of

being will make the coaching activity an intervention in itself, without the need to use positive psychology interventions.

3. It's tempting to focus on primary research in positive psychology, such as strengths or gratitude. However, the key is to use the entire potential of the field. By understanding the breadth of research in positive psychology, you can identify ways to apply it in coaching practice, thereby enhancing the effectiveness of your interventions.
4. The need to take an ethical approach to positive psychology coaching intervention practice. Even though increasingly many organisations are creating ethical guidelines for coaches, it is a widely unregulated field. It is, therefore, of utmost importance to ensure that when positive psychology coaching is practised, we follow the ethical guidelines established. After all, we are always dealing with human beings. This adherence to ethical guidelines, I believe, is what ensures the safety and wellbeing of our clients and instils confidence in our practice.

References

Biswas-Diener, R. (2020). The practice of positive psychology coaching. *The Journal of Positive Psychology*, *15*(5), 701–704. https://doi.org/10.1080/17439760.2020.1789705

Positive psychotherapy

Positive psychotherapy: A strength-based approach

The first time I met the author of this article, Tayyad Rashid from the Chan School of Public Health, Harvard, USA, was at a meeting to discuss co-writing a book, "Frontiers of Wellbeing Sciences". Until then, I have read his books about positive psychotherapy strength-based resilience programmes and other publications and marvelling at how innovative, practical, and deeply embedded in positive psychology the activities he created were. This article is no different.

Rashid (2015) introduces a complementary therapeutic approach that helps clients identify their strengths and use them to foster wellbeing. It shifts the therapeutic focus from clients' deficits and pathology to their inherent capabilities for growth and development. It addresses both symptom reduction and improvement in wellbeing. The therapy is based on Martin Seligman's PERMA Model of Wellbeing (2011), which comprises five elements: Positive emotions, Engagement, Relationships, Meaning and purpose, and Accomplishment. It also emphasises using strengths, such as gratitude, perseverance, or kindness.

In the paper, the author presents a 14-session programme, each focused on a different topic, such as good versus bad memories, satisfying versus maximising, hope and optimism, or positive communication. He describes each concept discussed and explains which character strengths are tapped into at each stage of the process.

For example, as part of the programme he introduces clients to the concepts of maximising versus satisficing when making decisions in life. Those who maximise weigh many options, trying to come up with the best solution. This often results in confusion, frustration, and regret for not selecting another choice. On the other hand, satisficers are satisfied with options that are good enough to allow them to make a decision. They tend to spend less time thinking about it and then move on without regretting their choice. The activity Rashid offers that week is helping clients create a plan to increase their satisficing when making decisions. The strengths that clients develop during this session are self-regulation and gratitude. This is just a description of one session on maximising versus satisficing. In this article, each session is described in a similar way.

This strength-based psychotherapeutic approach is deeply rooted in positive psychology and especially the science of character strengths. It explores the incidence of overusing and underusing strengths and provides concrete examples of what happens when we do it. For example, creativity refers to thinking of new and perhaps better ways of doing things. When creativity is underused, it could result in our disinterest or boredom. When it is overused, it could be perceived as nosiness. In this therapeutic approach, strength discussions happen from the beginning and continue throughout the programme. Clients are encouraged to recognise their strengths and develop them in a way that serves them well.

Finally, the author presents a series of pilot studies conducted which show a symptom decrease in such conditions as depression and anxiety disorders, and it has been since applied to patients with psychotic disorders. The programme offers an excellent opportunity to help clients reduce symptoms of illbeing and develop life satisfaction, optimism, and other wellbeing indicators.

References

Rashid, T. (2015). Positive psychotherapy: A strength-based approach. *The Journal of Positive Psychology*, *10*(1), 25–40. https://doi-org.elib.tcd.ie/10.1080/17439760.2014.920411

Seligman, M. E. P., Rashid, T., & Parks, A. C. (2006). Positive psychotherapy. *American Psychologist*, *61*(8), 774–788. https://doi.org/10.1037/0003-066X.61.8.774

The role of mental health in recovery from mental illness

One of the most impactful studies in the mental health field that has stayed with me for years is a longitudinal research conducted by Felicia Huppert and Joyce Whittington from the University of Cambridge, UK (2003). This research, which involved over 6,000 participants, demonstrated that wellbeing and illbeing are distinct but interconnected constructs. Over 35% of the participants experienced an overlap between the constructs, indicating that they simultaneously reported mental health issues and high levels of wellbeing. This pioneering study was the first one to demonstrate the distinct nature of wellbeing resources, as studied in positive psychology, from illbeing symptoms, such as anxiety or depression. It demonstrated the need for separate measurements of both.

Since then, two studies have been published, taking this concept further. Matthew Iasiello et al. (2019) led the first one from the South Australian Health and Medical Research Institute. He explored data from the MIDUS longitudinal study of relatively healthy individuals and showed that those who maintained high levels of positive mental health over 10 years were 27.6 times more likely to recover from an affective disorder during this time, such as anxiety or depression, compared to those who did not develop high levels of positive mental health. Similarly, those who gained high levels of mental health disorder were 7.4 times more likely to recover from an affective disorder than those who did not report high levels of mental health.

Another study, led by Marijke Schotanus-Dijkstra et al. (2019) from the University of Twente, The Netherlands, which was published in the same year, further explored this topic. This research focused on individuals diagnosed with an affective disorder, such as anxiety, for at least 12 months. The researchers found that 19% of individuals with anxiety disorders were also flourishing psychologically, indicating that flourishing and mental disorders are independent of each other. This finding also highlighted the importance of positive mental health in recovery, as those with positive mental health recovered from anxiety at a faster rate than those without it.

Following these research findings, healthcare systems urgently need to integrate positive mental health into their therapeutic approaches. These research findings show that positive psychological resources are crucial for recovery from mental illness and for maintaining overall health. When individuals go to their doctors with mental health issues, they are usually given assessments for chronic stress, anxiety, or depression. In addition to diagnosing mental health disorders, these studies show that patients should also be assessed for the presence of their positive mental health. This comprehensive approach would not only help reduce illness but also enhance positive mental health, leading to a healthier population and reducing the burden of mental disorders.

References

Huppert, F. A., & Whittington, J. E. (2003). Evidence for the independence of positive and negative well-being: Implications for quality of life assessment. *British Journal of Health Psychology*, *8*(Pt 1), 107–122. https://doi.org/10.1348/135910703762879246

Iasiello, M., Van Agteren, J., Keyes, C. L., & Cochrane, E. M. (2019). Positive mental health as a predictor of recovery from mental illness. *Journal of Affective Disorders*, *251*, 227–230. https://doi.org/10.1016/j.jad.2019.03.065

Schotanus-Dijkstra, M., Keyes, C. L. M., de Graaf, R., & ten Have, M. (2019). Recovery from mood and anxiety disorders: The influence of positive mental health. *Journal of Affective Disorders*, *252*, 107–113. https://doi-org.elib.tcd.ie/10.1016/j.jad.2019.04.051

Wellbeing therapy

For a few years, I have guest-lectured in Ireland's most prominent college for psychotherapists. During this time, I have explored a range of therapies incorporating positive psychology and shared them with our students. The approach to wellbeing therapy created by Giovani Fava and Chiara Ruini (2003) from the University of Bologna, Italy, was our students' favourite. They were particularly drawn to its simplicity and how seamlessly it could be integrated into their practice. Developed by clinical psychologists well versed in psychiatric conditions, it offered them comfort that it did not oversell positive psychology in therapeutic practice.

The programme is based on Ryff's Psychological Wellbeing Model, which has six dimensions: autonomy, environmental mastery, personal growth, positive relations with others, purpose in life, and self-acceptance. The programme's objective differed from traditional therapeutic approaches, which tend to focus on reducing symptoms. Instead, the researchers aimed to foster participants' wellbeing and their psychological functioning. It addresses some of the residual symptoms of psychological disorders that clients experience after attending months of therapy, and which therapists often overlook. As long as the symptoms of the clinical condition subside, the client is usually ready to leave the therapy. However, wellbeing therapy focuses on giving participants skills to go beyond a symptom-free life. It is designed for those in remission and aims to help individuals move from being well to enhancing their resilience and life satisfaction.

One of the most valuable aspects of this article is a practical rubric for practitioners. It delves into each of the six dimensions of the Psychological Wellbeing Model, identifying observable symptoms of impaired or optimal levels. For instance, when individuals exhibit an impaired level of environmental mastery, they may struggle with managing their daily tasks. They may feel powerless to change their environment and fail to recognise opportunities for exerting control over their external world. In such cases, our goal is to help them regain a sense of mastery and competence in managing their surroundings. We aim to help them identify and act upon available opportunities or create contexts that allow them to live according to their personal values. This is just one example of how the six dimensions can be practically applied in therapy.

The wellbeing therapy is rooted in cognitive-behavioural approaches and has been rigorously tested with participants experiencing various clinical conditions, including depression, anxiety disorders, and psychosomatic illnesses. Based on a robust wellbeing model that has been extensively researched, therapists can be confident in its positive impact. With its solid foundation in research, this evidence-based approach is undoubtedly worth considering as a supplement to traditional therapy.

References

Fava, G. A., & Ruini, C. (2003). Development and characteristics of a well-being enhancing psychotherapeutic strategy: Well-being therapy. *Journal of Behavior Therapy and Experimental Psychiatry*, *34*(1), 45–63. https://doi-org.elib.tcd.ie/10.1016/S0005-7916(03)00019-3

Positive technology

The field of positive cyberpsychology

Over a decade ago, I received an email from Alessandra Kostic, a social psychologist from Hungary, telling me about the new book she was putting together about the novel perspectives on positive psychology applications. She asked me what topics future researchers should explore in more depth regarding wellbeing. After reflecting on it, I decided to propose combining positive psychology with cyberpsychology, suggesting the creation of a new field – *Positive Cyberpsychology*.

Cyberpsychology is a field of research exploring our behaviours and attitudes online. I began reading cyberpsychology during my PhD to explore the possibility of designing an online wellbeing programme. I was aware that apart from the content, I needed to consider how the technology we are using and how we design it need to be adequate. As I explored this topic in more depth, I realised how little we knew at the time about this topic. I have also become aware of how negative the narrative about technological impact on our wellbeing was. This is why I decided that a chapter I will write for Kostic will be focused on raising people's awareness about the need for positive cyberpsychology (Burke, 2021).

Fast-forward a few years, and a new article on Positive Cyberpsychology was submitted to the *Frontiers in Psychology* journal. To my surprise, Pawel Fortuna (2023), an academic in Poland, had independently written on the same topic. It was a moment of serendipity when one of the reviewers brought my chapter to his attention. This unexpected connection across Europe highlighted the need for exploring this exciting field of research.

Fortuna's perspective was that a new sub-field within Cyberpsychology should be created, one that focuses specifically on exploring the impact of technology on human wellbeing. This new field would not only examine the "dark side" of technology but also its "bright side", encouraging psychologists to engage in a meaningful debate about the future of optimal human functioning within a cyber world.

While the field of positive cyberpsychology is growing, it has yet to progress at the same speed as technological advancements. Much more research is needed over the next decade to fully understand this area from a psychological standpoint. The deeper our understanding, the more effectively we can influence the impact of technology on human wellness.

References

Burke, J. (2021). Positive cyberpsychology: A conceptual framework. In A. Kostić & D. Chadee (Eds.), *Positive psychology: An international perspective* (pp. 85–101). Wiley Blackwell.

Fortuna, P. (2023). Positive cyberpsychology as a field of study of the well-being of people interacting with and via technology. *Frontiers in Psychology*, *14*, 1053482. https://doi.org/10.3389/fpsyg.2023.1053482

Positive technology

In his book *The Anxious Generation*, Jonathan Haidt presents the use of technology, especially in the context of young people impacted by the explosion of social networking sites in the early 2000s, as the most significant social experiment of our times. Would you enrol your child in an experiment you knew nothing about? You wouldn't know what it involved, you wouldn't know whether or not it adversely impacted your child, and you wouldn't know to what extent your child would be harmed by it. This is precisely what has been happening in the last 20 years, and slowly, we are seeing the impact of this experiment on young people.

Learning from some of the mistakes made in recent years, increasingly more technology designers are asking themselves how to improve end-users' experience. During one of the regional positive psychology conferences, a colleague posed an intriguing question: "Certain foods are labelled with quality stamps, would you like to see a quality rating for how much technology enhances your wellbeing and supports your positive functioning?" This question is the quintessence of the paper by Riva, who explores how technology can be designed not only for efficiency but also with a focus on enhancing wellbeing and positive functioning.

They have introduced the term "Positive Technology" to explain a scientific approach and practical applications of how technology could promote the quality of human experience. Positive Technology is essentially about designing and using technology to enhance our wellbeing and positive functioning. This could be done by structuring technology to assist in doing it, augmenting it, and, in some cases, replacing it if it does not improve positive outcomes. They connected positive psychology with information and communications technology (ICT) through some of the existing models to promote wellbeing, that is, by focusing on the emotional quality of technology, engagement, and connectedness.

Emotional quality reflected components such as emotional arousal of valence when using technology such as smartphones. This, in turn, led to influencing people at a hedonic level, further linking the use of technology with the theory of the Broaden and Build model of positive emotions (Fredrickson, 2001). The Broaden and Build model of positive emotions is a theory in positive psychology that suggests that positive emotions broaden an individual's momentary thought-action repertoire, which in turn can build their personal resources. This, in turn, was all related to such ICT topics as affective computing, emotional design, or engineering aesthetics.

Engagement is related to the extent to which technology challenges users and allows them to use their skills. This was linked with eudaemonic wellbeing and theories such as flow (Csikszentmihalyi et al., 2005) or Transformation of Flow (Della Fave, 2006). The Transformation of Flow theory is an extension of Csikszentmihalyi's original concept of flow, which suggests that flow experiences can lead to personal growth and development. The ICT topics relating to this dimension were persuasive computing, serious gaming, e-heath, and virtual reality therapy.

Finally, the connected aspect of technology is not to be overlooked. It relates to the social aspects of technology, drawing from theories such as social capital (Coleman, 1998). This dimension of technology impacts individuals on a social and interpersonal level, encouraging end users to connect with others through technology. The ICT topics relating to this dimension are social networks, social presence, and simulations, all of which foster a sense of connection and engagement.

The authors argue that technology and software designers can promote adaptive behaviours and positive functioning through technology. This would involve conscious engagement in design and tweaking it if needed to improve the impact of technology on users' wellbeing. This is how technology can not only harm, as illustrated by Jonathan Haidt, but also support people.

References

Coleman, J.S. (1998). Social Capital in the Creation of Human Capital. *American Journal of Sociology (Supplement)*, *94*, S95–S120. http://dx.doi.org/10.1086/228943

Csikszentmihalyi, M., Abuhamdeh, S., & Nakamura, J. (2005). Flow. In A. J. Elliot & C. S. Dweck (Eds.), *Handbook of competence and motivation* (pp. 598–608). Guilford Publications.

Delle Fave, A. (2006). The Impact of Subjective Experience on the Quality of Life: A Central Issue for Health Professionals. In M. Csikszentmihalyi & I. S. Csikszentmihalyi (Eds.), *A life worth living: Contributions to positive psychology* (pp. 165–181). Oxford University Press.

Fredrickson, B. L. (2001). The role of positive emotions in positive psychology: The broaden-and-build theory of positive emotions. *American Psychologist, 56*(3), 218–226. https://doi.org/10.1037/0003-066X.56.3.218

Riva, G., Baños, R. M., Botella, C., Wiederhold, B. K., & Gaggioli, A. (2012). Positive technology: Using interactive technologies to promote positive functioning. *Cyberpsychology, Behavior and Social Networking, 15*(2), 69–77. https://doi.org/10.1089/cyber.2011.0139

Positive education

Positive education

One of the first articles published about "Positive Education" was written by David Shernoff from Rutgers University, USA. Shernoff advocated for the use of the science of positive psychology in education, particularly in the context of STEM (science, technology, engineering, maths) education. He was particularly interested in how the concept of "flow", a state of complete absorption and involvement in an activity, could support STEM education. However, the article that gained popularity as one of the first on positive education was published by Martin Seligman and colleagues, who shared their insights on the integration of positive psychology and education.

The authors proposed a transformative shift in education, advocating for the integration of positive psychology to prioritise students' wellbeing over the traditional focus on achievement and cognitive skill development. They argued that positive psychology, when applied in the classroom, could significantly enhance both student wellbeing and academic performance. By fostering positive emotions, resilience, gratitude, and social skills, educators could pave the way for a more holistic and effective approach to student development.

It also encourages educators to embrace a range of classroom interventions such as teaching students about optimism, gratitude, mindfulness, and goal setting. For instance, teaching students about optimism can help them develop a positive outlook on challenges, while practising gratitude can enhance their emotional resilience. These interventions can become the foundation for student wellbeing. The authors highlighted the crucial role of teachers in implementing wellbeing. Years later, an article was published showing that the interventions implemented by teachers were more effective than those from outside the school. So many of the ideas presented in this early paper were later confirmed to be true.

Most importantly, however, reflecting on where we have come from since this article was published almost 20 years ago is exciting. We now focus on wellbeing in schools, with governments prioritising student wellbeing funding. Frameworks have been created that include some of the wellbeing concepts mentioned in this article and many more that have been developed since. It is lovely to read this paper from a perspective of years later to see how the vision of a few people turned into a reality.

References

Seligman, M. E. P., Ernst, R. M., Gillham, J., Reivich, K., & Linkins, M. (2009). Positive education: Positive psychology and classroom interventions. *Oxford Review of Education*, *35*(3), 293–311. https://doi.org/10.1080/03054980902934563

Shernoff, D. J. (2001). Towards a Positive Education for Adolescents: An Example from the Humanities. *NAMTA Journal*, *26*(3), 517–541.

SEARCH meta-framework

I recently visited the National Gallery in London, a place I used to visit once a week when I lived there, often to explore one or a few paintings in more detail. Art historians would guide us through various pieces, and I enjoyed their insights. The National Gallery has been a significant resource for me, providing a wealth of information and inspiration. Finding my way around it was usually straightforward because all the artwork is organised into different centuries. They are further organised into art styles, which are further organised into artists. If you compare the national gallery to how research works, the different centuries are like meta-frameworks that combine several art styles or theories within them.

SEARCH, a data-driven meta-framework for positive education, is an important tool in the field of education research. Its objective was to explore the literature, organise research on positive education interventions, and offer future directions to academics and practitioners. This task was vital as it helped schools explore the bigger picture of effective interventions delivered in schools.

The process began with a bibliographic search (see Rusk & Waters, 2015) that identified preliminary themes. This was followed by an action research project with ten schools, which identified three changes to the framework. Feedback from teachers, students, and administrators was crucial to this process. Subsequently, a further systematic literature review was conducted to identify the evidence that the selected dimensions improved wellbeing, school-based outcomes, and pathways for targeting them. The evidence-based nature of our interventions provides a solid foundation for their effectiveness.

The final meta-model, a culmination of our research, comprises six practical pathways for improving wellbeing in schools. These pathways are not just theoretical constructs but actionable strategies that can be implemented in educational settings.

1. **Strengths** are preexisting qualities that feel natural and are intrinsically motivating. Interventions that fall under this category include creating strength awareness, strength-use interventions, and strength-spotting interventions.
2. **Emotional management** refers to identifying and understanding emotions and managing them effectively. It also includes understanding the link between

emotions, thoughts, and behaviour. The types of interventions that fit into this category are emotional intelligence interventions that teach children how to recognise emotions in themselves and others and regulate them effectively. Also, gratitude interventions help students notice what is good in their lives.

3. **Attention** and awareness are about the ability to focus on either internal (e.g. own thoughts) or external (e.g. the teacher) stimuli while they occur. Meditation and mindfulness interventions fall into this category of pathways.
4. **Relationships** relate to the ability to build and maintain relationships and to use momentary social interactions to their full capacity. Mentoring interventions provide support on how to enhance one's sense of connectedness with others.
5. **Coping** relates to changing thoughts and behaviours to manage external (e.g. demands) and internal (e.g. overwhelming thoughts) challenges. Coping interventions change students' thoughts, emotions, and behaviour in the face of stressful situations to make them more effective. Resilience interventions support young people in developing the ability to maintain their mental health or recover following life challenges. These two types of interventions fall into the category of coping pathways.
6. **Habits and goals** – habits are patterns of behaviour and decision-making, whereas goals are goalposts that individuals aim to achieve. This pathway includes self-regulated learning interventions that develop self-evaluation, self-monitoring, goal setting, strategy planning, and monitoring fall into this category; and interventions for setting goals are also included in it.

This framework is a goldmine for practitioners. It is not prescriptive. Therefore, it offers educators, consultants, or other professionals interested in delivering well-being interventions for young people the freedom to customise the most applicable activities to the students' interests and needs. It offers flexibility, creativity in designing resources, and guidance in their direction. At the same time, it is essential to note that this framework is based on existing research and who knows what future interventions and approaches will bring.

References

Rusk, R. D., & Waters, L. (2015). A psycho-social system approach to well-being: Empirically deriving the five domains of positive functioning. *The Journal of Positive Psychology, 10*(2), 141–152. https://doi.org/10.1080/17439760.2014.920409

Waters, L., & Loton, D. (2019). Search: A meta-framework and review of the field of positive education. *International Journal of Applied Positive Psychology*, *4*, 1–46. https://doi.org/10.1007/s41042-019-00017-4

Growth in positive education over a century

I used to love going to school. For the first 3 years of my primary school, I had a wonderful teacher who lit a fire in my belly for education. She had almost 40 pupils in her classroom, yet I always felt like she "saw" me. She used to give us different levels of homework based on our interests. The basic level was for everyone, and the extra homework was for those who really enjoyed learning. I did my extra homework every day.

Roll on 40 years, I'm a lecturer at the Maynooth University Department of Education. I'm standing in front of 100+ students, all teachers and principals, discussing Positive Education. One school principal raises his hand and asks "is this not just education"? In his mind, my experience of primary school was the experience of all children. But it was not the case. Many children did not enjoy their homework; they did not thrive at school and some simply hated it. The question is, what can we, as educators, do to make education positive? This is our responsibility and we have the power to make a difference.

Was education "positive" before or is a recent phenomenon? Lea Waters and Daniel Loton traced back the growth of the Positive Education field. They explored the literature spanning over 100 years. The researchers used human and computerised approaches to review 74,496 academic papers. From the beginning, approximately 5% of articles published in educational research pertained to positive education. However, with the launch of the "positive education" field, the proportion of articles increased to 7% by 2013. While most research participants were from secondary (33%) and third-level education (36%), only 23% were from primary school and 7% from early learning.

The types of topics discussed in academic papers have decreased in volume since the launch of the positive education field related to performance, control, and achievement. The four new topics that have emerged in the top 20 topics in positive education were wellbeing, satisfaction, motivation, and engagement. Further, three topics that ranked significantly higher were emotion, health, and goals. Finally, a thematic analysis of all the quantitative research that emerged in this area highlighted nine themes. Well-being, strengths, connection, identity and personality, and school climate were of particular interest.

What does it all mean for practitioners? Firstly, positive education is not just education; its objective is different. The types of topics discussed in both vary. At the same time, it is heartening to know that positive psychology did impact the field of education by increasing the volume of research and changing the research trajectory. Significantly more research is published on topics that were not explored before, and more importantly, the researchers go deeper into such concepts as emotions, wellbeing, and health, which means that we are setting up a foundation for hopefully bringing up healthier children.

At the same time, the hard part to hear is the disregard of the early learning field within positive education research. Despite the children being in their formative years, characterised by the fastest neurobiological development, they are being ignored. This is the time to help them embrace the concepts of positive health; this is the time that could make the most difference; this is the time that we need to spend time with children to help them shape their positive future. More research is undoubtedly required to figure out how to do it best.

References

Waters, L., & Loton, D. (2021). Tracing the growth, gaps, and characteristics in positive education science: A long-term, large-scale review of the field. *Frontiers in Psychology, 12*. https://doi-org.elib.tcd.ie/10.3389/fpsyg.2021.774967

School-based interventions

We have a widely known wellbeing programme in Ireland that has yet to be empirically evaluated. The creators claim that they have done research but have not published it. My heart breaks when I see that wellbeing interventions are created and rolled out in schools without prior evaluation. It is like we are experimenting with children without their consent, and we don't even know how much these interventions may harm them. Just because our wellbeing programme's content relates to positive psychology, it does not mean it will improve their wellbeing. Over the years, I have read many studies demonstrating that wellbeing programmes caused children stress, did not demonstrate any improvement in wellbeing, or children found them so boring that they developed an aversion to wellbeing practice. How can we help children develop lifelong self-care practices when we are essentially shooting in the dark?

To shed light on this, Lea Waters from the University of Melbourne has reviewed the literature about positive psychology interventions that can be used in school. She explored the evidence behind each one of them. They cultivated such qualities in students as hope, gratitude, serenity, resilience, and character strengths. She has also encouraged educators to research the most effective implementation of interventions, such as frameworks developed to roll out positive psychology in schools or ensure that change is school-wide. She also highlighted that the school system plays an essential role in improving the wellbeing of students; therefore, the best change runs deep.

A team led by Claudia Tejada-Gallardo from the Universitat de Lleida Avinguda de l'estudi General, Spain, conducted a meta-analysis of a review of multicomponent interventions delivered with adolescents. These included programmes that ranged from 6 to 30 weeks. All of them had a control group, meaning they could pinpoint changes in wellbeing that occurred naturally in the school population. Their analysis showed that, on average, these interventions have improved young people's short- and long-term mental health, although the effect of the improvement ranged from minor to moderate.

Interestingly, the researchers explored some key factors that influenced the effectiveness of the intervention. For example, they found that the recent publications showed more effective interventions, meaning that researchers and practitioners have learnt how to improve the delivery of wellbeing programmes. Also, combining positive psychology interventions with other interventions has positively impacted young people's wellbeing. Over the years, many different psycho-social approaches have been developed to improve students' wellbeing or reduce their anxiety. Incorporating these can be useful for developing a more robust programme.

References

Tejada-Gallardo, C., Blasco-Belled, A., Torrelles-Nadal, C., & Alsinet, C. (2020). Effects of school-based multicomponent positive psychology interventions on well-being and distress in adolescents: A systematic review and meta-analysis. *Journal of Youth and Adolescence*, *49*(10), 1943–1960. https://doi-org.elib.tcd.ie/10.1007/s10964-020-01289-9

Waters, L. (2011). A review of school-based positive psychology interventions. *The Australian Educational and Developmental Psychologist*, *28*(2), 75–90. https://doi.org/10.1375/aedp.28.2.75

Flourishing classroom

One of my PhD scholars, Paul O'Donovan, has explored the concept of flourishing schools. We have had several discussions about what it means for a school to flourish. Is it based on the relationship colleagues have with each other, or does it relate to the success of student performance? While we've had many theories, we could not find a clear answer to address this question. The same challenge exists in the context of flourishing classrooms. This is why a team of researchers from the University of Melbourne led by Laura Allison et al. (2022) designed a study that focused on developing the *Flourishing Classroom System Observation Framework and Rubric*. It aimed to assess and promote wellbeing within the classroom environments. The study identified key elements and indicators of a flourishing classroom using the Delphi method, which is a structured, iterative process involving expert consensus.

The framework included the following dimensions:

Positive relationships: Exploration of the quality of interactions between students, teachers, and peers

Engagement and motivation: Exploration of the student involvement in the classroom and their enthusiasm for learning

Supportive environment: An exploration of the classroom climate, which included students' perception of emotional safety, and feeling included and respected by others

Purpose and meaning: Exploration of the school provides opportunities for students to find their meaning and make their learning relevant to them

Wellbeing promotion: An exploration of activities and practices that are designed to enhance psychological and emotional wellbeing

In addition to the framework, a rubric has been developed that helps schools assess each dimension. It provides specific observable behaviours and practices across all dimensions and a scoring system that allows schools to assess to what extent the classroom provides an adequate environment for students to flourish.

This framework and rubric is a practical tool that educators can use worldwide. It could guide classroom practice and support teacher-student relationships. Moreover, it is an excellent professional development tool, especially for new teachers who wish to help their students flourish. Given that it is a data-driven improvement tool, it could also be used by school principals to support school-wide wellbeing initiatives and monitor the process of creating flourishing schools.

References

Allison, L., Kern, M. L., Jarden, A., & Waters, L. (2022). Development of the flourishing classroom system observation framework and rubric: A Delphi study. *Contemporary School Psychology*. Advance online publication. https://doi.org/10.1007/s40688-022-00423-7

Workplace positive psychology

The what, how, and why of employee wellbeing

I have recently chatted with one of my English colleagues who half-jokingly said, "Do not talk to me about workplace wellbeing – it makes me mad!". Intrigued by her reaction, I asked her to elaborate. She explained that with all their good intentions, her organisation introduced an obligatory wellbeing assessment at the end of each week. All employees must reflect on their past week, rate their wellbeing on a scale from poor to excellent, explain their score, and elaborate on what they could have done differently. The idea is interesting, although not quite following the research recommendations, according to which reflecting on "why" we are happy can reduce our wellbeing. However, what frustrates my colleague even more is what happens next. Employees who do not complete it are pestered daily with reminders. Also, the results are forwarded to the HR team, which reviews them and contacts the line manager if the team's scores are low. The HR team then works with the line manager to address their team's wellbeing, and they must report their progress to HR. So, what was intended as a reflective, self-motivating tool to improve wellbeing became a beating stick for all staff involved? This example highlights how an organisation could have good intentions about supporting their staff's wellbeing but could also quickly get it wrong. Let us look at some articles that help us understand why and how we could implement it.

The article by Katherine Page and Dianne Vella-Brodrick (2009) explores the "what", "why", and "how" of wellbeing at work, which could be very useful for organisations such as my colleagues. It delves into the two main models of wellbeing, Subjective Wellbeing and Psychological Wellbeing, to establish the "what" of wellbeing. It introduces the "workplace wellbeing" concept, encompassing job satisfaction and work-related effects. Job satisfaction, a key component, spills over into other areas of life, including work-related satisfaction. It measures employee content with various aspects of their job, such as job security, recognition, work environment, and compensation. On the other hand, the work-related effect is the balance of positive and negative emotions experienced at work.

In relation to the *why*, they delve into a range of research that goes beyond doing wellbeing programmes to improve employees' benefits, but research that considers additional benefits for employers to have employees who are well. Some of the reasons proposed included better job satisfaction that leads to employee retention and increased performance of employees for employees with higher levels of wellbeing. Moreover, when employees experience psychological languishing, they are more likely to report distress and absenteeism at work. So, if organisations look after their employees' wellbeing, it will benefit not only their team members but also they could receive a financial return on investment.

The article explores the " 'how' of wellbeing, examining" a range of frameworks that can be used to introduce wellbeing at work. These frameworks, such as Gallup and VIA character strengths, offer practical strategies for increasing engagement.

Given that only a small portion of employees are fully engaged in their work, these frameworks allow many organisations to re-engage their employees. This concept has been previously explored in an article led by Lucy Hone et al. (2015), which found that employees with high awareness of their strengths were 9 times more likely to flourish compared to those who didn't. Those who used their strengths regularly at work were 18 times more likely to flourish than those who did not. These studies highlight the importance of using strengths at work as a pathway for workplace wellbeing, engagement, and performance.

Many years ago, I had a client to whom I wanted to apply this concept. He came to me because he wanted to quit his job and figure out what to do afterwards. However, when we started to discuss his strengths, he realised that he had yet to use any of his signature strengths at work. I remembered a study by Claudia Harzer and Willibald Ruch from the University of Zurich showing that using 4–7 character strengths are associated with perceiving one's job as a calling. Another study a few years later showed that encouraging people to use 4+ signature strengths at work increased their calling. Having read these articles, I decided to help the client by focusing on his strength development at work. We worked together for only a few weeks, and he managed to do this. Then, 2 years later, we were in touch, and he was still in the same job, except enjoying it much more. This is how these simple interventions can help clients grow.

References

Harzer, C., & Ruch, W. (2012). When the job is a calling: The role of applying one's signature strengths at work. *The Journal of Positive Psychology*, *7*(5), 362–371. https://doi.org/10.1080/17439760.2012.702784

Harzer, C., & Ruch, W. (2016). Your strengths are calling: Preliminary results of a web-based strengths intervention to increase calling. *Journal of Happiness Studies: An Interdisciplinary Forum on Subjective Well-Being*, *17*(6), 2237–2256. https://doi.org/10.1007/s10902-015-9692-y

Hone, L. C., Jarden, A., Duncan, S., & Schofield, G. M. (2015). Flourishing in New Zealand workers: Associations with lifestyle behaviors, physical health, psychosocial, and work-related indicators. *Journal of Occupational and Environmental Medicine*, *57*(9), 973–983. https://doi.org/10.1097/JOM.0000000000000508

Page, K. M., & Vella-Brodrick, D. A. (2009). The 'what', 'why' and 'how' of employee well-being: A new model. *Social Indicators Research*, *90*(3), 441–458. https://doi.org/10.1007/s11205-008-9270-3

Positive psychology interventions at work

Wellbeing at work programmes are everywhere, but a recent meta-analytical study by William Fleming from the University of Oxford, UK, examined the impact of resilience training, mindfulness training, and wellbeing apps in 233 UK organisations with 46,336 employees, and found that these interventions, on average, do not enhance employees' wellbeing as assessed by a range of self-report measures. More significantly, they do not increase the resources to a degree that they would compensate for employees' poor wellbeing. It's worth noting that the interventions

Fleming reviewed included a wide range of wellbeing strategies, such as time management courses, which extend beyond what positive psychologists typically define as wellbeing.

Another systematic review, led by Scott Donaldson from Rutgers Robert Wood Johnson Medical School, USA, revealed a glimmer of hope. The team's findings showed small to moderate improvements in work outcomes, particularly in reducing undesirable outcomes such as job-related experiences of negative emotions, job-related stress, emotional exhaustion, supervisor incivility, turnover intent, or anger. The desirable outcomes, including job performance, job-related experiences of positive emotions, organisation-based self-esteem, workplace trust, and calling, were all positively impacted using positive psychology interventions. This suggests that there is potential for these interventions to significantly improve workplace wellbeing.

These results highlight the urgent need for a paradigm shift in how we approach workplace wellbeing. Research consistently shows that individuals need intrinsic motivation to engage in wellbeing interventions for the best results. By creating organisational solutions and forcing employees to attend them, we inadvertently step into an employee's personal area that might be simply none of our business. The employees need to want to attend a programme, rather than be forced to do it. Perhaps an organisation should not reinforce the personal wellbeing of an employee. An organisation's role is to create an environment where the employees can thrive naturally and offer nudge interventions and programmes that encourage wellbeing rather than top-down programmes that force them to engage in meditation or other practices for which they might not be ready. All this is sometimes done for the benefit of an organisation to demonstrate that they support employees' wellbeing, rather than the employees themselves. A workplace environment is sometimes not where employees can freely open up about their wellbeing struggles, due to the potential impact of their openness on career opportunities in the future. More importantly, forcing employees to attend wellbeing programmes could slow down or even prevent their process of wellbeing improvement. We have yet to develop the best way to support employees' health and wellbeing in the workplace, but these findings should inspire us to continue searching for more effective strategies.

References

Donaldson, S. I., Lee, J. Y., & Donaldson, S. I. (2019). Evaluating positive psychology interventions at work: A systematic review and meta-analysis. *International Journal of Applied Positive Psychology*, *4*, 113–134. https://doi.org/10.1007/s41042-019-00021-8

Fleming, W. J. (2024). Employee well-being outcomes from individual-level mental health interventions: Cross-sectional evidence from the United Kingdom. *Industrial Relations Journal*, *55*(2), 162–182. https://doi.org/10.1111/irj.12418

Job crafting

When I was 25, I joined an organisation in a managerial position, but my role was made redundant within 3 months. Instead, I was offered a better position with higher salary and expanded responsibilities. Even though I embraced the change, after two years, I realised it was not the right fit for me. However, the experience allowed me to realise precisely what I wanted from my next job. I brought my perfect job "wish" list to a recruitment agent. After I finished describing my dream job, he laughed and told me that such a job did not exist. Three months later, he called me to say he found a position that might interest me.

It wasn't quite what I wanted, but I went with a flow.

I spent the first month in my new job learning about the organisation's needs and expectations. Then, I developed a strategy for best contributing to their goals. The management loved my plan, and 3 months later, when reviewing my original "wish" list, I realised that my new job had become my "dream" job. Even though the exact position I wanted did not exist, I crafted what was there to align it with my strengths. I was happy, and my employer was happy, too.

My experience is precisely what job crafting looks like. The concept was first introduced by Amy Wrzesniewski from the University of Pennsylvania and Jane Dutton from the University of Michigan Ross. They argue that employees can change certain aspects of their job that will allow them to tap into their motivation. There are three changes they can make, which relate to:

1. Tasks or duties that can be modified include the scope of tasks, reordering tasks, and altering how the tasks or duties are performed.
2. Relational modifications mean that the nature of a relationship with coworkers, clients, or others associated with the workplace could be altered. For example, an employee could expand their social network at work or deepen their relationship with existing colleagues.
3. Cognitive modification relates to changing how employees think about their jobs. This may include reflecting on the meaning of their work, beginning to consider work more significant than before, or focusing on parts of the job that provide more job satisfaction.

The authors argue that these changes do not only occur at an individual level but become part of an organisational structure. It could be a process an organisation encourages as part of the procedure. Given that the authors introduced this idea in 2001, it was incredibly innovative back then. Since then, a lot of research has been conducted that demonstrated a link between job crafting, wellbeing, and performance. It is significantly more embraced and practised nowadays.

References

Wrzesniewski, A., & Dutton, J. E. (2001). Crafting a job: Revisioning employees as active crafters of their work. *Academy of Management Review*, *25*, 179–201.

Positive leadership self-structure

I have coached leaders for many years. They ranged from junior leaders to CEOs. When we began working together, I saw leaders' capacity for depth and growth. Some leaders, however, were content with who they were, even when others had issues with their behaviour, expecting the world around them to adjust instead. Others were eager to change at a cognitive level, but we often hit a barrier that made the process of change difficult. Then, some embraced the change. They jumped with both feet into the messy intrapersonal world and were open and proactive in making all the adjustments needed to become the best leaders they could be. The article by Sean Hannah from Durham University, UK, and colleagues explores this concept further.

The researchers have expanded on the theory of positive leadership by exploring the role of a leader in developing a multifaceted structure of self. They argue that unless this happens, they will not be able to fully influence followers when dealing with complex situations in the workplace. These complex situations are part of leaders' lives. They perform a multitude of duties ranging from driving the organisational goals through to supporting individuals on their teams, dealing with uncertainty of the future, ambiguity, conflicting interests of a range of stakeholders, dynamic changes within the organisation and beyond, dealing with multiple departments at the same time, or balancing the personal value and organisational behaviours. All these tricky situations need leaders who can flex their style, tap into what is best in them and others, and then do what is right. Therefore, the authors have developed a model that addresses the leaders' self-structure needed to accomplish this.

It comprises four components:

Self-complexity: An ability for leaders to embrace a diverse range of self-aspects that enables them to be flexible across different contexts

Identity integration: Balancing leaders' values with situational demands in a way that feels authentic to them

Adaptive capacity: Leaders' capacity to navigate change and uncertainty

Positive outcomes: A leader's ability to be resilient, follow ethical guidelines, and engage with followers in a way that benefits them and the organisation

This model can be a useful approach for coaches and mentors to guide new and existing leaders in their development. The skills they gain will serve them as a basis for long-term growth and a foundation for becoming positive leaders.

References

Hannah, S. T., Woolfolk, R. L., & Lord, R. G. (2009). Leader self-structure: A framework for positive leadership. *Journal of Organizational Behavior: The International Journal of Industrial, Occupational and Organizational Psychology and Behavior*, *30*(2), 269–290.

Positive healthy organisations

A few years ago, I was involved in co-writing a book about Positive Leadership, and to prepare for it, I delved deeply into the literature around healthy leaders. An approach I enjoyed involved Aaron Antonovsky's Salutogenesis Theory from the 1970s, which focuses on understanding the origins of health. Recently, it was revived in the leadership literature, especially by German researchers, bringing together the idea of healthy leadership as a foundation for healthy organisations. Part of the model I wrote about in that book explored how healthy leaders look after their health, promote and reinforce healthy policies within an organisation, and enact them in their daily interactions with all stakeholders. After all, what is the point of creating health and wellbeing initiatives and policies and telling people to mind their health when balancing their work life with personal life and then piling up a lot of work on them, so that they work over the weekend to catch up on it? Annamaria Di Fabio from the University of Florence, Italy, in this article, explores why and how organisations can promote health and wellbeing.

The article advocates for the use of positive psychology as a means not only to mitigate negative aspects of wellness, such as stress or burnout, but also to foster the adoption of positive psychological concepts within organisations. The author primarily focuses on two such concepts, namely meaningfulness and psychological wellbeing. She provides practical examples of how these two domains can enhance employees' health and wellbeing and contribute to achieving organisational objectives and improving employees' performance.

The article combines research on positive health in organisations, blending positive psychology and organisational scholarship. It underscores that organisational sustainability should encompass not only environmental sustainability but also the sustainability of an organisational culture promoting employees' long-term health. This article is inspirational and crucial for any consultants reading it. It deepens our understanding of the need to prioritise employees' health and provides a solid foundation for further exploration. Its importance is undeniable, and it calls for our full engagement and commitment.

This article makes me think of an organisation as a tree. When the tree's roots are stable, they can weather storms and keep growing. Similarly, an organisation that invests in its employees and provides a solid long-term strategy for employees' health will create a culture that will sustain it regardless of the stormy weather of any political or social system. Just as roots nourish the tree, organisational policies and practices that support their employee's health and wellbeing can help the organisation survive and thrive.

References

Di Fabio, A. (2017). Positive healthy organizations: Promoting well-being, meaningfulness, and sustainability in organizations. *Frontiers in Psychology*, *8*, 1938. https://doi.org/10.3389/fpsyg.2017.01938

Psychological safety

Lucy Airs is one of my PhD scholars at the RCSI University of Medicine and Health Sciences. She is also a consultant in positive psychology and a coach working with leaders worldwide. When she came to me first with her project idea,

I hadn't considered psychological safety in the context of wellbeing programmes in the workplace. However, our discussions over the years have changed my mind. In her practice, Lucy noticed that sometimes, when she delivered positive psychology coaching or training to teams, it significantly improved the team's wellbeing. Other times, the improvement was modest. She tried to figure out why there were differences, and this is when she realised that it seemed to have stemmed from the level of the team's psychological safety. When their safety was high, their wellbeing soared after an intervention; when it was low, they were less open to and didn't trust in the benevolence of the intervention. Most importantly, their psychological safety seemed to be a barrier to impactful positive change. This is the area she is currently exploring as part of her PhD. Lucy's results of the study will be emerging soon. In the meantime, I wonder if psychological safety could be why some wellbeing programmes at work do not work. Could it be a missing link?

In her seminal work, Amy Edmondson (1999) from the Harvard Business School, USA, defined psychological safety as a shared belief that the team are safe to take interpersonal risks, such as speaking up without the fear of embarrassment, rejection, or punishment. When team members do not have psychological safety, they are hesitant to voice their opinions. Psychological safety is not about creating conflict but designing a work environment where people feel comfortable showing their authentic selves. It's about creating a culture where individuals feel safe to take risks, ask questions, and express their concerns without fear of retribution.

Following on from the original article, an abundance of studies was published to understand psychological safety and explore its impact on a range of outcomes. Edmondson and Bransby (2023) have recently reviewed over 190 studies, and their bibliometric analysis showed that the most common impact of psychological safety studied related to performance and the extent to which employees get things done. This was followed by the impact of psychological safety on fostering learning behaviours, improving the work experience and then, leaders and leadership in the context of creating psychological safety for their staff. The benefits of psychological safety in the workplace are numerous, including improved performance, enhanced learning, and a more positive work experience.

From this review, three leader behaviours emerged as facilitating their team's psychological safety: listening (paying attention to team members, comprehension, and having good intentions towards the speaker), competence (showing individual capability in performing their job), and transparency (sharing relevant information and being open to feedback). So, Lucy might be onto something very important. If, indeed, the research shows a link between the effectiveness of workplace wellbeing programmes and psychological safety, we can design a range of interventions that could be used to support the assimilation of wellbeing knowledge and skills.

References

Edmondson, A. (1999). Psychological safety and learning behavior in work teams. *Administrative Science Quarterly*, *44*(2), 350–383. https://doi-org.elib.tcd.ie/10.2307/2666999

Edmondson, A. C., & Bransby, D. P. (2023). Psychological safety comes of age: Observed themes in an established literature. *Annual Review of Organizational Psychology and Organizational Behavior*, *10*(1), 55–78.

Wellbeing arts

The role of arts and humanities in flourishing

When completing my PhD at Trinity College Dublin, Ireland, my office was right next door to the National Gallery. For three wonderful years, I would escape into the world of art whenever I needed a break from research, reading or writing. Sometimes, it was just a flying visit to sit and look at my favourite paintings for five minutes and relax. Other times, it was a more immersive experience involving an exciting talk or an exhibition. For the Irish, the arts were an important outlet through generations of struggle. Music, literature, paintings, and other forms of expression allowed them to share their hardships, hopes, and preserve their culture, even among those who have immigrated due to the political or economic situation. The article, led by Louis Tay et al. (2017) from Purdue University, USA, explores the contribution of the arts to human flourishing and offers a conceptual model as a pathway for wellbeing.

The authors begin by expressing concern over the devaluation of humanities over STEM education and highlighting the need for humanities in our lives. They explore some existing research showing the positive impact of humanities on well-being and they present a model according to which people engage with arts through modes of engagement or activities of involvement. **Modes of engagement** include creating something, performing, studying, consuming something, or critiquing a particular piece of work. **The involvement activities** are ways individuals get involved in the arts and humanities. This may include reading, writing, listening to sounds, watching something such as a film, analysing arts, acting, dancing, painting a mural or graffiti, singing songs, playing a musical instrument, and similar.

The mechanisms through which these engagement methods can lead to increased wellbeing are immersion, embeddedness, socialisation, and reflectiveness. Immersion refers to capturing attention and experiencing humanities using various senses. Embeddedness describes the socio-cognitive psychological process that maximises wellbeing through humanities. It is the process of developing new perspectives, habits, or skills associated with humanities. Socialisation refers to the individuals taking on new roles or identities within the community to enrich other people's lives. Reflectiveness is a process that results in abandoning some beliefs or aspects of ourselves through the involvement of arts and humanities. This whole process improves human flourishing outcomes such as physiological wellbeing, psychological competencies, self-efficacy, general wellbeing improvement, or development of character strengths.

Let me illustrate this process using dance as an example. I went to a burlesque dance class a decade ago, which was a lot of fun. My mode of engagement was immersion in the activities that led to a boost of confidence. My involvement activity was socialisation, which allowed me to meet many other people who did it for fun and even took part in an annual performance. We connected deeper and even began arranging social activities with the burlesque group. The whole experience led me to a boost of wellbeing for many months during my involvement in the burlesque community in Dublin.

References

Tay, L., Pawelski, J. O., & Keith, M. G. (2017). The role of the arts and humanities in human flourishing: A conceptual model. *The Journal of Positive Psychology*, *13*(3), 215–225. https://doi.org/10.1080/17439760.2017.1279207

Photography

While Martin Seligman spent decades developing the field of positive psychology, his wife Mandy has practised it through her love of photography. Her latest venture, *Seeing Happy*, a non-profit platform that aims to foster resilience and wellbeing through the joy of art and photography, made her realise how important arts could be for facilitating flourishing. This also connected her and Andrea Giraldez-Hayes from the University of Cambridge to explore the new subfield of positive psychology, Wellbeing Arts. Andrea, Mandy, and Martin spent hours discussing what it was and how it addressed a gap within the field of positive psychology. I was invited to join them because my research lab at RCSI explores ways in which to improve the effectiveness of positive psychology interventions, and I was interested in how art interventions can facilitate wellbeing. Together, we created the first *International Routledge Handbook of Wellbeing Arts*, the aim of which is to explore alternative ways to enhance wellbeing through arts. We defined Wellbeing Arts as "engagement with arts and everyday life aesthetics by producing or receiving them as vehicle to flourish". In it, you will find a kaleidoscope of ideas from thought leaders on how arts can facilitate wellbeing. One such exploration circles back to Mandy's passion for photography, which is what this section is about.

The study led by Laura McKee et al. (2020) from Georgia State University, USA, examines how a photography intervention impacts the experiences of positive emotions. Participants were asked to document their daily positive experiences by taking photographs of the little moments throughout the day and then report their emotional responses to the moments. The study found that daily reports created a greater awareness and appreciation of positive moments, and that led to sustained increases in positive emotions over time. The act of capturing in a photograph and reflecting on positive experiences amplified emotional wellbeing, meaning that it can be a valuable tool for enhancing happiness in daily life.

Daily photography and reflection are just two of the evidence-based approaches to wellbeing arts. This new area of research is bursting with interventions that have ample evidence for reducing the symptoms of illness and is now also growing in the evidence of improving wellbeing. We engage in wellbeing arts every day without realising it. For example, not a day passed when my grandmother did not hum or sing songs. Martin Seligman adores his garden, which is like wellbeing art to him. Barbara Fredrickson loves cooking. Creating food, when approached mindfully, can become a wellbeing intervention. Robert Biswas-Diener loves starting a day with drawing. These are just a few examples of positive psychologists using non-typical daily interventions that enhance their wellbeing. The evidence-based nature of these Wellbeing Arts interventions should reassure us of their effectiveness and inspire us to incorporate them into our daily lives, potentially making them part and parcel of positive psychology applications in the future.

References

McKee, L. G., Algoe, S. B., Faro, A. L., & O'Leary, J. L. (2020). What do daily reports add to the picture? Results from a photography intervention designed to increase positive emotion. *The Journal of Positive Psychology*, *15*(5), 639–644. https://doi.org/10.1080/17439760.2020.1789697

Music and dance

I must admit, I am a closet singer – I sing badly but I truly love the experience. I remember going to the cinema to see *Mamma Mia* and then coming home and singing my heart out in the sitting room, belting out all the ABBA songs so loudly that my husband had to jokingly excuse my behaviour to the passing neighbours. I love dancing too. It takes a lot to get me off the floor. I may not be good at it, but I absolutely love it. At my age, I've learned not to worry about what others think and just want to have a good time. Singing and dancing are part of our daily joyful moments. It's no wonder that they are slowly becoming recognised as wellbeing arts interventions.

The study by Maxine Campion from the University of York, UK, and Liat Levita (2013) from the University of Sheffield, UK, explored how dancing and listening to music can enhance positive affect and divergent thinking abilities. In the study, participants were put into four distinct conditions: dancing, cycling, listening to music, and sitting quietly. Participants completed a survey measuring their mood and creativity tests before and after engaging in these activities for 5 minutes. Results showed that while cycling and sitting quietly had little to no impact on participants, both dancing and listening to music significantly increased the experiences of positive emotions and reduced negative emotions and fatigue. Interestingly, dancing and listening to music also improved different aspects of creativity. Dancing improved verbal creativity (transforming language into new words and expressions), while listening to music influenced non-verbal creativity (using pictures). These findings suggest that even brief exposure to these activities can serve as powerful tools to boost emotional wellbeing and creativity, particularly in non-clinical setting.

These are just some of the initial interventions that can be used in this emerging field of research. These activities are part of our daily lives, and the potential impact they may have on our wellbeing is enormous. It's a potential pathway for improvement of mental health and wellbeing.

References

Campion, M., & Levita, L. (2013). Enhancing positive affect and divergent thinking abilities: Play some music and dance. *The Journal of Positive Psychology*, *9*(2), 137–145. https://doi.org/10.1080/17439760.2013.848376

Final word

As we reach the end of this journey through the key studies in positive psychology, I invite you to picture a vibrant forest. Each study discussed in this book represents a unique tree within that forest. As we moved through the book chapters, we stopped at some trees and ignored others. This doesn't mean that the ignored trees were any less significant. They have contributed to the field of positive psychology all the same and helped to develop it further. However, some trees stood out, for me and other contributors, who I have consulted when writing this volume. Their branches have grown so high and wide that they began to influence other trees nearby. These trees have been highlighted in this volume as key studies.

It has been a pleasure to guide you through this journey, but now it's time for you to spread your wings and explore the entire forest. I hope that the studies you've encountered have ignited a fire in your belly, inspiring you to keep reading, keep learning, and keep growing. The forest of positive psychology is vast and full of wonders, so don't hesitate to take the next step and continue your exploration.

DOI: 10.4324/9781003530596-6

Index

MIX
Papier | Fördert gute Waldnutzung
FSC® C083411

Kolibri 360 GmbH
Ferdinand-Jühlke-Straße 7
99095 Erfurt, Deutschland
produktsicherheit@kolibri360.de